A LAW GRADUATE'S GUIDE

NAVIGATING LAW SCHOOL'S HIDDEN CAREER AND PROFESSIONAL-DEVELOPMENT CURRICULUM

By Nelson P. Miller

Bridge Publishing Group LLC
Getzville, New York
2011

A Law Graduate's Guide: Navigating Law School's Hidden Career And
Professional-Development Curriculum

Published by:
Bridge Publishing Group LLC
39 Concetta Court
Getzville, New York 14068
United States of America
Phone: 800.758.3010
Email: mail@bridgepg.com
Website: http://www.bridgepg.com

Library of Congress Control Number: 2011920859
ISBN: 978-1-935220-39-8

Please note: *Special discounts are available for bulk orders. Please contact Bridge Publishing Group LLC for more information.*

Table of Contents

Foreword

As the dean of placement for the nation's largest law school, I am passionate about the need for this guide written by a colleague of mine. I supervise 13 placement officers on four law school campuses and spend all of my professional time working on the career and professional development of law students. For 27 years, I practiced law as an appellate judicial law clerk, prosecuting attorney, at a large firm, and until fairly recently as a partner of a medium-size law firm. During the course of these positions, I hired and mentored many new lawyers. I am also the immediate past president of the State Bar of Michigan, meaning that I spent the past year meeting with lawyers and law-firm managing partners from all over the state and country, and in other parts of the world. I used a good portion of that time to learn more about what lawyers expect from new associates. The simple answer is that they expect a lot from new associates. And they deserve it. Law practice is an incredible privilege. There was hardly a day that went by during my law practice that I did not sense the depth of that privilege. New lawyers should be prepared for practice.

I am convinced that practice preparation takes a lot more than what law students experience in the classroom. The premise of this guide that there is a second curriculum to law school is, to me, perceptibly obvious. Lawyers are not like doctors or dentists, whose skills are, by comparison, relatively narrow (still in the best of senses). Lawyers serve in so many different practice settings doing so many different kinds of legal work. I discovered again in my travels last year as State Bar president what I already knew well, that for lawyers the choices are nearly endless. Because of the variety of practice settings and legal fields in which lawyers work, law students have a special opportunity and obligation to evaluate in law school what will be their best career choices. Law students can learn a lot in the classroom about various practice settings, but there are many more opportunities to learn more about those practice settings outside of the classroom. Additionally, during law school students can explore and sharpen their skills in networking, communication, research, negotiating, and other essential qualities for successful placement.

The activities that this guide recommends are not unusual. Law students have been selecting courses and concentrations, preparing resumes, interviewing, and doing the other recommended activities for many years. What is unusual about this guide is that it organizes those activities based on the knowledge-skills-ethics construct used in the Carnegie Foundation's report *Educating Lawyers.* My law school has been using that construct to good effect for many years, well before the Carnegie Foundation report's authors adopted it. I am delighted to see that same construct applied explicitly for career and professional-development activities. That design gives this guide comprehensiveness and an order that career and professional development warrants. Every law student deserves to find their best career and be as fully prepared for it as possible when they graduate. Law students invest too much energy, time, and money to settle for anything less. I firmly believe that this guide will contribute to that important goal.

— *Associate Dean Charles Toy*

Acknowledgments

The author drew much of the text in this book from materials developed by a team of career and professional-development co-ordinators at Thomas M. Cooley Law School. Cooley Law School is an Internal Revenue Code §501(c)(3) tax-exempt nonprofit educational organization. The nation's largest law school, Cooley has an access, diversity, and practice-preparation mission. The success of that mission requires Cooley to place a special emphasis on career and professional development. Broad access of a diverse population to legal education plays a profound role in the nation's welfare. A democratic republic depends on an informed citizenry capable of meaningful participation in and control over government. The common law, that great engine of liberty and economic prosperity, depends on its private enforcement. Lawyers play critical roles in keeping government responsible, liberty secure, and the economy prosperous. The author acknowledges and celebrates Cooley's mission to help more individuals overcome greater obstacles to gain and exercise a lawyer's knowledge, skills, and ethics. There is no more precious mission within legal education.

The author wishes specifically to acknowledge and thank the board of directors of Cooley for establishing and maintaining so vital of a mission. They also wish to thank Cooley's visionary President and Dean Don LeDuc, who shapes and carries forward that mission. To support its career and professional-development functions, Cooley recently established the position of Associate Dean of Career and Professional Development and appointed Charles Toy as the first occupant of that post. Dean Toy is a past President of the State Bar of Michigan, longtime partner and civil litigator in a major law firm, and summa cum laude Cooley graduate. The author acknowledges Dean Toy for supporting the drafting of this book and as a tireless and effective advocate for the career and professional development of lawyers. The author also acknowledges Career and Professional Development Office Director Lisa Fadler, Coordinators Danielle Hall, Alana Glass, Bradley Merritt, Karen Poole, Shari Lesnick, and especially Administrative Assistant Kaleena Kowalkowski who compiled resources for this book and Coordinator Danielle Hall who prepared a draft of the checklist appendix. Because Cooley graduates three classes every year, its placement professionals are among the most skilled and experienced in the country.

The author also wishes to acknowledge Cooley's Center for Ethics, Service, and Professionalism, which plays a substantial part in the professional-development activities of the school's students. The author developed text and patterned exercises in this book after the Center's Professionalism Portfolio, to which many Cooley faculty members contributed. The author thanks Associate Dean of Students and Professionalism Amy Timmer and Center for Ethics, Service, and Professionalism Director Heather Spielmaker and Assistant Director Karen Rowlader, each of whom are inspiring innovators in developing professional-development resources and opportunities for the school's students. The author also thanks Associate Dean of Enrollment and Student Services Paul Zelenski who worked with Dean Timmer to develop the Pathway to Success elective course from which the authors drew other inspiration and materials. The author also acknowledges and thanks Associate Dean of Foreign Study Programs William Weiner for his review and support. The author, whose role is Associate Dean of Cooley's Grand Rapids campus, works closely with Deans Toy, Timmer, Weiner, and Zelenski on the career and professional development of the school's students.

The author also wishes to acknowledge and thank the Cooley faculty. Faculty advisors can play a critical role in supporting and shaping law students' career goals. All Cooley faculty members practiced law before teaching, some as managing partners of law firms recruiting, evaluating, and hiring associates. Their ability to instruct in practical legal skills and the contacts they maintain within the professional community make them the most skilled and effective of faculty advisors. The author relied heavily on the wisdom and experience of Cooley's faculty in writing this book. Particular recognition goes to Grand Rapids-campus Professors James Peden, Paul Carrier, Paul Sorensen, Devin Schindler, Marjorie Gell, Chris Hastings, Tonya Krause-Phelan, Don Petersen, Heather Garretson, Derek Witte, Cindy Faulkner, and Sherry Batzer, Lansing-campus Professors Gary Bauer, Kim O'Leary, and Chris Shafer, and Ann Arbor-campus Professor Gina Torielli. The author also acknowledges and thanks Grand Rapids-campus Assistant Dean Tracey Brame, Campus

Director Cynthia Kruska, Deputy Director Joan Rosema-David, and Administrative Assistants Cheryl Scott and Tracie Simons.

The author also wishes to thank the judges and practitioners who contributed quotes. Several of them are adjunct professors at Cooley, where they give their time and share their skills and experience to train the next generation of great lawyers. There is no more dedicated group of professionals. Most of all, the author wishes to acknowledge and thank the Cooley graduates and students whose ambition, growth, maturity, and success inspired this book. The quotes at the end of the sections are all from Cooley graduates. Particular thanks go to Pathway to Success course students Melood Abugasea, Monique Howery, Steven Metcalf, Joel Schacchar, Laurie Schmitt, Kason Smith, Steven Vargo, and Clay Wittman, for their insight, encouragement, and, above all, their professionalism. Thanks also to the recent Cooley graduates whose quotes follow and illustrate each section of this book. They are lawyers today becoming the leaders of the profession tomorrow.

Introduction

Law school has a hidden curriculum. The courses that the school requires and the electives you choose are only a part of what you should be expertly navigating through law school. While you are registering for courses, studying, completing course requirements, and making progress toward your law degree, **you should also be deliberately planning your career and professional development.** Beyond your coursework, law schools and the legal profession offer you many tools to plan and pursue your career while you are in law school. You should be identifying and employing those tools throughout your time in law school if you want to give yourself the widest choice of career options, make the best choice of careers, and have the greatest success after you graduate.

Your pursuit of a job and career should not mean periodically reaching into a disorganized bundle of discrete tools. **Your approach to career and professional development should be** like the law school curriculum itself, **an organized set of disciplined practices that serve your career and placement goals.** One advisor suggests treating law school not like school but like law practice itself. *See* DENNIS TONSING, 1000 DAYS TO THE BAR 5 (William S. Hein & Co. 2010). Read and follow this guide if you want to increase your prospects for gainful employment and a meaningful career after graduation from law school. This guide is to help you get from law school into a meaningful career. It draws on the experience of some of the most effective career advisors in legal education. It also connects the law school curriculum with your preparation for a legal career. It is also the product of substantial research on legal education, career and professional development, and law practice. Given your substantial investment in law school, **your career and professional development should not be a hit-or-miss proposition**.

Your law school's career and professional-development staff and resources can help you connect your legal education with your law career. Law schools maintain career and professional-development offices and employ trained staff for those functions. Staff can provide substantial valuable career guidance and advice. They will have worked with other students having similar interests to yours and will know of lawyers and law firms with practices like the one you wish to enter. Staff can also direct you to career and professional-development materials. Even if you already have a job when you graduate, interacting with career staff can help prepare you for that job by helping you understand, appreciate, and equip yourself for what your future employer values. **Get an early start with your law school's career and professional-development staff.** Get to know their services before you think you need them. Doing so can make a substantial difference in the quality of your legal education and its outcome. Your law school's career services likely include:

- career planning and advice;
- career programs and workshops;
- career-and-professional-development library;
- handouts, checklists, forms, and samples;
- compensation surveys and information;
- employment statistics;
- job bulletins and postings;
- job fairs, conferences, and symposia;
- on-campus interviews;
- on-campus recruitment programs;
- classified advertisements;
- national employment directories;
- database access;
- judicial clerkship listings;
- law-firm internships, externship, and clerkship listings;
- grant and fellowship information;
- work-study and other part-time employment postings;
- excursions to the legal community;
- volunteer and pro-bono opportunities;
- copying and faxing;
- training to use online services; and
- resume and cover-letter review.

This guide helps you identify, organize, and make the best use of career and professional-development advice and resources. To get the most out of this guide, read it in your second to third term of law school, and return to it periodically thereafter.

Entering law school involves an adjustment. The author wrote *A Law Student's Guide* (Carolina Academic Press 2010) to help you make that adjustment. The *Law Student's Guide* maps the law school curriculum for you, making it transparent so that you can navigate it more readily to achieve your educational purposes. Yet once you enter law school and complete the first term or two, you will have made many of the adjustments necessary to earn your law degree. Your challenge changes. The new challenge becomes to **link your education with a meaningful career**. Instead of looking forward at law school from the point of entering it, you begin to look back at law school from the point of leaving it. This *Law Graduate's Guide* gives you that perspective when you most need it, which is early enough in your legal education to make the most of your career and professional development opportunities. After you read the *Law Graduate's Guide* in your second or third term, periodically evaluate your progress against the guide's recommendations. If you are reading this book later, even after graduating from law school, then it should still be helpful to you.

The *Law Graduate's Guide* has three parts organized around **knowledge, skills, and ethics**. The reason for this organization is that the Carnegie Foundation for Higher Learning's groundbreaking two-year study of legal education *Educating Lawyers* identified knowledge, skills, and ethics as legal education's three dimensions. Your law school should be instructing you in what lawyers (1) know (knowledge), (2) do (skills), and (3) become (ethics). **Employers are interested in the same three areas**. You must know law, be skilled in its use, and be fit for its practice, and then be able to show your readiness for practice to clients and employers. If they are to be effective, then the career and professional-development activities that this guide describes should fit the same paradigm. Read any text on how to get a law job, and you will recognize that you could readily organize what it describes around knowledge, skills, and ethics dimensions. We are doing that organization for you, which is the first step in helping you fashion the right career for you.

Each of the *Guide's* three parts on knowledge, skills, and ethics has three parts of its own on: (1) school (the law school curriculum); (2) tools (professional-development resources); and (3) transitions (career paths and opportunities). Law school offers courses, programs, and activities that focus on each of the three dimensions of legal education knowledge, skills, and ethics. You should **know how those curriculum components and co- and extra-curricular**

activities strengthen your career and professional development. Yet there are also specific tools like portfolios, resumes, networks, and memberships that tend to capture, promote, and reflect your professional development in each of these three dimensions knowledge, skills, and ethics. Each part of the *Guide's* three parts identifies and describes those tools because you should **know how to use those tools to translate your accomplishments into career opportunities**. Beyond the law school curriculum and the tools that you use to reflect your accomplishments, school and its tools can help you connect your knowledge, skills, and ethics with your preferred career pathway. These pathways involve variables like state bars, practice niches, firm size, and size of the metropolitan area in which you want to practice. Each of the *Guide's* three parts describes related pathways because you should **develop a clear sense of your career pathway**.

In short, what we have done is to give you a matrix within which to reflect on and confirm your professional development as a lawyer while exhibiting that development to employers and others. You may be familiar with the Myers-Briggs Personality Test® and other indicators of personality type and career preference. Those tests are useful. We also offer you here a way of mapping your professional personality, preferences, and accomplishments across the dimensions of legal education and law practice. We take all three dimensions of the rich law-school experience and help you translate them through specific professional-development tools into your career pathway. Law school is an exciting time holding great career prospects. It is also a time when you want to **take control over those prospects** so that you do not end up living another professional's dream. Law school holds powerful influences, not all of them toward your individual pathway. We have organized this information about school, tools, and transitions for your greatest use and benefit.

This guide has some other features to increase its usefulness to you. Simply reading about practices is not always the best way to learn how effective they can be. The guide includes a graduate success story illustrating each practice that the guide recommends. The guide includes career and professional-development advice from dozens of judges, lawyers, and law school deans and professors. It also includes exercises for each recommended activity. Appendix A then lists in alphabetical order the activities that each section of the guide describes, making for an index. Appendix B lists the same activities in roughly the chronological order in which you might explore them, recognizing that many of the activities are continuous and overlapping. The guide does not itself treat the activities in chronological order because the greater value is in seeing them in their relationship to one another. Law school is effective because of its coordinated curriculum and integrative nature.

Ultimately, the author hopes that the *Guide's* rich and thoughtful design helps you in your transition from graduate to great lawyer. Law holds the prospect for you of being the best of professions. Only, you must make it so. Here is another resource for adding to your professional wisdom.

Knowledge

Knowledge remains the basis for law practice. Law is a learned profession. Law practice requires knowledge of rules and procedures. Law firms, their clients, and other employers of lawyers hope to retain lawyers who know a lot of law. They also hope that you know something about the professions, businesses, industries, and other fields in which law operates. In general, the more law that you know, and the more that you know about the fields within which law operates, the better you are able to serve clients. **Clients want smart lawyers**, not necessarily book or grades smart but smart about the law and legal world. This part of the book shows you how law school's curriculum reflects the knowledge base that you use in practice. It then shows you the professional-development tools that you can use to connect your knowledge base with career transitions.

Law School Curriculum

There are a variety of ways that law school prepares your knowledge base for law practice. The law school curriculum requires that you take certain doctrinal courses. You also have the choice to take doctrinal electives. Your school may offer concentrations around general law fields. You also have the opportunity to work on law review or law journals on scholarship relating to specific subjects and fields. There are also graduate and dual-degree programs that enable you to deepen and enrich your studies of specific fields. Finally, you have the opportunity to conduct a portion of your law studies in other countries in ways that expose you to different perspectives on law subjects and legal fields. This section explores how you can connect your doctrinal courses, concentration, graduate and dual degrees, and foreign study to your career and professional development. **Keep this knowledge list in mind:**

- required and elective courses involving doctrinal subjects;
- concentrations organized around legal fields;

- working on law review and journals;
- completing graduate and dual degrees; and
- traveling for foreign study.

Doctrinal Courses—*Connecting*

A first way to connect the law school curriculum to your law career is to consider the courses you take. The courses that you take in law school are so obviously the foundation for your career and professional development that we sometimes miss the implications. There are a couple of reasons that we overlook courses when thinking of ways to capture evidence of your law knowledge and translate it into career opportunities. One reason is the mistaken assumption that all law students take basically the same courses. In fact, **there are relatively wide differences in required-course curricula** from law school to law school. Some schools have relatively few required courses all in the first year, while other schools have many more required courses covering all of the first two years. Some schools devote six credits to each of Torts, Contracts, Property, Constitutional Law, and Civil Procedure, while other schools devote only three credits to each of those courses or even offer them only within integrated courses centered around international law, comparative law, or case studies.

> "Developing an expertise in a specified field can be very valuable and rewarding, assuming you are confident in your continued interest in that field, as well as in its future marketability. Don't limit your options, however. When I was in law school, I selected courses based on certain assumptions about what I was going to do with my law degree. None of those assumptions materialized, however. I couldn't be happier with the unexpected path my career took, but I wasn't as prepared for it as I might have been had I selected a more diverse curriculum. It is also important to be a well-rounded lawyer. Challenge yourself."
> **Assistant United States Attorney Phil Green**

Value your doctrinal-knowledge base. While it is certainly true that law school teaches a set of transferable skills allowing lawyers to learn new fields, graduates can still be qualified or unqualified for specific career opportunities based on their required-course curriculum. Even though not all law schools require them, many lawyers find essential courses in Evidence, Business Organizations, Securities Regulation, Sales, Taxation, and Wills and Trusts. Other broadly helpful courses that may be required or elective include Family Law, Employment Law, Administrative Law, Pretrial Skills, and Intellectual Property Law. Here are a few other examples of how your doctrinal instruction in required courses can make a difference to your career opportunities:

- The graduate who took six credits of Torts instruction is likely to be more knowledgeable about the premises-liability, products-liability, medical-malpractice, no-fault, and worker's compensation claims that are the bread and butter of a personal-injury practice than the graduate who had only a three-credit survey course or no instruction devoted exclusively to tort law;
- The graduate who took Secured Transactions as a required course is likely to be far better prepared to represent lenders, debtors, and creditors in a consumer or collections practice than the graduate who avoided the course because the school did not require it and other students said it was a difficult course; and
- The graduate who took Taxation as a required course is likely to be far better prepared to help a retiring owner plan the sale of a small business to an adult child with the most favorable tax treatment than the graduate who avoided the course because the school did not require it and it involved some basic math concepts.

The variety in the knowledge base with which students graduate from law school multiplies when one considers elective courses. Most schools offer dozens of different electives and some over 100. Some schools offer a core of electives that satisfy concentration requirements. Schools offer other electives based on a variety of factors including student demand, the availability and expertise of full-time faculty members interested in teaching an elective, the interest and availability of prominent adjunct professors, recent developments in the law, demands and opportunities within the profession, and the school's mission. Examine the elective courses you have taken or are planning to take. **Elective courses distinguish your knowledge base**. Law firms and other employers of lawyers sometimes hire graduates based on special elective courses that they took in law school. Here are a few examples of how your doctrinal instruction in elective courses can make a difference to your career opportunities:

- The graduate who just took an elective course in E-Discovery is likely to prove highly valuable to a large firm that conducts substantial civil litigation defense but whose partners are unfamiliar with electronic document retention law, technology, and practices;
- The graduate who just took an elective course in Family Law is likely to prove highly valuable to a senior partner whose practice in that field developed before recent federal legislation on domestic violence, marriage, taxation of alimony and retirement accounts after divorce, parental kidnapping, child-support enforcement, termination of parental rights, foster care, and adoption; and
- The graduate who just took an elective course in Military Law may be a distinguished candidate for the Judge Advocate General Corps or for a law practice located near a large military base serving military members and their families.

The connection between your knowledge base and career has not only to do with the courses you took in law school but also **who taught those courses**. Some full-time faculty members have deserved reputations for helping to develop legal talent in specific fields. Practitioners may recognize them as masters of their field. Adjunct faculty members are typically judges or full-time practitioners prominent in the fields in which they teach. Your full-time or adjunct professors teaching required or elective doctrinal courses may have:

- helped to place a highly successful graduate in a specific job like one that you seek;
- helped to draft uniform laws in a specific field relating to a career opportunity you wish to pursue;
- taught judges and practitioners in continuing legal education courses relating to your preferred field; or
- co-authored an authoritative treatise on a law subject of interest to your prospective employer.

The fact alone that you received instruction from a certain professor may distinguish you from other graduates. You may also know that professor's specific thoughts or general perspective on subjects within the doctrinal field, or have interacted with that professor in ways that highlight your doctrinal knowledge and subject-matter interests for prospective clients and employers. **Do not overlook the connection between your doctrinal-course professors and the career path you are discerning.**

The other reason we overlook doctrinal courses as the foundation for career and professional development is the myth that all law students learn the same things in the same courses. Actually, there can be significant differences in what students draw from specific doctrinal courses. Some graduates will have engaged a doctrinal course and its professor in a manner that takes them **well beyond ordinary learning**. It is not necessarily that you may have received the highest grade in the class, although that may also have occurred. Rather, you may have engaged and experienced a doctrinal-course subject in a way that makes your knowledge of it uniquely valuable to you, clients, and employers in your career and professional development. Every professor experiences students whose vital interest in a certain subject combines with such insight that the professor wants to say:

- "You could easily pass the bar today with your knowledge";
- "You are already so competent that I would retain you as my lawyer";
- "If you were licensed, then I would refer trusted clients to you";
- "A law firm would profit with you as an associate and partner";
- "You are going to lead the bar in this field some day"; or
- "You could be a scholar in this field if you wished to do so."

Exercise. Later in this chapter we will explore how to capture, preserve, organize, and share evidence of your doctrinal-course knowledge. For now, answer these questions to help you reflect on your doctrinal-course instruction and begin to identify its value to your career pathway:

> ➢ If you had an opportunity to describe your best doctrinal-course experience to a listener considering law school, what would it be?

> ➤ What doctrinal-course subject seemed to come easier to you than to classmates?
> ➤ What was the best doctrinal-course exam or paper that you wrote, without regard to the grade that you received?
> ➤ What doctrinal-course professor, full-time or adjunct, would be able to recall something favorable about your knowledge and experience?

Sara Haas, J.D. 2006

"My undergraduate degree was in engineering. I had a clear goal from the start to connect my legal education with career opportunities in the intellectual property field. So, I focused my coursework on related fields, making sure to take Patent Law, Federal Administrative Law, and Intellectual Property Law among my doctrinal courses. I was also on Law Review and won the Alumni Association Distinguished Student Award. My academic focus helped me join an intellectual property firm right after graduation."

Concentrations—*Focusing*

Another way to connect the knowledge dimension of the law school curriculum to your career opportunities is through concentrations. Law schools do not generally offer major and minor fields of study in the manner of an undergraduate degree. The law school curriculum is significantly more unified than an undergraduate program, with a more specific goal of educating professionals capable of providing legal service. However, some law schools do offer concentrations in specific fields of law. Concentrations help a student organize studies around the particular field of the student's interest. The faculty determines what courses a student must complete to satisfy a concentration's requirements. The graduate's transcript then certifies completion of the concentration, enabling the graduate to publicize that fact to potential employers, clients, and others. Common concentrations include:

- Solo Practice, focusing on law-office systems to serve individual consumers in family law, real estate, small business, and estate planning;

- Litigation Practice, focusing on pretrial, trial, and appellate skills to serve individuals, private corporations, and prosecutor and public-defender offices;
- Transactional Practice, focusing on forming and advising business organizations and negotiating, structuring, and documenting their transactions;
- International Practice, focusing on norms, treaties, and conventions to serve global organizations and government relating to trade, travel, and immigration;
- Administrative Practice, focusing on constitutional and civil rights and administrative procedures to serve individuals, public-interest organizations, and government.

> "I interviewed many applicants to the Criminal Division of the U.S. Attorney's Office over the years and was always drawn to the ones who took courses reflective of their interest in litigation in general and criminal law in particular. Taking courses that demonstrate an interest in litigation and an externship in a prosecutor's office where a student gets hands-on experience, doing pro-bono work for an appellate defender office, and completing other criminal-law programs demonstrates to a prosecutor's office that your interest is long term and deep seated."
>
> **Former United States Attorney's Office Criminal Division Chief**
> **Alan Gershel**

Concentrations can influence your pathway from law school into a legal career. Some focus can certainly be appropriate within a legal education. Even without pursuing a concentration, you can focus your law studies and begin to develop your own expertise by taking one or more electives involving a specific legal field. As the concentrations listed above suggest, **you can select your elective courses based on the type of lawyer you want to become**. Lawyer and law-firm consultant Gerald Susskind suggests in his 2008 Oxford University Press book *The End of Lawyers?* that the five types of lawyers who will thrive in emerging new markets for legal services include:

- expert advisors who can impart complex new solutions to their corporate clients;

- enhanced practitioners who convey standardized products to clients at reduced costs;
- knowledge engineers who develop standard corporate documents and procedures;
- risk managers who develop methods and systems to help clients control and reduce liabilities; and
- multi-disciplinary hybrids who integrate their law knowledge into their client's or employer's business.

You would likely choose a different set of elective courses depending on which of these lawyer types you want to become:

- expert advisors would select business-organization, secured-transactions, taxation, and other transactional courses;
- enhanced practitioners would select estate-planning, bankruptcy, and other drafting courses;
- knowledge engineers might take drafting, administrative, and compliance courses;
- risk managers might take products liability, malpractice, environmental law, and other regulatory courses; and
- multi-disciplinary hybrids would focus on procedure courses and interdisciplinary courses related to their field.

Yet it is not necessary that you select and complete a concentration or even make a concerted effort to focus your elective courses in certain fields. Some employers recognize and value concentrations. Others do not. There is value to keeping your legal education varied and broad. You might concentrate in one area but by graduation find that your interests and opportunities lie elsewhere, or you might find a job in your concentration but later decide to pursue another field. Clients and firms value specialists, but they also value generalists who can act as trusted advisors across a range of fields. Also, bar exams require broad knowledge. Taking elective courses on bar-tested subjects should increase your bar-exam performance on those subjects. **Do not feel compelled to narrow your law studies if you cannot discern a clear reason to do so**.

"A required-course curriculum can force students to take classes they would never choose. Students end up with such a strong foundation of legal theory that they have the tools to take their careers in any direction that circumstances dictate after graduation. The film *The Devil's Advocate* calls being a lawyer 'the ultimate backstage pass.' A law degree opens so many doors that it is mindboggling. So I tell students not to concern themselves with whether they made the right decision of concentration in law school, just do well at whatever path you choose."

Professor Gary Bauer

Exercise. Reflect on the following questions, and then write and save answers to which to return as you evaluate your career and professional development:

> ➢ Look again at Gerald Susskind's five types of future lawyers listed above. Which type of lawyer will you be: expert advisor; enhanced practitioner; knowledge engineer; risk manager; or multi-disciplinary hybrid?
> ➢ List the courses that you have had that will help you be the type of lawyer that you want to become.
> ➢ List the courses that you could take that will help you be the type of lawyer that you want to become. Consult with your faculty advisor about those courses and other courses.
> ➢ List co- and extra-curricular activities that you could pursue that will help you be the type of lawyer that you want to become. Consult with your school's career coordinator about those activities and other activities.

Kimberly Royster, J.D. 2006
"I was a paralegal for a bankruptcy trustee for several years before going to law school. I knew that I wanted to draw on my skills in that field after graduation. So in law school, after completing my required courses, I focused my elective courses on a business-transactions concentration. The concentration helped to prepare me for an associate position in a bankruptcy practice after law school. Concentration was a good way to connect my experience with my career goal."

Law Review and Journal—*Writing*

Participating on law review or journal is another way to connect the knowledge dimension of the law school curriculum to your career opportunities. Law schools support publications run by students with a faculty advisor. Law reviews and journals serve several functions including:

- providing a forum in which faculty can publish to improve legal education and satisfy tenure requirements;
- providing the courts, legal profession, and lawmakers with a body of scholarship from which to draw to address and decide legal issues;
- hosting symposia, bringing scholars to the law school, and attracting attention to and improving the reputation of the law school; and
- providing opportunities to students for leadership, teamwork, and training in research, writing, editing, and other scholarship skills.

It is primarily the last point immediately above, your opportunity for training in a variety of scholarship-related skills, that connects law review or journal to careers.

Most schools have two or more student-run journals beginning with a law review. In most schools, law review is competitive, meaning that only students with superior grades (perhaps the top 5 to 10 percent of the class) after the first year of law school qualify to participate. Some law reviews give students with borderline grades the opportunity to boost their chances to participate through a write-on competition. **Some employers**, especially judges seeking law clerks and large law firms offering associate positions, **look at class rank and law review as key qualifiers for employment**. Law-review participation tends to qualify students for:

- summer-associate and post-graduate associate positions at larger law firms;
- judicial externships and clerkships, particularly in the federal and appellate courts;
- student research-assistant positions, post-graduate fellowships, and full-time teaching positions in law school; and

- writing and editing as a practitioner, for bar journals and continuing-legal-education publications.

"Research and Writing may be your most important class in law school. Law school is, after all, learning how to teach yourself the law. Your doctrinal classes help you to learn the law and rules. The research portion of Research and Writing teaches you how to find those specific rules that apply in your clients' cases. When finding those specific rules, you are using the teach-yourself-the-law lessons you learned throughout law school. The writing portion of Research and Writing teaches you how to communicate your research results accurately, clearly, and briefly so that anyone can understand them. While you will have lawyers with whom to collaborate in practice, you will not have lawyers who will teach you every aspect of the law. Research and Writing classes give you the confidence to be self-reliant."

Professor Evelyn Calogero

Law reviews are usually general in their subject matter, meaning that they attract and publish articles on a wide variety of subjects. If you are on law review, then you may spend many hours editing a small number of articles written by experts on specific law subjects, meaning that you can learn a great deal about those specific subjects. You tend not to have a choice in what articles you edit. You do, on the other hand, usually have an opportunity to choose your own subject on which to write your own article. Student articles are often called *notes* or *comments* to distinguish them from articles written by law professors. Writing a note or comment on a specific subject can further your career goals, giving you specific knowledge in a field that may interest prospective employers looking for that expertise. **Some students write notes and comments to attract specific employers**.

Schools offer other journals for students who do not qualify for law review or who do not wish to serve on law review for its general research, writing, and editing experience. Those other journals tend to be devoted to specific fields such as public policy, clinical law, law and economics, and environmental law. **Students choose journals** for the general training in scholarship and to improve their knowledge of the specific field, including **to attract prospective employers**. A judge, law firm, or other employer who typically seeks students with law-review experience may also accept students with journal experience, given that the research, writing, editing, leadership, and teamwork experiences are similar.

> "A Law Review credit on a resume looks glamorous. But its real value is in telling employers that the applicant has experience doing a variety of things that aren't glamorous at all: meeting deadlines, getting quotations right, checking citation form, checking punctuation, checking usage, and the like. The practice of law is about deadlines and details, so these things matter to employers."
>
> ***Professor Mark Cooney***

Although the research, writing, editing, and other skills you learn on law review or journal can create opportunities and serve you throughout your career, **law journals are not for everyone**. They require substantial time commitment. Participation typically begins with second-year students serving as the editorial staff for a requisite number of hours throughout the school year and perhaps part of the summer. After laboring over the minutiae of footnote and citation style, participants move up in their third year to the editorial board, where they train and supervise the new second-year students joining the review or journal. The editorial board appoints an editor in chief and other officers, each of whom devotes substantial time to organizational matters including reviewing and winnowing dozens of submitted manuscripts for publishable matter. Some schools give academic credit for law review or journal, while others do not.

Exercise. Reflect on these questions to help you decide whether to pursue a writing opportunity in law school for career and professional development:

> ➢ Do you qualify for law review? If so, then would it serve your career and professional-development goals for you to participate? Interview a law-review editor. Then, consult with your faculty advisor and career coordinator, telling them what job or career track you are thinking of pursuing, and asking them whether you should pursue law review.
>
> ➢ Whether or not you qualify for law review, what other journals are available to you? Would it serve your career and professional-development goals for you to participate on one of those journals? Interview a journal editor, and then consult with your faculty advisor and career coordinator.

> **Sameer N. Bhimani, J.D. 2007**
> "On my school's Law Review, I took a lead role in organizing its annual Symposium. I spent untold hours recruiting and communicating with speakers and authors while working with the Law Review's faculty advisor and the school's Communications Department. My experience on the editorial board of Law Review served as a great icebreaker during several job interviews. Participation on Law Review later helped me obtain a year-long, post-graduate clerkship with a prominent judge in the U.S. Court of Appeals—the opportunity of a lifetime."

Graduate and Dual Degrees—*Enriching*

Graduate law degrees can help connect the knowledge dimension of the law school curriculum to your career. A Juris Doctor (or J.D.) degree from an American Bar Association-accredited law school satisfies state-bar requirements for licensure. Employers of lawyers practicing in most fields have traditionally required or encouraged no other professional or graduate degree. Yet law continues to grow increasingly complex. With the increasing complexity of law especially in certain fields, lawyers have increasingly specialized in those fields. Lawyers specializing or wishing to specialize in those fields will on occasion pursue a Master of Laws (or LL.M.) degree beyond the Juris Doctor. The number and type of Master of Laws degree programs are rapidly expanding. Master of Law degrees are available in many fields including:

- taxation;
- intellectual property;
- insurance law;
- health law; and
- legal education.

If you have a strong interest in one of those specific fields in which a Master of Laws degree is available or common, then **consider whether you should plan for that additional graduate degree** while completing your Juris Doctor degree, especially if the Master of Laws degree will open additional career opportunities. A Master of Laws degree typically involves an additional 24 or more credits of study beyond the 90-credit Juris Doctor degree. Many, but not all, schools will permit a student who studies for both the Juris Doctor and Master of Laws degrees simultaneously to overlap credits, in effect reducing the credits requirement for the Master of Laws degree. Some students complete their Master of Laws degree immediately after they complete their Juris Doctor degree studies. Many other lawyers who earn a Master of Laws degree do so after having completed the Juris Doctor degree and having practiced for some years, when they find that their specialization warrants the additional investment in legal education within their practice field.

Some law schools also coordinate their Juris Doctor degree requirements to allow you to earn a graduate degree from another university or another school within the same university, in a non-law field. These dual-degree programs typically allow an overlap of up to six credits between the dual degrees, in effect reducing the required credits for the Juris Doctor degree and other graduate degree by that number of total credits. For example, if you pursued dual 90-credit Juris Doctor and 60-credit Master of Business Administration degrees, you could earn the Juris Doctor degree by completing 84 credits and the Master of Business Administration degree by completing 54 credits, provided that the law school approved and accepted 6 business school credits and the business school 6 law school credits. You may find dual Juris Doctor degree programs with the following degrees:

- Master of Business Administration;
- Master of Public Administration; and
- Master of Social Work.

"Do your research when choosing a graduate-degree program. Some programs are better at educating future academics, while others focus on providing practice skills and substantive expertise. Some programs provide an interesting course of study but one that the job market does not yet recognize. Also, consider how you learn best when selecting a program. Some schools offer online programs that, while convenient, may not be your best delivery system. Consult the director of the program that you are considering to be sure that it is right for you. Confirm that the program provides placement and career services to its degree candidates."
Master of Laws Program Director Gina Torielli

While you should consider a graduate degree's cost, graduate-degree programs can offer several practical benefits supporting career goals. Where a Juris Doctor-degree graduate has not found a suitable job opportunity, a graduate-degree program can provide a smoother transition into a law career. Sometimes, discerning the right field and locating the right opportunity just takes more time. Then again, some law jobs now either prefer or require a graduate degree beyond the Juris Doctor, so that earning a graduate degree may open new opportunities not previously available. Research job postings to see if a graduate degree is required or preferred for the work you want to do. Then again, some employers do not have the staff to train lawyers in the specialized skills that they require and so instead rely on graduate-degree programs for professional development of their lawyers. Holding a graduate degree in addition to your Juris Doctor degree may help you serve certain clients, especially corporate clients whose business is within the industry or field represented by your other graduate degree.

Exercise. Use the following questions to help you decide whether to pursue a Master of Laws degree or other graduate degree at the same time or after your Juris Doctor degree:

> ➤ If your undergraduate major was in a field other than pre-law, then consider what graduate degrees that field offers. Are there dual-degree programs for one of those master degrees?
>
> ➤ As you explore legal fields, research the education of master practitioners in that field. Do they have Master of Laws degrees? If so, then in what law field? Do they have other graduate degrees? If so, then in what non-law fields?

Philip Admiraal, J.D. 2007

"My undergraduate major was in history, but a personality test pointed me toward tax law. So I focused my legal education on taxation and found that I enjoyed and was very good at the studies. While still completing my Juris Doctor degree, I entered my law school's dual Master of Laws degree program in taxation. When I completed the Juris Doctor degree, I joined a global Fortune 100 company as an associate tax counsel while completing my Master of Laws degree. I now also teach taxation."

Foreign Study Programs—*Broadening*

Foreign study can help you connect the knowledge dimension of your legal education to your law career. **Law schools operate foreign study programs in which their students are able to earn academic credit studying law in another country.** The programs operate for a semester or a period shorter than a semester, often (though not always) in the summer when traditional law school programs are not offering courses. Tuition is like that for the traditional law school curriculum. Financial aid is often available on terms similar to the terms for traditional law school enrollment and courses. The programs typically offer housing and may offer limited or discounted transportation and food plans. They also commonly offer orientation programs and special events in addition to the law school coursework for academic credit. Completing academic credit in a summer foreign study program enables you to take fewer credits during the traditional school year, freeing up your time for internships, clerkships, and other career and professional development.

In today's globalizing legal, business, and social environment, foreign study have a way of helping you stand out to prospective employers. Yet studying foreign and international law is not solely a matter of making your skills peculiarly attractive to certain employers. It is also a matter of basic competence. As recently as 20 years ago, you may have been able to graduate from law school and enter practice without any exposure to foreign and international law, and be fully prepared to enter law practice. **Law is increasingly global.** Courts give increasing consideration to international law sources. The Supreme Court has recently looked to international norms to decide domestic constitutional issues. Cross-border and international disputes bring foreign law into state and federal courts under choice-of-law rules. Family-law disputes, tort claims, and consumer disputes may require resolution under foreign law or may be influenced by international-law norms. Business transactions are so commonly global in nature that lawyers serving larger corporate clients often cannot avoid foreign and international law. For example, a corporate lawyer may face foreign or international law questions over:

- treaties and tariffs on trade;

- compliance with foreign regulations on product quality and safety;
- compliance with United States restrictions on export of technology;
- reporting of foreign financial transactions;
- taxation of repatriated foreign earnings;
- registration of corporations doing business in foreign countries;
- choice-of-law, choice-of-venue, and jurisdiction provisions in contracts with foreign suppliers;
- visas for overseas travel of business executives;
- work permits for foreign employees; and
- retention of foreign counsel for defense of foreign claims.

> "Foreign study should be foreign in the classroom and not just in the pubs and clubs. Cooley's foreign study courses are overwhelmingly taught by lawyers and law faculty from the host countries. In Canada, Australia, and New Zealand, you can gain personal insights into other legal systems every day by interacting with lawyers from those countries."
>
> **Foreign Study Program Director Dean William Weiner**

To meet the needs of law graduates for global law knowledge and skills, foreign study programs teach foreign law, meaning the law of other countries. Foreign study programs tend to focus on the legal issues and law most relevant to the world region in which the law school conducts the program. For example, a program in New Zealand may offer a course in Antarctic and Southern Ocean Legal Studies. Foreign study programs also teach comparative law, meaning to compare foreign to United States law for better understanding of both legal systems. For example, the same New Zealand program may compare the law of Pacific Rim nations including Korea, China, Japan, Vietnam, New Zealand, and Australia to United States law. Foreign study programs also teach international law, meaning the international system of treaties and conventions, customary international law, and general principles of law that bind nations and restrict the domestic law of nations. You may also be able to complete some of your law school's required or popular courses at the same time that you study foreign, comparative, and international law. **Programs**

offer rich mixes of foreign, comparative, and international law courses. You may find courses in:

- Bills of Rights & Civil Liberties;
- Comparative Corporate Theory and Governance;
- Comparative Criminal Law;
- Comparative Torts;
- International Economic Law and Institutions;
- International Environmental Law;
- International Human Rights;
- Migration, Immigration, and Refugee Law;
- North American Free Trade Agreement Overview;
- North American Free Trade Agreement Dispute Settlement;
- Trade and the Environment;
- Transnational Criminal Law.

Yet the attraction of foreign study programs is not simply that they teach different courses. It is also that law schools conduct the programs in foreign countries, enabling you to gain skills in the language and an appreciation for the people and culture of those places. Sponsoring United States law schools tend to hold the programs at established law schools in the foreign country, with courses taught by a mix of law faculty visiting from the United States and law faculty and practitioners local to the foreign country. You need not know the foreign language of the country in which you study. Faculty teach in English from materials written in English unless otherwise specified in program materials. Even though a law school may only conduct one, two, or a small number of foreign study programs, law schools also belong to consortia through which their students are able to earn academic credit from foreign study programs conducted by other law schools. **You may have a wide choice of foreign study programs enabling you to study at a location literally around the world,** fitting your foreign study to your legal field and geographic region of interest. Among other places, there are popular foreign study programs in:

- Melbourne, Australia,
- Barcelona, Spain,
- Cambridge, England
- Cape Town, South Africa,

- Dublin, Ireland,
- Florence, Italy,
- Galway, Ireland,
- Istanbul, Turkey,
- London,
- Madrid,
- Mexico City,
- Montreal,
- Moscow,
- Christchurch, New Zealand,
- Oxford, England,
- Paris,
- Shanghai, China,
- Tokyo, and
- Toronto.

The point is that the value of foreign study is not simply that lawyers in the United States need to help local clients with foreign and international law concerns. It is also that there are increasing numbers of foreign clients with United States interests requiring assistance from lawyers licensed in the United States. **You may have the opportunity and need to represent foreign individual and corporate clients.** Many law firms have foreign clients. Your knowledge of a foreign country and its laws, and your knowledge of international law, can make your services attractive to law firms. It can also make your services attractive to foreign clients. In addition to the foreign and international law issues, lawyers face cultural and language barriers when helping both domestic and foreign clients in global matters. Foreign study give you the opportunity to remove those barriers through your increased language skills and cultural knowledge. Consider the value of foreign study when planning your connecting your legal education with your career and professional development.

Exercise. Use the following activities to help you decide whether to pursue foreign study while in law school:

➢ List the foreign countries you have visited. Is there anything in the activities that you conducted in those countries, like speaking the language, employment, service or mission work, education, training, or guiding tours, that you would list on a resume?

➢ List the foreign countries that you would like to visit. Is there anything in what attracts you to those countries, like family and friends, language skills, cultural interests, property interests, nonprofit organizations, business contacts, or industry or professional skills, that you could connect to your law career?

➢ List the legal fields in which you would like to practice. Is there anything in those fields, like industries or economies, legal disputes, social movements, or populations or major clients, that you can see would connect that field with specific foreign countries?

➢ Now take any connections that you made to specific countries in the above activities, and find out what law school foreign study programs are available in those countries. If your law school does not have a program in that country, then inquire of your school's foreign study office as to your options.

> *Brandon Petelin, J.D. 2007*
> "Through my law school's study abroad program, which allowed me to study in Durham, United Kingdom, I explored the possibility of studying and potentially working in Europe. Based on this experience, I decided to pursue an LL.M. in the United Kingdom, which ultimately led me to the London School of Economics and Political Science where I specialized in international economic law. I am now working in the international trade arena for the United States Department of Commerce in Washington, DC. Thus, I can honestly say that my school's study abroad program directly contributed to my early career choices."

Professional-Development Tools

What you do in law school should not only increase your law knowledge but create and preserve evidence of that knowledge. To enter law practice and thrive, you need not only knowledge of the law but proof that you are knowledgeable. If you cannot show that you know, then you may never get that opportunity. Having the knowledge base is not enough. You must also be able to readily demonstrate it in an organized and attractive manner. Law school should help you create useable evidence of your knowledge, so that you can demonstrate your knowledge in ways that promote your career and professional development. Your class standing is a good example. High class standing reflects a comprehensive knowledge base. Portfolios are another example. They help you organize and exhibit your knowledge base to further your career and professional development. Student-organization leadership and professional memberships can also reflect your fields of interest. Career and professional development has its own knowledge base. There are abundant resources to help you shape your career and professional development. This chapter helps you identify those resources. As we go through them one by one, **keep these connections in mind:**

- class standing to reflect your knowledge base;
- portfolios to demonstrate your knowledge base;
- student-organization leadership to reflect your knowledge base;
- professional memberships to reflect your knowledge interests; and
- resources to build your professional-development knowledge.

Class Standing—*Achieving*

Your class standing is a first tool to connect the knowledge dimension of the law school curriculum to your law career. Many law schools disclose to each individual student their class rank based on cumulative grade-point average. **Class rank has several uses.** It allows students with comparatively high grade-point averages to tell prospective employers that they rank first out of 150 students in the class, or are in the top ten percent of their class, or are in the top quarter, whatever the ranking indicates. Class rank can, in other words, be **a marketing tool**. Law schools do not publish class standings. It would violate federal educational privacy rights to do so. Yet the availability of a class rank tends to make employers expect its disclosure and, in the absence of disclosure, assume a lower rank. It is acceptable not to disclose class rank, but doing so may leave an implication of a lower rank. One seldom sees students listing below-median ranking, such as 137 out of 150.

> "Although class standing is certainly not the only measure of law school success, it is a strong hiring barometer for many employers inasmuch as many of the skills involved in being a successful law student are relevant to becoming a successful lawyer. These skills include long hours of dedicated study, knowledge of the law, keen analysis, and an ability to communicate through skillful writing."
> *Former United States Attorney's Office Criminal Division Chief Alan Gershel*

Class rank has other uses. Class rank can also reward and reassure high academic performers, while cautioning and challenging low academic performers. It can also help all students relate their school performance to probable bar passage. Law school grade-point averages tend to correlate well with bar results. In general, high grades mean a greater likelihood of passing the bar, while low grades mean a lesser likelihood. Students who graduate with high or low class ranks can thus gauge their bar-passage prospects to help them prepare for the bar exam and results.

Your academic class standing can influence your pathway into a legal career, although not always in ways that you might expect. In general, high grades can create opportunities. Some of the opportunities most likely to require high grades or where high grades will be given more emphasis than other accomplishments include:

- law review;
- research and teaching assistant positions with law professors;
- scholarships;
- summer-associate positions particularly with larger firms;
- fellowships;
- judicial clerkships;
- employment with large law firms; and
- teaching full-time in law school or other higher education.

High grades can be important to pursuing these opportunities. If you have high grades, then consider pursuing these career and professional development opportunities.

On the other hand, prospective employers recognize that class standing is only one performance indicator. Employer needs vary widely. **Some employers give little or no credence to grades** and instead use other performance measures. Some of the opportunities where high grades mean less, mean nothing, or may in rare cases even be unusual and questioned include:

- competitions;
- student government;
- student organizations;
- internships;
- clinics;
- externships;
- pro-bono and other volunteer service;
- public-defender offices; and
- small-firm and solo practice.

Note that most lawyers practice solo or in small firms, where high grades in law school may be largely or entirely irrelevant. Whether your grades are high or low, keep in mind that few clients ever ask their lawyer their law-school grades or class rank or care what law school their lawyer attended. Clients tend to value current skills and attributes, not academic performance.

Law students tend to receive their lowest grades in the first two terms of law school. Law school requires adjusting to its different methods of studying and instruction and different forms of assessment. Adjustments can take time. Grades tend to improve after the first two terms. There are exceptions. Students who do well initially may put in less effort later, resulting in declining grades. You earn grades. Professors do not award them based on status, standing, reputation, or potential. Courses and forms of assessment can change from term to term, presenting different challenges and resulting in different grades. Physical, mental, and emotional health, social and financial support, and other outside conditions can also change term to term, influencing grades. It is important to remember that grades reflect performance in specific courses at a specific time, not one's general merit or capability.

Surprising as it may seem, high grades can also inadvertently influence you to pursue opportunities that do not fit with your career goals and personality. Law students who earn very high grades may feel that they should pursue a traditional career track into a judicial clerkship and large firm serving corporate clients rather than small-firm or solo practice or public service that they had planned before high grades earned them those additional opportunities. It is generally unwise to take easier courses simply for high grades while avoiding harder courses that would build knowledge and skills. Too much focus on earning high grades through classroom work might also cause you to avoid potentially more valuable service-learning opportunities, unwisely sacrifice family, work, and community responsibilities, or sacrifice peer relationships in favor of competition.

Still, high grades are better than low grades, and so set a goal to earn the highest grades you can while keeping the above cautions in mind. Although this book is not about how to succeed in law school, **here are some practices within your control that could improve your grades:**

- take responsibility, setting your goal for the highest grades;
- assess whether you worked as hard as you should;
- if you did all that you could without success, then change practices;
- write your own case briefs and outlines;
- complete all of your professor's practice problems and exercises;
- attend all professor and teaching-assistant review sessions;
- use computer-aided legal instruction and other online resources;
- review unclear concepts with your professor outside of class;
- consult hornbooks and other secondary sources on unclear issues;
- review exam banks to determine test format and content;
- write practice exams on all major concepts;
- evaluate your practice exams against model answers;
- review practice answers with your professor;
- rewrite practice answers until you get an excellent score;
- consult the school's academic resource center staff;
- consult with a psychologist about testing for learning disability;
- request accommodations if you have a learning disability.

If you have done less well than you had hoped in a specific course, then ask exam administrators to review your exam. Read your professor's comments and review scoring to see what you can learn. Check the professor's numeric calculations to be sure that they are correct. Professors, secretaries, and exam administrators do make mistakes in tabulating, transferring, and posting scores. Bring incorrect calculations to the attention of exam administrators, following your school's administrative appeal procedures. Review your exam for substantive scoring errors, where the professor did not give you credit for responsive work meeting scoring rubric and model answer criteria. Bring scoring errors to the attention of exam administrators, following your school's substantive appeal procedures.

After you complete any appeals, if you still have questions about your exam performance and the professor's scoring, then **meet with your professor**. Professors are generally adept at diagnosing error patterns in student exams. You can learn a great deal about your exam performance with the professor's help. Professors may also be adept at helping you correct common errors, by explaining the errors and directing you to practice resources. You can find additional help from academic resource personnel to evaluate exam performance.

If low grades put you on academic probation, then know that **students succeed in getting off probation to graduate from law school**. Your school designed probation not as a trap toward dismissal but to give you a path toward better grades. Determine your school's probation terms. Know the steps and timetable for getting off probation. Stay positive and active. Work with professors and academic resource personnel to plan for your improvement and graduation. They want to help you. Your professors may not know that you are on probation. Although you may have the choice whether to disclose your probation to your professor, consider doing so. The professor may be able to direct you to resources or otherwise help you plan to improve.

Academic probation does not have to negatively impact your career. Overcoming academic probation demonstrates that you can meet challenges. Lawyers lose cases and face other challenges in practice. If a prospective employer asks about your former academic probation reflected on a law school transcript, then you can use it to show that you have the skill to adapt and character to persevere. Other candidates may not be able to show that they have faced and overcome professional challenges. Clients also face challenges. Proving that you can overcome adversity also indicates that you can help clients believe that they can also do so. Many lawyers find that your abilities to believe in yourself and convey that belief to others are critical skills for attracting, gaining the confidence of, and competently serving clients. Academic probation is not failure. Failure would have been quitting law school.

Exercise. Use the following questions to help you use your class rank as a career transition tool:

> ➤ Determine your class rank through your school registrar's office. Do you think that it accurately represents your current capabilities? If your class rank is lower than you think it could be, then identify why. Are the matters you identified within your control? How can you address them to improve your class rank? With whom would you consult for advice on improving your class rank?

> ➤ Consider whether you would disclose your class rank to prospective employers before asked. Would you put it in a cover letter to a prospective employer and in your resume? Identify the career coordinator at your law school with whom you would consult about whether and how to disclose your class rank.

> ➤ Keeping in mind that class rank is only one measure among many measures of performance, what opportunities do you think it most qualifies you to pursue? What opportunities might it discourage or foreclose? Identify two of your law school administrators, faculty, or staff members with whom you would consult to find out more about how your class rank affects your career opportunities.

Emily Coyle, J.D. 2010

"I graduated summa cum laude. I was not the only one of my classmates to get a good job at a large statewide law firm. In fact, I received and accepted my job offer before my last year of law school, well before learning that I would graduate first in my law school class. Yet I would not have had the interviews that I did for summer-associate positions if I had not done so well at the beginning of my law school career. My ability to tell my future employer that my grades would get me on Law Review made a difference, and my high grade-point average throughout law school gave my law firm confidence in me."

Transfer—*Leaving*

Some students transfer from one law school to another rather than completing their education at the school they entered. Transfer patterns indicate that **students transfer primarily to gain entry to law schools that rejected their initial application and refused them admission.** Law schools reject students initially and then accept them after their first year at another law school in part to manipulate and improve their rankings. Rankings rely in part on admission indices like median LSAT score and undergraduate grade-point average and in part on rejection rates (ratio of applications to acceptances). Rankings do not count transfer students when evaluating admission indices and rejection rates. Higher-ranked law schools maintain their higher rankings in part by letting rejected students with lower admission indices transfer in after their first year at a lower-ranked law school. If you wonder why those schools take transfers in the second year at all, then consider that tuition revenue is important to all law schools, including public law schools, especially in today's climate of decreased tax revenues and funding for public higher education. These law schools need and budget for the additional tuition revenue from transfer students. By rejecting you initially and then letting you in the back door, these schools improve their rankings and tuition revenue.

Students give several reasons for transferring to a school that initially rejected them. One reason they give is to improve their employment prospects. **Unless you break into the putative national top ten of law schools, moving up in the rankings ladder is unlikely to significantly improve your employment prospects.** Employers want skills. They do not hire based on entitlements. They do not want lawyers who think that they are better than other lawyers simply because of the law school that they attended. Pride and a sense of entitlement are the first steps toward a fall, especially in a service profession like law where success depends on what you are able to actually do for clients. In nearly all cases, simply because you graduated from a certain law school does not guarantee you a job. Even if it did get you an interview, then you would still have to win and hold the job based on your performance.

Employers have their own evaluation of law schools, published rankings aside. If your law school does not train you as a lawyer, then its ranking does you no good and may instead have misled you. Moving up the rankings ladder is generally not a good reason to transfer. Indeed, **firms and other employers value and depend on loyalty.** They lose a substantial investment in you (estimated at six figures) when you bolt for another employer. Your decision to transfer to another law school may do nothing more than show a prospective employer that you will leave them, too, when you perceive an advantage to doing so. The lawyer interviewing the transfer student for a job may even have graduated from the school out of which the student transferred. It happens.

> "Be true to your school. If you transfer schools, then employers will assume that you will leave them, too."
>
> *Dean Amy Timmer*

Be careful that you do not lose valuable professional-development opportunities if you consider transferring to move up a few spots in the rankings ladder. The Law School Admission Council gives the following advice. **When you transfer, you may lose your grade-point average, class rank, and opportunity to participate on law review.** You may also lose your opportunity to serve as an officer or on the board of the student bar association and student organizations. You may also fail to qualify for moot-court and mock-trial competitions or for leadership positions on the student boards that plan and operate those competitions. Law schools treat transfer students differently. If the other school does not give you a class rank until you graduate, for instance, then you may lose the opportunity to show an employer that you have superior academic standing. If you are considering transfer, then confirm how the other school treats the grade-point average and class rank you earned at your present school. Also, find out whether you can qualify for law review, bar-association and student-organization leadership, and competitions and competition leadership.

You may also lose valuable relationships that you have established with students, administrators, faculty, and staff at your school. The first year of law school builds bonds among students. **Law-school-peer relationships, professional and personal, can last a lifetime.** Law-school classmates can be a source for information, support, referrals, references, and recommendations throughout one's career. When you transfer to another law school after your first year, you must make new relationships. It is harder to do so when the class you are joining has already formed relationships through the challenging first year of law school. Some transfer students report feeling isolated, shunned, and outcast from their new classmates, especially if their new school and its student organization did not permit them to participate or to earn leadership positions.

"Attending law school, in addition to the intellectual challenge, is a lot about gaining momentum within the curriculum and co-curriculum, and in developing relationships with faculty and peers. When one transfers, that momentum is disrupted and can be difficult to recapture at another location."

Dean Paul Zelenski

In your first year, you also come to know deans, faculty, and staff, and we come to know you. We are skilled at guiding your career and professional development. Our work with you during the first year of law school gives us a basis on which to guide, employ, refer, and recommend you. In your second year, we can employ you as research and teaching assistants, find you work study, place you in a judicial internship or other special program, and work one-on-one with you on directed study of your choosing. Our calls and letters to judges, lawyers, and other employers of graduates in your second and third years can make differences in your career opportunities. It can be harder for deans and professors to understand, guide, hire, recommend, and otherwise help you when you spent your first year at a different law school.

The school that you leave also loses something. Second- and third-year students make a difference in law school programs. They lead law review and journals, write competition problems, serve as research and teaching assistants, and lead existing student organizations or form new ones. Considering returning your services to those who gave you and others the opportunity to attend law school. Second- and third-year students also volunteer in the community, do foreign study programs overseas, serve in judicial internships and externships, and take law-firm externships and clerkships, representing their law school to the larger community. Consider giving that credit to the school that gave you those opportunities.

Avoid false buyer's remorse when it comes to your legal education. Study of lawyer happiness indicates that graduates of lower-ranked law schools report greater career satisfaction than graduates of higher-ranked law schools, even when controlled for other factors like law firm size. NANCY LEVIT & DOUGLAS O. LINDER, THE HAPPY LAWYER: MAKING A GOOD LIFE IN THE LAW 14-15, (Oxford Univ. Press 2010). **Graduates of fourth-tier law schools report the highest job satisfaction.** *Id.* At 117-118. After indicating that following rankings is the wrong way to pick a law school, the authors of the book just cited indicate that "[b]y far the best indicator of a good law school match for you is how well you like, respect, and trust the students who will become your peers and whether you are stimulated by them." *Id.* at 117. They also recommend to choose a law school that cares about you and that fosters a supportive educational culture. *Id.* at 118-119.

Like Groucho Marx, do not fall into thinking that you should not associate with any institution that would admit you as a member. Avoid marketing pitches. Instead, **make a careful cost comparison, including any scholarships you would lose by transferring. Compare bar-passage rates and placement data.** If after graduation you want to live and work elsewhere, then find out if your law school has alumni and externships in that area to help you establish a professional network there. Search your school's alumni and externship databases, and network among your professors, for local contacts. Make contacts there through your school, and then visit. Your school may let you establish a new externship in that area where you can spend your last term, getting you to the place you want to go without the costs and disruption of transfer.

If you continue to believe that transfer may be best for you, then visit the school to which you are considering transfer. **Interview the students, dean, and faculty members, and attend some classes.** Ask about academic support, faculty accessibility, curriculum scope and depth, pro-bono and clinic opportunities, and career and professional-development services. Program cost and quality can be good reasons to transfer. Yet students who transfer often report that their first school's professors were more accessible and supportive, the staff friendlier, and the student services better. Schools that work hard to recruit rather than reject you also work hard to serve and keep you. Schools that grant entry to students with lower admission indices (LSAT and undergraduate grade-point average) have trained and equipped their professors and staff, and designed their curricula, to support those students. Not all schools have the same academic- and instructional-support staffs and services.

Consider these circumstances carefully before transferring. Above all, get counsel about transfer. See your faculty advisor and law school dean, discussing openly the pros and cons. There may be programs and opportunities about which you were not aware. You may not need to transfer to find the career and professional-development opportunities you most want. Your law school may be able to help you in ways that you did not know. The students who most regret transferring are generally those who did not investigate it sufficiently and instead relied on myth or gossip.

Exercise. Use the following questions to help you evaluate whether transfer is a career and professional-development tool for you:

> ➢ If you are considering transferring to another law school, then identify the law school to which you would transfer, investigating it in the ways suggested above (data comparison, visit, interviews). Then rank each of the following factors in order of your priority before rating your school against the other school on each factor:
>
> ➢
>> o   cost including scholarships;
>> o   class rank and grade-point average;
>> o   law review and journal opportunities;
>> o   student organizations and competitions;
>> o   foreign study opportunities;
>> o   professor accessibility and support;
>> o   academic resources support;
>> o   peer relationships;
>> o   counseling and mentor relationships;
>> o   library and facilities;
>> o   externship and clinic opportunities;
>> o   career and professional-development office and staffing;
>> o   alumni network.

Portfolios—*Organizing*

A professional-development portfolio can be another tool to connect the knowledge dimension of the law school curriculum to your law career. A portfolio can help you find employment and succeed in law practice. Learning law is one thing. It is another thing to be able to **display evidence of your learning** to prospective employers, clients, co-counsel, and others. A portfolio helps you collect, organize, and reflect on evidence of your learning and then select items for various uses. **A portfolio is not extra work. You have to store your work somewhere,** in some fashion. You may as well recognize and embrace the opportunity to think of the way in which you store your schoolwork as your portfolio. Professionals benefit by reflecting on their work to change and improve it. They also benefit by being able to demonstrate it to others. A portfolio promotes your ability to reflect on your developing skill, while making it easier and more effective to assemble evidence of your skill.

> "As I help law students build their portfolios, I see a similar construction developing in their minds of their own work. Students begin to see that what they are learning in law school lays the foundation for their chosen career. Portfolios do double duty. They help students see how they are becoming whole and talented professionals, while also reflecting to others everything that a student offers as that professional."
>
> **Dean Amy Timmer**

Put simply, you should organize your career and professional development activities. Career and professional development require that you continuously pursue multiple different activities in overlapping time periods. You may all at once be planning for and taking courses, engaged in student organizations, volunteering, conducting informational interviews, attending bar meetings, working part time, and doing several other things to promote your career and professional development. **Let your portfolio organize your career and professional-development activities by tracking:**

- job opportunities;
- job applications you made;
- draft and completed cover letters;
- draft and final resumes;
- interview preparation;
- interview notes;
- thank-you and follow-up notes;
- a telephone log; and
- job contacts and networks.

You can make an electronic professional-development port-folio simply by using your computer operating system's folders, stored on hard drive and flash drive, and accessible to you through the Internet. An electronic portfolio allows you to collect, organize, study, and maintain files, photographs, video, and other indications of your skill. The key is to **start your portfolio now and use it consistently**, storing your schoolwork and evidence of your law-related co- and extra-curricular activities in a manner that causes you to reflect on it. Here are some other tips for creating your professional-development portfolio:

- store everything that you do related to your legal education and professional development in your portfolio;
- organize your portfolio into Knowledge, Skills, and Ethics folders, representing the three dimensions of legal education;
- sort your course-work and co- and extra-curricular work into those three dimensions, to help you balance your education;
- as you do so, turn your files into Portable Document Format (pdf) files so that prospective employers can open them without conversion;
- create a folder for Vision in which you store thoughts and inspiration about your career as they occur to you;
- create a folder for Career in which you store everything directly related to your job search; and
- back up everything so that you do not lose your accumulated work.

Plan periodic reviews of your professional-development portfolio, for example, at the end of each term or school year. Schedule the review with your faculty and career advisors, mentor, and a peer, in a classroom or conference room. Wear professional attire to the review, and take your place at the podium or head of the conference table. Plan to speak for 10 minutes about your professional development. Include academic accomplishments, co-curricular activities, concentration, law-related work, and volunteering. Acknowledge areas where you need to work to improve. Be sure to address any character-and-fitness issues such as school discipline, criminal charges, financial issues, and substance abuse. End with your plans for future development. Then listen for a longer period to your review panel's comments and suggestions. A review of this kind, while challenging, will improve your ability to speak publicly about yourself in a way that demonstrates your commitment to your professional development.

You can then provide to prospective employers a flash drive, other electronic storage device, or link to your **public portfolio, in which you have placed the best examples of your work**. You can assemble and reassemble in your public portfolio what you wish to display to match the interests and needs of specific prospective employers. Prospective employers can then peruse a wide variety of your work such as course outlines, practice exams, and scholarly papers, or with one click see examples of legal memoranda, motions, briefs, and correspondence that you have written, and even video files of you using your law knowledge. **Work with your school's portfolio administrator, faculty advisor, career advisor, and mentor to assemble in your public portfolio the best examples of your work.** Here are some specific steps to create your public portfolio:

- create a folder named Public Portfolio on your flash drive, hard drive, or other electronic storage device where you have your professional-development portfolio;
- create and place in your Public Portfolio folder a master text file named Cover Letter or Executive Summary;
- create other subfolders in your Public Portfolio for Knowledge, Skills, and Ethics;
- write the text for your Cover Letter or Executive Summary for the specific employers you are approaching;
- as you describe in the Cover Letter or Executive Summary examples of your work, create hyperlinks to specific files that you move into the Knowledge, Skills, and Ethics subfolders of your Public Portfolio;
- describe a wide range of evidence of your knowledge, skills, and ethics, while at the same time being selective in choosing the highest-quality work product;
- copy your Public Portfolio onto an unused flash drive, DVD, or other electronic storage device, or create a link to it that the prospective employer can access;
- mark the flash drive, DVD, or other electronic storage device with your name and contact information, in a professional manner, so that the prospective employer does not misplace it;
- describe in the Cover Letter or Executive Summary how the prospective employer can open your Public Portfolio and hyperlink to the files;

- show your materials to your mentor and other professionals to ensure that they are appropriate; and
- test your Public Portfolio on someone else's computer to be sure that the prospective employer can access it using common computer software and equipment.

Always print a hard copy of the Cover Letter or Executive Summary to provide to the prospective employer along with the electronic version of your Public Portfolio. When you do so, use high-quality bond paper. You may also wish to print your Public Portfolio rather than provide it to your prospective employer solely in electronic format. If you do so, then the quality of your portfolio binder and the paper and print format that you use becomes important. Photographs and other images look better in glossy formats using color printing. Get the help of a copy shop or office supply store to produce a professional-quality portfolio.

Exercise. Use the following questions and suggestions to evaluate whether to use an electronic portfolio and, if so, how to start it:

> ➤ Where do you store your schoolwork now? Is it organized? Does its organization help you reflect on your professional development?
> ➤ On your flash drive, computer hard drive, or other electronic storage device, create the set of folders described above for your professional-development portfolio.
> ➤ Begin saving and sorting all of your work into your professional-development portfolio.

Daniel Ufford, J.D. 2010

"During law school, I participated in a career and professional-development course that helped me create a portfolio of my law school work and experience. The coursework, including working on a portfolio throughout law school, helped me discern my preferred career. It also helped prepare me for a job search and interview. I passed the bar on the first try and received and accepted a job offer at a law firm in my desired location, I feel in large part because of that coursework and my portfolio."

Memberships—*Joining*

Membership in student organizations and bar associations can also help you connect the knowledge dimension of the curriculum to your career goals. Law schools support student organizations with funding, office space, professional contacts, staff support, and facility use. **Forming or joining a student organization can promote your career and professional development** in a variety of ways including:

- helping you meet and work with school administrators, faculty, and staff, giving you guides and mentors within the school;
- helping you meet and develop networks with practitioners outside the school, within fields interesting to you;
- helping you develop peer relationships that maintain and increase your academic, social, and emotional support;
- increasing your participation in speaker, mentor, panel, training, service, and other professional-development events;
- providing you with leadership, teamwork, and other organizational opportunities interacting with peers; and
- increasing your knowledge of specific legal fields and law-practice disciplines.

There are several types of student organization, each serving somewhat different combinations of the above several professional-development activities. Students form and participate in organizations around **subject-matter fields**, linking specific required and elective courses or concentrations with the practice discipline. If you become a leader of one of these groups, then the organization's members may ask you to identify and invite practitioners in the field to speak at organization events, **giving you professional contacts within your desired field**. In general, judges and practitioners like to speak to groups of law students. When as a student leader you give a professional that opportunity, you stand in special relationship to that professional. Student members of your organization attending speaking events learn about the field from those practitioners, including whether the students want to pursue a career in that field. Among many others, these organizations can include:

- Sports Law Society;

- Entertainment Law Society;
- Intellectual Property Law Society;
- Tax Law Society;
- Constitutional Law Society;
- International Law Society;
- Immigration Law Society; and
- Animal Law Society.

Students also form organizations around ethnic, religious, cultural, and affinity groups. These groups can provide you with **peer support, leadership and teamwork opportunities** within the school **and professional networks** outside of it. If you lead an affinity group, then its members may call on you to identify and invite prominent practitioners sharing that affinity to speak at the school, giving you access to prominent mentors. Professionals network through affinity groups. Identifying yourself with a student affinity organization can help connect you with the larger formal or informal professional affinity group outside of school. These organizations can include:

- Black Law Students Association;
- Hispanic-Latino Law Society;
- Asian-American Law Society;
- Christian Law Student Association;
- Muslim Law Student Association;
- Jewish Law Student Association;
- Caribbean Law Society; and
- Gay, Lesbian, Bisexual, and Transsexual Law Society.

Students also form organizations around professional, public-education, political, public-interest, civil-rights, and service commitments. **Judges and practitioners share these commitments**. Your membership in these organizations can connect you with the larger professional organizations outside the school through which judges and lawyers network. They can also provide substantial learning opportunities. These organizations can include:

- Federal Bar Association Student Chapter;
- Federalist Society;
- Military Servicemembers and Veterans Group;
- Republicans Society;

- Democrats Society;
- American Civil Liberties Union Student Chapter; and
- Disaster Relief Legal Association.

Membership in bar associations and other professional organizations can also help you connect the knowledge dimension of the curriculum to your career goals. As a law student, you may join national, state, and local bars, usually at reduced cost and sometimes for free. Those bars have magazines, newsletters, e-journals, and other current resources for law-practice information, and hold educational events. They also have sections for specific areas of practice like negligence law, intellectual-property law, real-estate law, family law, and many other fields of practice. Even as a student, you can join those sections to receive their journals and notices, and attend their educational events. Law-practice fields can change quickly. **Practitioners use bars and sections to stay current on practice developments.** Employers with whom you interview are interested in your currency. At bar and section events, you may learn the current law, language, practices, and issues that tell your prospective employers that you know the field. It also shows your interest in your own professional development.

Membership can also make a difference in finding employment opportunities. **Bars and sections post job openings and offer networking events.** Membership introduces you to a network of professionals who know where the opportunities are. Membership in bars and sections, and attendance at bar and section events, gives you standing within that network. **Attend bar and section meetings and events.** Introduce yourself and give your business card to practitioners at those meetings and events. Ask them how their practice is going, and listen to their answers. Lawyers attending professional gatherings will often speak much more openly and reflectively about the challenges and successes of their law practice than in proceedings in which they represent a client. List your memberships on your resume as an indication of your interest in the field and your recognition that professional fellowship improves your skill.

"Getting involved in state and local bar associations may appear a little daunting and intimidating at first, but most associations are very interested in attracting student members who may join their organizations as lawyers after admission to the bar. These organizations are wonderful networking opportunities for students to begin to get to know lawyers and judges in their area. Many of these organizations are developing pro-bono opportunities for their members and often involve interested students in these programs, providing volunteer opportunities that contribute to our ethical obligation to serve those who cannot afford legal services, while providing another great networking opportunity. These contacts can lead to internships, externships, references for employment applications, and employment, and are well worth the effort required to develop them."

Dean John Nussbaumer

At the national level, the American Bar Association is the largest professional organization of lawyers. It has a student section with abundant resources and also has multiple practice-area sections many of which are open to student members. There are also national affinity bars such as the National Bar Association founded by and primarily for African-American lawyers and those interested in increasing their professional opportunities. Student membership in the National Bar Association can introduce one to a network of mentors and models among minority lawyers. The state bar and local bars in larger metropolitan areas are also likely to have law-student divisions and multiple sections organized around practice areas. **Consider joining these bars and the sections in your field of interest.**

The American Inns of Court deserves special mention. The Inns of Court is a national organization with local chapters. Its purpose is to maintain and improve professionalism. Local Inns chapters hold meetings throughout the year at which local judges and lawyers make presentations on issues related to professionalism. The meetings often involve an elegant luncheon or dinner where judges and lawyers have an opportunity to network around the educational program. **Inns meetings tend to attract the acknowledged leaders of the local legal community.** You may not learn as much at an Inns meeting about your specific field of law as you would if you attended a section event. Yet you will meet judges and lawyers who lead and influence the local bar, learn about the professional norms they follow, and become a part of their professional network. Consider joining the nearest Inns of Court chapter.

Exercise. Use the following questions to help you evaluate whether to join, create, or lead a student organization or to join a bar association and, if so, which one or ones:

> ➢ Locate and review the list of student organizations at your law school. What subject fields do the organizations represent? Which of those subject fields most interests you? Identify one of that organization's student members, and contact and interview that student about the organization's activities and value.

> ➢ To which affinity groups did you belong before entering law school? To which affinity groups do your favorite professors belong? To which affinity groups do the judges and lawyers with whom you want to work belong? Which group would you consider joining in law school? Who are its members? Who is its faculty advisor?

> ➢ Which of your school's student organizations represents a cause, perspective, or service commitment that you share? Identify one of that organization's student members, and contact and interview that student about the organization's activities and value.

> ➢ What student organization do you feel your school should have but does not have? Contact the school administrator who is responsible for assisting students in forming new student organizations. Interview that administrator about the steps and time commitment for forming a new organization. Do you know other students who would join your organization?

> ➢ Go to the American Bar Association's law-student-division web page to investigate the cost and benefits of joining. Also, explore the web pages for the American Bar Association section for your field of interest.

> ➢ Check your local bar association to determine whether it offers student memberships, and if so, at what cost and offering what benefits. Does your local bar association have a section for your field of interest?

> **Michael Lichterman, J.D. 2009**
> "As graduation neared, I decided to focus my law practice on pursuing my passion—estate planning. I joined an esteemed nationwide estate-planning association to improve my knowledge of and connections within the field. It turned out to be one of the best moves that I could have made, increasing the quality and sophistication of the estate-planning products and services that I am able to offer in my new solo practice."

Informational Interviews—*Meeting*

As the above mention of networking suggests, informational interviews can help you connect the knowledge dimension of your legal education with your law career. Informational interviewing is a form of networking that helps you learn from practicing lawyers about career options while also developing job knowledge and leads. You can learn a lot about legal fields from written materials, but interaction with a lawyer who practices in the field can give you a clearer sense of its challenges and opportunities. Lawyers treat law students as fellow professionals. They know that they share responsibility for your professional development. They also like to talk about what they do. **To arrange and manage an informational interview:**

- identify a local practitioner in the field of your interest. Your faculty advisor and school's career staff can help. You can also use your school's alumni database and local bar and public listings for lawyers;
- contact the practitioner making it clear that you are not asking for a job but to meet briefly for information about the practitioner's legal field;
- arrange to meet the practitioner at the practitioner's office where you can get a sense of what the work environment is like and may be able to meet the staff and other lawyers;
- wear business attire for the informational interview and conduct yourself at all times as if the practitioner was evaluating you for employment;
- although you are asking the practitioner for information about the legal field, also talk about your work experience, law school success, and career interest;

- when the brief time that the practitioner has offered you ends, offer to leave whether or not you and the practitioner have completed the interview;
- ask if there are other individuals, firms, associations, or organizations to whom the practitioner can refer you for similar informational interview, other resources, contacts, or information, and, especially, potential job opportunities and interviews; and
- send a thank-you letter immediately after the interview.

The heart of the informational interview is the list of written questions that you bring to the interview and ask of the lawyer. Be sure to ask your questions. Remember that in an informational interview, you are interviewing the lawyer, not the other way around. Informational interviews give you a chance to experience some of the formality and conditions of a job interview but without the pressure to perform. You, not the lawyer, are in control. The lawyer answers your questions. Take written notes of the lawyer's answers if the circumstances of the interview permit it. **Ask the practitioner to tell you about:**

- the practitioner's specific job, including typical responsibilities, hours, day, legal issues, clients, work products, supervision, and most and least satisfying work;
- the law firm or other organization for which the practitioner works including the practitioner's role in it, the organization's challenges, the institutional culture (formal or informal), and the organization's history, future, and mission;
- the organization's clients including their legal needs, service and communication expectations, relationship with the organization including its duration and fee terms, and obstacles or limitations;
- the practice field including the practitioner's path into it, its rewards and challenges, the strengths and talents that it rewards, the practitioner's likes and dislikes, current issues and trends, and the job market; and
- the practitioner's specific advice for you in entering the field including how to prepare in law school, what associations to join, and who to contact for job leads at an appropriate time.

As soon as you have completed the interview and written the lawyer a brief thank-you letter, record in an electronic file marked Informational Interviews the three things that the lawyer said or that you observed during the interview that made the greatest impression on you. **Record and investigate any job leads that the lawyer gave you.** Also, record your impressions about how meaningful and desirable the lawyer's work looked and sounded. Record any impression you drew about the lawyer's work life, mental health, and balance, and the law firm atmosphere and culture. Think deliberately about whether you would like to engage in the same kind of work within that legal field under similar conditions or, if not, then what you would want to change to find more meaningful work. Then, send an email or make a telephone call to the lawyer with whom you interviewed every month or two to maintain the contact and learn of any new job opportunities the lawyer may be able to share with you.

Exercise. Use the following suggestions to help you use informational interviews for your career and professional development:

➤ Set an objective for yourself of conducting at least four informational interviews over the course of the next term of law school. Interview practitioners in at least two different fields.

Erin McAleer, J.D. 2009

"I wanted an externship to equip me for solo practice in my hometown across the country from my law school. So, I researched, identified, and interviewed two solo practitioners in the area, choosing the one with the stronger practice and reputation, even though he told me that he would not offer me a job at the end of my externship. It worked perfectly. Near the end of my externship, he offered me a job at nearly double the salary that I expected, but I still ended up in solo practice and am loving it."

Career Transitions

Identifying and developing your knowledge base while using tools to capture and reflect it are important steps in your career and professional development. Yet you must then use those tools to connect your knowledge base with specific career opportunities. For example, one way that you connect your knowledge base to careers is to identify the specific bar of which you plan to be a member. Another way is to identify the type of firm of which you should be a member and the legal field in which you prefer to practice. You may also find a judicial externship or clerkship beneficial as a way to observe a wider variety of practitioners and survey a variety of fields. You might also want to know something of the economics of practice within various fields. This chapter helps you begin to reflect on and identify your preferred bar, firm, and field. As we go through them one by one, **keep these connections in mind:**

- the bar of which you should be a member;
- your preferred type of law firm;
- the legal field in which you might prefer to practice;
- whether a judicial externship or clerkship would aid your transition; and
- how the economics of law practice may influence your career choice.

State Bars—*Licensing*

One of the first career connections that you must navigate is **choosing the bar from which you will seek a license.** Because state law requires a license to practice law, and state bars (rather than any national organization) grant those licenses, before practicing law you must determine from which state to seek a license. Your bar license depends on where you will practice, just as where you are allowed to practice depends on your bar license. Because individual state bars license lawyers, the law practices of individual lawyers tend to remain within the state in which they are licensed. A case that a lawyer files in the state in which the lawyer is licensed may require travel for meetings and depositions all over the country. Conduct rules tend to permit those activities without licensure within those other states. Conduct rules may also permit a lawyer to file and try a single case in another jurisdiction with court permission when associating with licensed local counsel. Many lawyers also hold licenses in more than one state, particularly when their practices are located in metropolitan areas that cross state borders. Yet on the whole, lawyers conduct their practice in the single state in which they are licensed.

In short, **licensure makes the state in which you intend to practice an important consideration.** The state where you have a job to practice law after graduation is obviously a state from which to seek a law license. Some students know from the moment that they enter law school the state in which they will practice. They may have no plans to practice in any state other than the state of their current residence or may have a job waiting for them in another state. Other students gradually discern the state in which they intend to practice as they gather information and make career and personal decisions, and as job opportunities arise. Still others graduate with two or more opportunities in different states and no clear direction as to where to seek licensure.

You may wonder how to go about choosing a state from which to seek a license if you do not yet have a job offer from a specific employer. The challenge of choosing a state bar from which to seek a license is especially great if you must register with that state bar when you enter law school or at another point well in advance of graduation, when your career plans and job prospects would be clearer. The decision is made only a little easier in that some state bars offer reciprocity where, if you have passed another state's bar and perhaps also practiced for a certain period, then you may qualify for licensure without repeating the bar examination. If you do not have a specific job offer already in place when it comes time to seek a license, then **consider seeking a law license from the state where:**

- you attend law school;
- you most anticipate that a job offer will arise;
- your professional network is strongest;
- economic indicators are most favorable;
- your practice-area interests are most prevalent;
- reciprocity works in your favor for joining more than one bar;
- your closest family members reside;
- your social network exists;
- you most prefer to live; and
- your affinity for the bar is the greatest.

As to the last point above, it may help you to keep in mind when selecting a state bar that each bar can have its own history, culture, and dominant practice. **Bars differ in their professional culture.** Because of their large size and more transient membership, some bars are more anonymous and impersonal. You may like that openness, in which you get to prove yourself again in each new professional encounter. Smaller bars may be more closed (tight-knit), giving greater emphasis to personal history and professional reputation. You may prefer the relational and inter-dependent nature of practice in those bars. **Bars can also differ in their practice areas.** Bars in rural states may support law practices in mining, agriculture, environmental law, game regulation, water rights, and land use. Bars in urban states may support practices in banking, securities, media, sports, and entertainment. Use your studies and interaction with professionals to discern those differences and determine your preference.

While you select a bar from which to seek a license, recognize that **licensure takes time and effort.** All bars require some form of examination plus character-and-fitness review. Common steps associated with licensure, each addressed in greater detail below, can include:

- research into the requirements of the particular state bar from which you intend to seek licensure;
- registration with the state bar when you enter law school or during your time in law school;
- formal application to the bar including providing exhaustive information demonstrating character and fitness;
- completion of a commercial bar-review course over a period of weeks or months leading up to examination;
- taking and passing the multiple-choice format Multistate Professional Responsibility Exam (MPRE) drafted and administered by the National Conference of Bar Examiners;
- taking and passing the multiple-choice format Multistate Bar Exam (MBE) also drafted and administered by the National Conference of Bar Examiners;
- taking and passing essay testing focused on the state's specific laws;
- completing and passing a performance exam involving legal drafting;
- waiting a period of weeks or months for bar-examination results; and
- a formal ceremony taking the attorney's oath of office before a judge.

As just indicated, **some state bars require that you register** with them before completing your law degree and applying to take the bar exam. In those states, you first register and then later apply to take the bar exam, updating the information you submitted with your early registration. Registration helps state bars predict and plan for the number of applicants for the bar exam and also to begin the investigation process. **State bars**, or in some cases the National Conference of Bar Examiners on behalf of state bars, **investigate registrants' character and fitness.** Some state bars require that you register with them while in your first term of law school. Several state bars that require registration also require that you pay a much higher fee if you register later. Other state bars permit you to register but do not require that you do so.

Research your state bar as soon as you enter law school to see if it requires registration. You can find out from the state bar itself or from registration information compiled by the National Conference of Bar Examiners in its *Comprehensive Guide to Bar Admission Requirements.* If you do not know your state bar yet, then research your two or three most probable state bars including the bar of the state in which your law school is located. You may wish to register early at a low fee even if you are unsure of your final destination. Consult with your school's career coordinator if you have questions about registration. Do not rely on word from others for your state bar's registration requirements. State bars change their registration requirements from time to time, making unreliable the experience of others. **Nearly all state bars require that you pass the Multistate Professional Responsibility Exam** (MPRE) in addition to the state bar examination. Find more information about the Multistate Professional Responsibility Exam in the Ethics section of this book.

Then there is the bar exam. **Nearly all states require that you pass the Multistate Bar Examination.** The Multistate Bar Examination is a 200-multiple-choice-question, 6-hour examination. The National Conference of Bar Examiners develops the Multistate Bar Examination. State bars requiring the Multistate Bar Examination administer it twice each year on one day in late February and one day in late July, in 100-question, 3-hour morning and afternoon blocks. Unlike the Multistate Professional Responsibility Exam for which you register with the National Conference of Bar Examiners, you register for the Multistate Bar Examination by registering and applying for your state bar. The Multistate Bar Examination covers Constitutional Law, Contracts, Criminal Law and Procedure, Evidence, Real Property, and Torts, with about an equal number of questions in each of those six subjects. The National Conference of Bar Examiners offers online subject-matter outlines for each of those six subjects. It also offers study aids and information guides for the exam.

> "Deciding which state bar from which to seek licensure involves foresight, strategy, and a little sense of adventure. The first thing that you should do, particularly if you are not sure where life and career will eventually take you, is compare and contrast the state bars that interest you most. If you are looking at two states, determine which state has the best reciprocity policy. For example, if you are deciding between Michigan and North Carolina, you may want to think about the North Carolina bar as a first option because Michigan accepts MBE scores from other jurisdictions, but North Carolina does not. BarBri has an excellent digest that summarizes state bar requirements. Other commercial bar preparation courses should as well. Above all, keep in mind that you will have a long career and that you do not have to decide right now where you will be forever more. Just make the best decision that you can with the information that you have before you."
>
> ***Assistant Dean Tracey Brame***

Many state bars require that you pass state-specific essay questions in addition to the Multistate Bar Examination. Because the Multistate Bar Examination tests fundamental legal principles general to all states, some state bars use an added essay portion of their exams to test legal rules specific to the state. In those states that administer an essay portion of the bar examination, you must adjust your bar-exam preparation to study the state's specific rules, which may be different from general rules tested on the Multistate Bar Examination and taught in your law school. You should take a commercial bar-preparation course offered for that state to help you learn those state-specific rules. State bars that require that you pass state-specific essay questions usually administer that portion of the bar examination with the Multistate Bar Examination, making bar examination a two-day affair. **Research whether your state bar requires that you pass state-specific essay questions. If so, then research, register, and budget for a commercial bar-preparation course for that state.**

Many state bars require that you pass the Multistate Performance Test (MPT). The National Conference of Bar Examiners develops the Multistate Performance Test, which state bars then administer in conjunction with the Multistate Bar Examination and any state-specific essay questions. The Multistate Performance Test involves two 90-minute skills tests requiring you to review a collection of practice materials such as cases, statutes, pleadings, other court papers, memoranda, and reports, and to prepare a pleading, motion, brief, or other court paper, legal memorandum, or other common attorney work product. The National Conference of Bar Examiners offers online study aids, information guides, and descriptions of past performance tests.

No matter what your state's bar-examination scope and format, **plan and budget to take a commercial bar-preparation course.** A commercial bar-preparation course is a course offered by a private, for-profit company over the last few weeks or months before your bar examination. Instruction typically involves a combination of paperback and online outlines of bar-tested subjects, fitted to the state of your bar examination, together with classroom or video lectures, online exercises, and practice tests. Courses can cost from several hundred to several thousand dollars, with some companies offering steep discounts for early registration. A single, national company may offer many different courses each modified for a different state. Financial aid may be available to help you pay the cost of the course.

Bar examination is different from law school examination. Law school teaches you fundamental legal knowledge, skills, and ethics, and prepares you to practice law. It may not teach you the specific laws and rules of the state from which you will seek a law license. Also, you will have learned some of those laws and rules as much as three years or more before your graduation, meaning that you may need refresher studies. You learned those subjects in individual courses with individual examinations, while the bar examination will mix all subjects in a single examination. Your state's bar examination may also test subjects that you did not study in law school. Commercial bar-preparation courses help you learn or recall all bar-tested subjects. They can also help prepare you for the mixed subjects and particular format of your state's bar examination. **Consider these factors when choosing a commercial bar-preparation company:**

- cost including available discounts and payment schedules;
- quality of materials, online resources, and instruction;
- fit of materials to your specific state's laws and rules;
- fit of materials to your specific state's bar-tested subjects;
- flexibility of course and class offerings to meet your availability;
- frequency and quality of practice tests and assessment;
- individual feedback on practice tests and assessments; and
- success of course reflected in bar-passage rates.

When it comes to actually preparing for the bar examination, **budget and plan to take time off to study for the bar examination.** You may need to work for financial reasons. Some work, especially early in your bar preparation, may actually help you stay disciplined and structured in your studies. Yet in the last few days and weeks before the bar examination, stop working and devote your full time to bar studies if at all possible. If you have extra time, then rest and recuperate so that you have more energy for final preparations. The little that you might gain financially by working right up to the bar examination you can quickly lose if you fail the bar examination and have to wait an additional six months before taking the examination again. Help your family and friends appreciate the challenge you face and the time you need alone to study. Above all, **appreciate the singular quality of bar studies.** There may be no other time in your life when you so readily justify devoting all of your energies to such a worthwhile intellectual endeavor.

The exercise below shows in summary how you best plan and prepare for bar examination before you graduate from law school. **Research bar-exam requirements, scope, and format** for the state in which you plan to take the bar. Find that information online from the state bar itself. Check online with commercial bar-exam-preparation companies for additional helpful information. **Do not rely on word from others for your state bar's examination requirements.** State bars change their bar-examination requirements, scope, and format from time to time, making unreliable the experience of others. Save the information that you discover so that you can review and use it later.

Keep the bar exam in perspective. All professions have licensing examinations of some kind. That your law school admitted you into law school and you remain in good academic standing are reliable indications that you can pass the bar exam. **Most state bars pass 70% to 80% of first-time takers,** giving you a substantial opportunity to pass on the first try. Reasonable planning and preparation are keys. Devotion to your law school studies is another important measure. Law school grade-point averages tend to correlate with bar-passage rates, meaning that the better are your grades, the better is the probability that you will pass the bar exam. When you start to stress over the bar exam, remember that those who fail are more likely those who did not adequately prepare over either the short or long term, or perhaps having had something interfere. Persistence pass rates tend to be significantly higher than first-time pass rates. Ultimately, your probability of passing the bar may be well over 90%. If you do not pass on the first try, then there remains a reasonable prospect of passing on a second or subsequent try. Yet plan for success, not failure. Be satisfied that you gave it your all on the first try.

Exercise. Learn and store in a single electronic file the answers to the following questions, so that you can follow a sound plan to obtain your bar license:

> ➤ When are the earliest and latest dates that you may apply for your state's bar examination?
> ➤ Does your state bar require that you pass the Multistate Professional Responsibility Exam (MPRE)? If so, then:
>> ➤ What score does your state bar require?
>> ➤ When must you take the exam relative to your bar licensure?
> ➤ Does your state bar require that you pass the Multistate Bar Examination (MBE)? If so, then:
>> ➤ May you pass your state's bar examination based on your Multistate Bar Examination score alone?
> ➤ Does your state's bar examination require that you pass a state-specific essay portion of the exam? If so, then:
>> ➤ What state-specific subjects do the essay questions cover?
> ➤ Does your state bar require that you pass the Multistate Performance Test (MPT)?
> ➤ What percentage weight does your state bar assign to each portion (e.g., MBE, state-specific essays, and MPT) of its bar exam?
> ➤ What bar-review courses does your school offer?

- ➤ What commercial bar-review companies offer state-specific studies for your state bar's examination?
  - ➤ What is the cost of those commercial bar-review courses?
  - ➤ Does early registration save on those costs?
  - ➤ Will financial aid help you pay those costs?
- ➤ Budget and plan to take time off from work for your final bar studies.

Law Firms and Clerkships—*Practicing*

Another career transition for you to navigate is to **learn about, evaluate, and prepare for law practice within a law firm.** The great majority of lawyers work in law firms. The law firms in which lawyers work vary widely from solo practices and small firms of a few lawyers, where the majority of lawyers work, to vast international firms with hundreds of lawyers in worldwide offices. Many other lawyers work for government including for administrative agencies and legislative bodies, as judges, referees, and court staff, and in prosecutor's and public defender offices. Other lawyers work in corporate counsel offices, while others work in academia, the nonprofit sector, and law-related or non-law jobs. Study of lawyer happiness suggests that lawyers are on the whole more satisfied working in the public sector, small firms, or solo practice than in large firms, *see* Nancy Levit & Douglas O. Linder, The Happy Lawyer: Making a Good Life in the Law 9 (Oxford Univ. Press 2010), but each setting has its own attraction. Lawyers who do not work in law firms often retain, monitor the work of, and interact professionally with lawyers in law firms. Whether or not you plan to work in a law firm after graduation, it makes sense while you are in law school to **gain a clear understanding of how law firms work, as part of your career and professional development.**

You should first know how law firms organize and why they organize as they do. Law firms are the dominant legal-service providers in part because of ethics rules prohibiting lawyers from providing legal services to the public through organizations controlled by non-lawyers, and discouraging lawyers from mixing legal services with investment advice or other professional services. Lawyers must provide independent advice. If accountants, investment brokers, or other non-lawyer professionals employed and supervised lawyers to provide legal services to the public, then the interests of those employers might influence the advice of those lawyers. If it were not for those ethics rules, then lawyers might provide legal services to the public through large organizations that offered a mix of legal, financial, investment, and insurance services. Law firms employ legal assistants, secretaries, bookkeepers, messengers, and other non-lawyers. Yet **the professionals who own and control law firms are all lawyers.** Law firms organize as partnerships or other corporate entities like limited partnerships, professional corporations, or professional limited liability companies that have the characteristics of partnerships, in which all partners, shareholders, or members are lawyers.

The fact that you and other lawyers will control, supervise, and manage your work within a law firm has important consequences to your career and professional development. Lawyers think of themselves as professionals, regulate one another as professionals, and treat one another as professionals. Although business models are important to the economic survival of law firms and have their own effect on lawyers' careers, professional norms like respect for authority, respect for one's fellow professionals, honesty and integrity in all matters, loyalty, trust, confidentiality, and competence imbue law firm culture. **Your attention to professional norms within a law firm can be equally or more important than your attention to economics.** Law firms are fundamentally conservative more so than competitive institutions, meaning that adherence to rules of professional conduct and to professional norms comes first. That adherence makes law firms special places to work.

> "Have realistic expectations when you graduate from law school. A law degree was never designed to be a ticket to the life style of the rich and famous. You still have to pay your dues. You may find yourself working 80 hour weeks for a large firm or struggling for clients when you hang out your own shingle. But decide what you want to do and give it complete effort. Success is built over time."
>
> *Former State Court Judge Jeff Martlew*

Know how law firms analyze and maintain profits. Employers appreciate employees who know and respect the employer's finances. Law firms tend to pay attention to several factors including rates, utilization, leverage, expenses, and speed. A lawyer's hourly billing rate, whether high, low, or in between, matters to profits. The greater the demand for a lawyer's services and the higher the hourly rate, the greater the profit. Utilization typically involves the number of hours a lawyer bills. A lawyer with a high hourly rate but fewer billable hours may not generate as much revenue for the firm as a lawyer with a lower rate but more billable hours. Leverage involves the amount of work that a partner generates for associates of the firm to complete and bill. A partner who bills relatively fewer hours but generates lots of billable hours for associates can generate more revenue for the firm than a partner who bills lots of hours but generates little work for associates. Expenses are what the firm must spend to support the lawyers' billing. The lower the expenses, such as rent and non-billing staff, the more firm profit. Speed involves how quickly the billings result in realized revenue. Some clients pay more quickly and completely than others. *See* Michael Downey, Introduction to Law Firm Practice 107-120 (ABA Law Practice Management Section 2010). **Keeping these basics in mind can help you understand how law firms evaluate legal talent.**

You should also know how law firms employ and compensate their lawyers. Many law firms employ lawyers in a two-tier hierarchy of partners and associates. Partners own and control the firm, paying its debts and dividing up its profits. With risk comes reward. Partners tend to share liabilities such as for office rent, a line of credit for expenses, or malpractice, while also sharing in windfall profits from unexpectedly large fees. Partners also choose, develop, and maintain the client relationships. By contrast, associates have little risk and so have fixed reward, and often select, develop, and control few or no client relationships. Associates work as employees of the firm, earning fixed salary and benefits with the possibility of an annual bonus for especially effective individual work or for the general success of the firm. **Associates do the work assigned to them by partners.** Partners pay associates at rates that allow the partners to pay the firm's expenses and earn profits for the partners. Partners compensate themselves with draws that provide them with higher compensation than associates.

Although law firms sometimes hire new associates off partnership track, **law firms are generally interested in hiring associates whom they believe will make partner.** You should know the criteria on which law firms promote associates to partner. Law-firm economics affect whether an associate will progress to partner. Law firms typically have an expected partnership track that may range from five to eight years of service as an associate before the partners determine whether to promote the associate to partner. Completing the associate track does not guarantee promotion to partner. Law firms do not make partners of associates simply based on years of service. **Partnership tends to depend most on two factors: (1) your relationships with the partners and (2) your ability to develop and maintain your own client base,** a practice lawyers within firms call *rainmaking*. When partners interview you for employment as an associate, they are evaluating whether you can develop and maintain strong relationships with them, meaning primarily whether you can do quality and timely work on their assignments.

> "When I was a new associate, I would walk into the office of my most frequent work-provider with questions, and he would smile at me, address my questions, and smile at me again as I left his office. When I came to know him better, I realized that this smile meant he was entertaining the notion of ripping my head off. Later in my career, I remember a new associate who made a habit of coming into my office to ask procedural questions. Annoyed, I would smile at him, and make a big show of pulling the rulebook off my credenza, looking up the controlling rule, and having him read out loud the answer to his question. I smiled at him as he left, confident that I had taught him to look at the rulebook. I had not. He always returned with another question he should have answered for himself."
>
> ***Professor Christopher Hastings***

Partners are also evaluating whether you can bring new clients to the firm, preserving and enlarging its income. There are exceptions. Some firms have longstanding institutional clients such as insurers, municipalities, or utilities, where an associate's value has nothing to do with bringing in new clients and everything to do with quality work for trusting partners. Yet in most firms, **associates should expect to attend to their business development.** Business development or rainmaking among lawyers varies widely. Keeping and updating contact lists helps. So does making deliberate lunch and coffee plans with your network. Community and bar involvement can help greatly, as can publications in trade journals and organizing conferences and workshops. Know some of the practices recommended in DOWNEY, *supra*, at 194-196, for when you interview with firms that have business-development expectations for their associates:

- do quality and affordable work, always good marketing;
- develop a specialty in which you are a recognized expert;
- treat everyone as a potential referrer of new business;
- plan business-development opportunities;
- work on business development at all times, not sporadically;
- communicate with clients frequently; and
- be patient even while you persist in these good practices.

Given these interests, probably the most important skill a new associate must acquire is the ability to get frequent quality work assignments from influential partners. **Working as a law-firm associate can be exciting and meaningful work,** giving you an immediate opportunity to do work that you would not have had the opportunity to do on your own right out of law school. You can quickly acquire significant responsibility doing high-level work on large and important matters, although partners will supervise and (in many instances) receive credit for your work. You also get to work immediately for clients with whom the firm has a longstanding relationship and whom you would not get to serve on your own in a solo practice. Because you need strong relationships and (eventually) your own client base to do the best within your law firm, you need to learn relevant law-practice skills in law school.

You also need to develop relationships within the law firm to get quality assignments and develop a reputation outside in the community to attract new clients. Law firms employ associates on an at-will basis. If it looks to the partners like an associate is not progressing, then the firm may terminate the associate's employment at any time, even a year or two into the employment. If an associate does not make partner within the firm's established time period, then the law firm is likely to terminate the associate's employment, meaning that the associate must start a solo practice or find employment with another law firm. **Law firms are constantly recruiting new talent and evaluating current associates toward partnership.**

Keep these partnership considerations in mind when evaluating and interviewing with a law firm. Also, appreciate that partnership arrangements vary among firms. Some larger firms have two or more partnership levels. Some firms require new partners to buy into the partnership. Some firms accept lateral partners from other firms. Partners and associates within one firm sometimes leave together to start a new firm. No matter the variation, though, appreciate that a lawyer's employment and advancement within a firm tends to depend on the lawyer's ability to attract clients and serve them in a manner that retains their loyalty, leading to referrals and additional future service. **When a lawyer interviews you for a job within the firm, the lawyer may well be thinking:**

- "Is this candidate someone with whom I can work well?"
- "Can I expect this candidate to do timely and quality work?"
- "Will this candidate get along with the firm's lawyers?"
- "Will this candidate get along with the firm's staff?"
- "Will this candidate get along with the firm's clients?"
- "Will this candidate soon bring new clients to the firm?"

Before you graduate from law school, consider pursuing the opportunity to experience some of what it is like to be a law-firm associate. **Many law firms hire law students as law clerks,** either part time during the school year or full time in the summer. **A law clerk is not a secretarial, staff, or administrative position.** A law clerk is a law student whom the law firm treats in several respects like an associate. A law clerk must not practice law, meaning that the law clerk must not give clients advice or make court appearances. Yet a law clerk will perform many other tasks usually performed by lawyers, such as legal research, drafting legal memoranda, drafting pleadings and court papers, preparing legal forms, and reviewing and summarizing depositions, documents, reports, and files. **Law firms bill clients for a law clerk's work,** meaning that law clerks record their time and work, and contribute to the law firm's income, in exchange for fixed compensation.

Some firms, particularly the larger ones, have formal summer-associate programs for law clerks, which they use to evaluate and recruit law students for permanent employment after law school. Students participating in those programs work full time for the firm throughout the summer with other summer associates, while the firm decides whom to invite back for a second summer if it is a first-summer program or whom to offer a job after graduation. There are fewer summer-associate positions for students after their first year than for students after their second year. Second-going-on-third-year students have more knowledge and skill, and thus greater value to the firm. They are also more likely to return for permanent employment the following summer after graduation. Students who find a summer-associate position after their first year may try a different firm after their second year. Summer-associate programs often involve more than supervised work, mixing in training sessions and social outings both to impress and to evaluate the students. **Everything is a test. Conduct yourself accordingly.** Do not enjoy the social outings so much that you forget that the firm is evaluating you.

Your law school may have rounds of interviews on campus for summer-associate positions. Investigate and participate in on-campus interviewing for summer-associate positions. Doing so can be a relatively low-cost and –risk way of educating yourself to the employment market while gaining experience at interviews. **Firms compete for talented students, interviewing on campus and making summer-associate offers earlier than you might expect in the school year.** Students also compete for summer-associate programs at premier firms. Depending on the economy, the firm, and the performance of the summer-associate class, firms may make offers of permanent employment to most of their summer associates. The economy affects summer-associate programs, which can be one of the first places law firms will cut back in slow times. Summer associates are not always the most productive of workers. Productive work involves a learning curve. Do not fret if you find few on-campus-interview opportunities for summer-associate positions. Many law students find their own summer-associate opportunities the old-fashioned way, by reviewing law-firm listings, submitting cover letters and resumes, networking, and interviewing off campus.

Other firms use law clerks year round without significant expectation of permanent employment. Either opportunity, premier summer associate or routine law clerk, can be worthwhile. Firms without summer-associate programs, usually smaller firms, may hire law clerks at any time during the summer or school year, whenever they lose another law clerk or have excess work. A law clerk may work 10, 15, or 20 hours a week during the school year and full time on breaks and over the summer, substantially increasing income and reducing borrowing. Law clerks can also gain substantial law-practice experience, making relevant their classroom studies while helping to integrate those studies into a professional identity in what amounts to an old-fashioned apprenticeship of much the type that existed before law schools. **There may be no more effective and sensible preparation for law practice than to work year round as a law clerk while completing law school.** It is no longer law school. In many firms, you can expect your first and every work as a law clerk to have an immediate impact on client matters, even though partners supervise clerks to ensure the reliability of their work. Well-educated and -trained law clerks can do much of the work of a lawyer including:

- reviewing and analyzing agreements;
- assembling and drafting wills and other documents;
- researching and writing memoranda;
- reviewing and analyzing case files;
- reviewing and summarizing depositions;
- drafting pleadings;
- drafting trial-court motions, responses, and briefs;
- drafting appellate motions and briefs;
- drafting deposition questions;
- accompanying partners to depositions;
- accompanying partners to court hearings;
- creating trial notebooks and folders;
- preparing and organizing trial exhibits;
- participating in mock trials;
- assisting partners with documents at trial;
- creating manuals, checklists, and templates; and
- improving other office systems.

Many law firms also accept law students as volunteer interns or for-academic-credit externs. Your law school may have a program to place volunteer (unpaid) interns in law firms, part-time for one term or an even shorter time period. To comply with federal wage laws, unpaid interns must not do work that replaces the work of compensated employees. They must serve on projects that contribute to their education rather than do routine, non-educational work that is a regular part of the work of the firm's compensated staff. **Law schools also have externship programs that place law students in law firms full or part time for an academic term for credit.** Externship programs provide students with ongoing academic supervision in evening classes or through electronic communications, while a lawyer within the firm supervises the extern's daily work at the law-firm site.

If the state's practice rules permit it, then the extern may be able to act as a lawyer, including making court appearances.

Working as a law clerk, interning as a volunteer, and externing for academic credit are all highly valuable experiences. They give practice context to your academic studies. They also give you practical experience helping to build your practice skills and introduce you to mentors and models within the law firm. They also give you the opportunity to prove your worth to specific law-firm employers. Your work as a law clerk or intern or extern in a law firm may convince the law firm to make you a job offer. Even if it does not, then lawyers within the firm may write you recommendation letters, act as references, and give you job leads through their professional network. Lawyers recognize that law clerks are preparing for a career. They will treat you as a fellow professional while giving you opportunities to observe their work at trial and in depositions and client meetings, in a manner that they would not treat the firm's paid non-lawyer staff. Legal assistants may do some of the same work that you do as a law clerk, but the roles and expectations are distinctly different. You are preparing to be a lawyer. Lawyers within the firm will expect more of you and give you the opportunity to show it. Respect the opportunity.

Work as an associate within a law firm can be satisfying and rewarding. Yet **there are alternatives for law graduates for whom the partner/associate law firm model holds no attraction.** Nearly half of all lawyers work as solo practitioners or in very small law firms, without the formality of partner/associate arrangements. They do so for good reasons. Among those reasons is that solo practice preserves the full reward for one's efforts. Uniquely skilled lawyers may not wish to share the fruits of their gifts and labors with other lawyers. Some of the most gifted of lawyers operate as solo practitioners, even while working within an informal professional network on which they can draw for the support of other lawyers, often in co-counsel relationships on larger cases. Many lawyers in solo practice share office suites, staff, and expenses with other lawyers, without sharing clients or legal work. Office sharing can significantly reduce expenses. It can also increase referrals and the kind of informal office interaction with other lawyers that improves practice. Law students can prepare for solo or small-firm torts practices by taking courses like Law Office Management and taking academic credits in clinics set up like small firms. There can be benefits to working for yourself, especially when you have entrepreneurial skills, good sense, and strong work habits.

Some lawyers have no direct client contacts and do not work in law firms but instead work on a **contract basis with established law firms.** Those lawyers may work at home on flexible hours, often to be able to care for family members or engage in other service, business, or activities outside of law practice. Law firms benefit by having contract services available. It gives them the flexibility to expand and contract their labor base without having the cost and disruption of hiring and firing permanent associates. By contracting certain tasks, they can quickly complete unexpectedly large assignments that their partners and associates could not alone manage. Contract work does not involve substantial interaction with other lawyers. Contract lawyers often work alone on more mundane tasks like document review, although **contract assignments can involve challenging and creative work such as researching and writing appellate briefs.** Some lawyers prefer contract work to formal employment within a law firm.

Consider modifying your law school curriculum choices to better fit the type of law firm you prefer to join. If your career pathway is into solo practice, then modify your course selection to include Law Practice Management and to take clinical courses where you represent actual clients. If, on the other hand, you expect to work in a large law firm, then you may benefit by identifying the special knowledge that would best serve the law firm where you hope and expect to work. Larger firms tend to have practice groups focused around an area of law. Large firms may have practice groups in real estate, family law, mergers and acquisitions, bankruptcy, taxation, intellectual property, municipal law, civil litigation, criminal defense, and other practice areas. Your choice of electives, externships, and directed study in law school can equip you with the knowledge and skills base to work in one of these practice groups. Even in small firms, lawyers within the firm will specialize in practice niches requiring a focused knowledge base. While generalist lawyers with broad knowledge bases remain valuable to clients and firms, you may wish to consider focusing your knowledge base while in law school.

When evaluating firms, realize that each firm also has its own professional-development methods and culture. **Some firms offer substantial professional-development opportunities for their lawyers,** such as travel to law and business conferences, in-house training and seminars, continuing legal education materials, member-ship in professional and industry associations and social and net-working organizations, support for charitable and pro bono work, and formal mentor programs. Other firms do not, taking more of a sink-or-swim approach to the success of their lawyers. Law-practice expertise can take years to fully develop. Attending a local trial-skills program or a national conference accelerates professional development. Some firms encourage bar service and pro-bono service in ways that enhance the skills, reputation, and career satisfaction of their lawyers. Other firms do not. Training and various forms of legal and law-related service outside the firm can quickly enhance practice exper-tise, broadening one's professional contacts and resources, improving interpersonal skills, and expanding practice-area knowledge.

Ask lawyers how their firms manage their professional development. Look for opportunities with organizations that budget and plan to enhance your career and professional development. Keep in mind when evaluating law firms for employment opportunities that law-firm culture differs in other ways beyond professional develop-ment. Small firms may be less impersonal and hierarchical, making for less competition and pressure within the firm, and greater autonomy of its lawyers, but possibly more standardization and repetition within the work. *See* JEAN STEFANIC & RICHARD DELGADO, HOW LAWYERS LOSE THEIR WAY—A PROFESSION THAT FAILS ITS CREATIVE MINDS 71 (Duke Univ. Press 2005). **Study firms in the geographic area where you want to practice.** Learn about the firm before you leap. *See* GEORGE W. KAUFMAN, THE LAWYER'S GUIDE TO BALANCING LIFE & WORK—TAKING THE STRESS OUT OF SUCCESS 53 (ABA Law Practice Management Section 2006). Job interviews are to learn about the firms, not simply to tell the firms about you. There can be 20 to 30 different criteria against which you may wish to measure the qualities of a job in a particular firm. *See id.* at 60-61.

Exercise. Rate the following for your ideal law firm job opportunity, with a 5 for the most important considerations, 3 for neutral considerations, and 1 for matters that make no difference to you. Save your answers in an electronic file for when you choose firms with which to interview. Use your answers to evaluate firms with which to interview and to evaluate job offers:

➢ expectation as to number of hours of worked each week;
➢ compensation level;

- ➤ benefit package including insurances;
- ➤ vacation time each year;
- ➤ availability of bonuses for especially effective work;
- ➤ variety and challenge of the work;
- ➤ predictability of the work;
- ➤ level of responsibility for new associates;
- ➤ client demographics (individual, corporate, etc.);
- ➤ opportunity for frequent client contact;
- ➤ practice areas and specialties;
- ➤ opportunity for travel;
- ➤ opportunity for advancement within the firm;
- ➤ quality of supervision and mentor opportunities;
- ➤ job terms and security;
- ➤ reputation of the firm within the professional community;
- ➤ reputation of the firm outside the professional community;
- ➤ opportunity for pro-bono and other public-service work;
- ➤ opportunity to serve the bar association and profession;
- ➤ stability of the firm's governance and finances;
- ➤ level and qualifications of support staff;
- ➤ geographic location of the firm;
- ➤ library and other research resources of the firm;
- ➤ technology resources of the firm;
- ➤ billing method (hourly, contingency, fixed-price, etc.).

> *Jeremy Nastoff, J.D. 2010*
>
> "I gave some real thought to the kind of law firm in which I wanted to practice. Externing for two federal judges gave me an opportunity to see lawyers from various firms and to hear the judges' career advice. When one of the firms I had grown to admire offered me a job in one of its satellite offices in a great community, it was a perfect fit for me and my family."

Judicial Clerkships—*Judging*

Judicial clerkships, internships, and externships, like law-firm clerkships, internships, and externships, can help you in your transition from law school to law career. A judicial clerkship is a paid position a law graduate accepts for a limited period, often one year immediately out of law school, to work for a judge. Appellate-level judicial clerks primarily do case-file review and legal research, writing bench memoranda to help prepare the judge to hear oral argument and interact with other judges to decide appeals. An appellate-level judicial clerk may also cite-check and proofread opinions and write draft opinions for the judge's consideration. Trial-level judicial clerks will also do research and case-file review but may also draft orders and spend more time in the courtroom observing motion hearings and trials to help the judge identify and research novel legal issues.

A judicial clerkship can distinguish you from other job applicants. Some law firms, particularly larger firms, recruit candidates who have served judicial clerkships. In that recruiting, there tends to be a hierarchy in which employers prefer federal-court clerkships over state-court clerkships, and appellate-level clerkships over trial-level clerkships. Serving a premier federal appellate clerkship could be your ticket to a large-firm job offer, if that is your goal. Competition can be fierce for the premier federal appellate clerkships, requiring stellar grades and recommendations. On the other hand, hierarchies can be misleading. Federal appellate clerkships can involve substantial work on very narrow issues with very limited professional interaction. By contrast, state-court trial-level clerkships can give you a broad picture of day-to-day law practice and the opportunity to observe a broad range of practitioners exercising foundational law-practice skills. If you want a job at a premier large firm serving corporate clients, then pursue a federal appellate clerkship. If you want to be an effective lawyer serving individuals on a broad range of ordinary legal needs, then consider a state trial-court clerkship.

Judicial clerkships, internships, and externships can greatly aid your professional development, particularly in expanding and developing your knowledge base. Judicial clerkships can be isolating. You often work with a small court staff. You may watch lawyers argue, but it is unlikely that you will have substantial contact with those lawyers. You will have no client contact and may not even be able to observe lawyers interacting with their clients, particularly if your clerkship is for an appellate court. The value to a judicial clerkship is instead in the research and writing that you do, and the way in which that work and your interaction with the judge whom you serve develops your law knowledge and instincts. **A judicial clerkship can significantly improve your legal research, reasoning, and writing.**

"It is often said that a judicial clerkship is the equivalent of a Master of Laws degree. That is true, but it can be much more than that. With the right judge, it is an opportunity to gain true insight into the value of serving the law, and not just profiting from it. I had the privilege of clerking for the first African-American to sit on the United States Court of Appeals for the Eighth Circuit. He had grown up amid bigotry and segregation, and he had risen above it with dignity, optimism, and a keen sense of the inherent goodness of humanity. I learned a lot more from him than just the law, and I will carry those lessons with me the rest of my life."

Assistant United States Attorney Phil Green

Locate judicial clerkships through your law school's career office. Law schools have specific courses or programs, or informal initiatives, to identify, recruit, qualify, prepare, and promote students into judicial clerkships. Faculty advisors, especially those who have served clerkships or developed and maintained other connections with judges, can be particularly effective in helping you locate, evaluate, and apply for judicial clerkships. Law schools benefit in their reputations and relationships from having graduates go on to judicial clerkships, just as students benefit. Investigate and request your law school's assistance. You can also do your own research to locate judicial clerkships. If you know of a specific community in which you hope to do a judicial clerkship, then contact the court administrators or judicial clerks to find out about the application procedures for that court. If you do not have a specific court in mind, then check online sites like judicialclerkships.com and lawclerks.ao.uscourts.gov.

Once you locate a judicial clerkship for which you wish to apply, be sure to **rely on faculty advisor and career staff advice to court the judicial clerkship.** Federal judges use the Online System for Clerkship Application and Review (OSCAR) to evaluate clerkship candidates. In most cases, you must apply for federal clerkships using the OSCAR system. Using the OSCAR system, you can submit multiple applications at once, and your recommenders (law professors and others) can submit multiple recommendation letters. State appellate and trial courts have their own systems, from online to the more traditional posting and resume submission. Obtaining a judicial clerkship can involve more than the usual politics, networking, and sensitivity. It can particularly involve recommendations from the right individuals who know your qualities and the judge's preferences. Judges can rely heavily on judicial clerks. They certainly work closely with them, often forming mentor and protégé relationships. Appreciate and respect those sensitivities.

> "The courthouse staff can make you or break you. Treat them with courtesy and respect."
>
> ***Former State Court Judge Jeff Martlew***

Some judges, particularly in the state trial courts, will also accept law student volunteer interns and for-academic-credit externs through law school programs. Your law school may have an internship program in which it places you part-time for a term with a judge or an externship program in which it places you full or part time for a term with a judge for academic credit. **Interns and externs can do the same research and writing work as post-graduate judicial clerks,** although without the pay and status. Judges may also encourage their interns and externs to watch more of the court proceedings and to circulate through the courthouse watching other judges and courts. A volunteer internship or for-credit externship can give you once-in-a-career insight into how courts work and judges think. Lawyers are relatively isolated from judges. Judicial clerks, interns, and externs are not. A judicial clerkship, internship, or externship can also give you a premier recommender (your judge) when pursuing other job opportunities.

Exercise. Reflect on the following questions to determine whether you might obtain and benefit from a judicial clerkship, internship, or externship:

> ➢ Do you have the higher academic standing that many judges prefer to qualify you for a judicial clerkship, internship, or externship?
> ➢ Do you expect to practice litigation so as to get the greatest benefit from a judicial clerkship, internship, or externship?
> ➢ Do you someday wish to be a judge?
> ➢ Do the law firms that you want to approach for job opportunities require or prefer candidates who have had a judicial clerkship, internship, or externship?

> **Roumiana Velikova, J.D. 2007**
>
> "I completed a judicial externship while in law school, hoping for a judicial clerkship after law school. The appellate judge for whom I externed gave me a wonderful recommendation that led to a year-long post-graduate clerkship with the chief justice of my state supreme court. I liked the work so much that I have since pursued a career as a judicial clerk at the trial and appellate-court level."

Legal Fields—*Specializing*

The knowledge you acquire in your law studies connects with practice areas and specialty niches. Many lawyers are general practitioners, drawing on the broad knowledge base that the law school required-course curriculum imparts. Other **lawyers work within practice areas** like civil litigation, criminal defense, and business transactions, drawing on concentrations within law school's curriculum. Still other **lawyers develop narrow specialty niches** focused around a particular industry, where the lawyers draw on special electives, seminars, directed study, or externships that they had in law school or knowledge that they acquired and perfected after law school graduation. What follows is a way to explore your preferences for a legal field.

First, appreciate the breadth of law and the number and variety of legal fields. Consider reviewing the National Association for Law Placement's *Official Guide to Legal Specialties* for its comprehensive list of practice specialties. Know that each practice specialty has its own challenges and rewards, and that lawyers are finding satisfaction and meaning in each specialty. **Consider the following list of a few popular specialties,** as a reminder of the options you have to choose any one of a much larger number of law-practice specialties and legal fields:

_ Admiralty / Maritime Law	_ Insurance Law
_ Antitrust Law	_ Intellectual Property Law
_ Appellate Practice	_ International Law
_ Banking and Commercial Finance	_ Labor and Employment Law
_ Bankruptcy Law	_ Legislative Practice
_ Civil Litigation	_ Military Judge Advocates / JAG
_ Corporate Law	_ Municipal Finance Practice
_ Criminal Law	_ Public Interest Law
_ Education Law	_ Real Estate Law
_ Entertainment and Sports Law	_ Securities Law

__ Environmental Law   __ Solo, Small Firm, General Practice
__ Family Law   __ Tax Law
__ Government Practice   __ Telecommunications Law
__ Health Care Law   __ Torts—Personal Injury & Property Damage
__ Immigration Law   __ Trusts and Estates Law

Begin by considering whether you are attracted to **litigation on one hand or transactional work on the other hand.** Litigators, whether in the civil or criminal law field, are expert in advocacy and procedure. They tend to be quick studies, knowledgeable in the many fields to which their litigation takes them even if masters in few fields or none. They tend to be extroverts, comfortable with their own identity and with others, at ease with public speaking, and at home in the courtroom. They deal well with change and uncertainty, thriving on new and unpredictable challenges, willing to test and prove themselves over and over again with new clients, always ready to adapt. By contrast, transactional lawyers help clients evaluate and avoid risk. They prosper in stable, long-term client relationships. They develop deep knowledge and subtle skills, the value of which they confer in consultative relationships that may last for an entire career. **Meet litigators and transactional lawyers, comparing and contrasting how they view and appreciate their practice.**

Next consider whether you prefer civil or criminal law work. **The subject matters, roles, and client relationships within the civil and criminal-justice systems are fundamentally different.** The criminal-justice system involves the government's responsibility to deter and punish crime. Lawyers either represent the government or defend those whom the government charges with crime. Lawyers on both sides may work for the government (prosecutor's and public defender offices), or defendants may retain defense lawyers who practice in law firms. By contrast, the civil-justice system typically involves private parties seeking to enforce individual rights. Lawyers involved in civil litigation typically work in law firms, representing litigants on retainers or under contingency-fee agreements. Lawyers develop an affinity for one field or the other, and only occasionally both. Crime fascinates some of us while abhorring others of us. Civil litigation captures the passion of some of us while boring others. Meet civil litigators, prosecutors, public defenders, and defense lawyers, comparing and contrasting how they view and appreciate their practice. Consider the side you would choose, prosecution, plaintiff, or defense.

> "Make a decision. If it turns out to be wrong, then make a different decision. Don't wallow in indecision."
>
> **Dean Amy Timmer**

Next, **consider whether you are drawn to a particular practice field or specialty.** Some lawyers do nothing other than collections work. Others do nothing other than handle worker's compensation or Social Security disability claims. Others handle nothing but construction cases while others nothing but business or insurance disputes. As you read cases in law school, see if you have an affinity for one or a small number of law fields, or whether you might appreciate engaging them all. Draw on your undergraduate or other graduate education. Practice areas matter. Each has its own conditions. Litigation is competitive, producing adrenaline or, some would say, testosterone. *See* AMIRAM ELWORK, STRESS MANAGEMENT FOR LAWYERS—HOW TO INCREASE PERSONAL & PROFESSIONAL SATISFACTION IN THE LAW 41 (Vorkell Group 3d ed. 2007), *citing* J.M. Dabbs, Jr., E.C. Alford, & J.A. Fielden, *Trial Lawyers and Testosterone: Blue-Collar Talent in a White-Collar World,* 28(1) Journal of Applied Social Psychology 84 (1998); Isaiah M. Zimmerman, *Stress and the Trial Lawyer,* 9(4) Litigation 37 (1983). Family law can be emotional. Choose conditions that match your skills and personality, and you will find the work more meaningful and less stressful. Choose poorly, and you will find more stress.

Once you know your target legal field and employers, **use your law studies to achieve knowledge of the field, fluency in its language, and skill in its procedures.** Prepare your skills for competent and successful practice, and to impress potential employers. As you do so, think of which courses you most enjoy. Consider in which courses you received the best grades. Keep in mind the reason that you first decided to pursue a law degree. **Review your preferences with your faculty advisor and law school's career staff,** who may know about aspects of the fields in which you may have an interest. Meet with faculty members who practiced in those fields before teaching. Ask them to introduce you to practitioners who can tell you more about the field.

Read the National Association of Law Placement's *Official Guide to Legal Specialties* for details about the practice fields that most interest you. Then, complete informational interviews with lawyers who practice in those fields. Consider drawing on your law school's alumni database for lawyer candidates for those interviews. Watch for speaker events at and outside of your law school, where lawyers speak about your fields of interest. Check with your law school's volunteer program for opportunities to explore those fields. Use your law-school breaks to meet with lawyers in your hometown to learn about their practice fields. In the end, if you are unable to identify a specific legal field in which you should practice, then relax. The fields will find you.

> "The law will take you where it wants to take you. Few attorneys envision what they will be doing career-wise while in law school. Most will tell you, 'I never thought I would be doing employment law, litigating, doing transactional work,' and so on. It can be virtually impossible to predict what specialty you will be engaged in after graduation. The employer or the client walking in the door dictates your legal path. Unless you have a family member ready to hire you into a firm that specializes in a particular area of the law or if you came to law school with a specialized background (like working in an area recognized as a legal specialty), sit back and enjoy the trip. Of course students graduating at the top of their class will have some choice if invited to work in a large firm with multiple specialties. But even that is subject to change when one of the partners needs someone to defend a client in a criminal matter. And at the appointed hour, the new lawyer may enjoy criminal defense work and have a knack for it."
>
> **Professor Gary Bauer**

Exercise. Go quickly down the following list, choosing one or the other as your preference without significant reflection. Then go down the list again, thinking more deeply about each of your choices:

➢ Litigation or transactional work;
➢ Civil justice or criminal justice;
➢ Prosecutor or public defender;
➢ Plaintiff's personal injury or insurance defense;
➢ Courtroom appearances or office work;
➢ Individual or corporate clients;
➢ Long-term or short-term clients;
➢ Many clients or few clients;
➢ Technical matters or social matters;
➢ Drafting or negotiating;
➢ Negotiating or advocating;

> ➤ Advocating or mediating;
> ➤ Dealing with experts or dealing with lay persons;
> ➤ Dealing with judges or dealing with lawyers;
> ➤ Dealing with lawyers or dealing with clients.

Toan Chung, J.D. 2009

"I had many interests when I started law school. To get a better sense of the field in which I wanted to practice, I read about legal fields, met with my faculty advisor and professors, and listened to practitioners speak at the law school. It was when I volunteered at a legal self-help resource center that I began to realize that family law was my field. I confirmed that decision by completing two terms at my school's family-law clinic and a clerkship with the family court. I joined a small firm right after graduation and have been enjoying practicing family law ever since."

Law-Practice Economics—*Marketing*

Knowledge of law-firm economics and particularly law-firm time-keeping and billing practices can help your career and professional development. When partners interview you for an associate position in a law firm, they are considering whether you have the skill, judgment, and discipline to work productively within the firm's service-pricing system. Can you turn your legal knowledge and skill into effective legal service to clients who are willing to pay for it? In a large firm, you may be able to disguise your inefficiency at billing for a little while, although not long. Partners turn a sensitive eye toward such things. Yet if you are in solo practice, then you must much more quickly learn how billing works. If you know how lawyers convert services to billings, then you can better understand the skills that you must possess in solo practice or that a law firm would need from you in order to be able to pay your compensation. If you know in advance, then you may plan and interview better, and work smarter from the start. You may also make better choices in your legal education and a smoother transition into practice.

Most law firms use one or a combination of three basic methods for pricing legal services: (1) time (hourly fee) billing; (2) set-price fees; or (3) contingency fees. Time billing requires the lawyer to keep track of the time the lawyer spends on each client project and the client to pay for that time at an established hourly rate. Some lawyers, especially newer associates in larger firms, criticize time billing, saying that their firms use it to create unreasonable demands on them to meet hours targets. Firms track and compare their lawyers' hours, using comparisons to decide whom to retain or fire, whom to reward with bonuses, and whom to promote. Time billing can become the proverbial rat race for lawyers who lack perspective and balance or who work in firms that do not value the long-term health and development of their lawyers. Clients also criticize time billing for encouraging waste. When a lawyer bills for time instead of a finished product, the time can become the lawyer's incentive and goal rather than a providing the client with a fairly priced product.

Be sensitive to the challenges and vagaries of time billing. The subject of hourly billing expectations may arise in a job interview. **Many lawyers consider 2,000 annual billable hours to be at the top end of reasonable.** Depending on your efficiency in the office, only about 80% of the time that most lawyers spend in the office converts into billable hours. There are other things to do in the office, like meetings and marketing. The 80% figure means that to bill 2,000 hours per year, you must work consistent 48-hour weeks for 50 weeks of the year with 2 weeks of vacation—perhaps a bit of a grind as labor expectations go but not wholly unreasonable when starting a new career. A figure of 1,800 annual hours would suggest to many lawyers a more humane firm that is concerned with the welfare of its associates. At the other end, figures well above 2,000 annual hours can be common in more-competitive and demanding, higher-pay positions.

It is a fair question to ask in a job interview what are the firm's billing expectations, although you might not want it to be your first question if you wish to impress a prospective employer with your commitment. You may want to reserve that question for an associate in the firm rather than the hiring partner. For all its criticism, time billing remains a widespread method of pricing many legal services, particularly in areas like civil litigation where uncertainties in the scope and course of a case can make it hard to estimate time and budget accordingly. Time billing also has its advantages. It establishes clear expectations. You tend to know when you have done what the firm expects of you or, in a solo practice, when you can turn off the lights and go home satisfied that the practice will be there tomorrow. Time billing tends to reward the disciplined, determined, and diligent, and in that respect is a laudable system. **Develop and share with prospective employers evidence of your discipline and productivity.** Their hiring partners are likely to appreciate it when thinking of your capacity and willingness to meet time-billing targets.

> "A law school extern was bemused by her supervisor's sudden push to work very, very hard, after a semester of being fairly lackadaisical in his approach to billable hours. This change of attitude came at the end of October. I explained to the extern, 'What you are witnessing is probably the effect of what many private practice lawyers call "the nut." The nut is the total cost of running a law office for the year. On that day when your receipts more than equal the nut, you have "cracked the nut." Until you crack the nut, you work to meet your payroll, pay the rent, keep the lights on, and keep the door open. On that great come-and-get-it day when you crack the nut, you are finally working, fully and unabashedly, for yourself and your family. If you bill and collect $300 an hour, you GET $300 an hour, unlike before, when all you got was your draw. Until now, you were working against fear—now you are making money.'"
>
> ***Professor Christopher Hastings***

An increasingly popular alternative to time billing is the practice of setting fixed fees for specific legal products or services. Set fees work best for standardized products like a consumer bankruptcy or an estate plan for a low- to middle-income client. Set fees are obviously an advantage for clients. They know what to expect in the bill and may even be able to shop and compare prices among lawyers. Set fees can also be an advantage for lawyers who have the skill to create efficiencies by developing systems and templates, innovating, and leveraging technology. Firms that price their legal services at set fees would look for those qualities in job candidates. **Develop and share with prospective employers evidence of your technology skills, innovation, and efficiency.**

Many lawyers in certain fields work on contingency fees. The primary field for contingency fees is personal-injury practice, where clients are often unable to pay on an hourly or set-fee basis for the t services necessary to pursue litigation. Worker's compensation and Social Security-disability claims also typically involve contingency fees. Some lawyers are able to construct and offer contingency fees in business litigation that lawyer and client expect to result in a lump sum payment or the reduction of a lump sum owed. The primary skill in contingency-fee practice is to attract and choose the more valuable cases, meaning the cases that have the highest return for the fewest hours. Efficiency in the use of one's time is also important to contingency-fee practice. Lawyers can earn reasonable returns by handling many smaller-return cases that each take very few hours, or fewer larger-value cases that take more hours but still produce a reasonable rate of return. Lawyers who choose small-value cases that take many hours or large-value case that take enormous numbers of hours will not be long in practice. **Develop and share with prospective employers evidence of your good judgment, efficient work, and ability to engage clients.**

Global economic trends and improvements in technology will continue to affect the terms on which law firms employ lawyers and the methods by which they price and deliver legal services. Do not overlook that **there are economic pressures on law firms,** just as there are on employers in other professions, businesses, and industries. While the traditional pricing models described above continue to serve most clients, recognize that **law firms are constantly looking for ways to improve the delivery and pricing of legal services.** Recognize, too, that their search means an opportunity for you to demonstrate that you have the skill and commitment to find more efficient ways to deliver higher quality legal services in a competitive global environment. You may not yet have the knowledge and skill to make those innovations, but when you recognize that law firms have the continual need to do so, you demonstrate a quality that is highly valuable to prospective employers. Improve your networking and interviewing skills by gaining a sense of these seven trends that law firms currently face, as identified in David Galbenski, Unbound: How Entrepreneurship Is Dramatically Transforming Legal Services Today 18-19 (Lumen Legal 2009):

- new ways for clients to learn about legal services, like the Internet making the marketing and pricing of services more transparent to the purchaser;
- new ways for clients to buy legal services, forcing firms to improve quality, increase the speed of delivery, and reduce the price of legal services;
- new ways for law firms to provide legal services, helping firms to globalize and standardize services making them more affordable and useful to clients;

- new ways for law firms and clients to organize legal services, unbundling services into discrete products and tasks for clients to better manage costs and delivery;
- more pressure to consolidate law firms, as globalization, client cost reductions, and competition force firms to find new talent, markets, and efficiencies;
- new providers of legal and law-related services, as the legal profession grows more diverse and global, and clients and other professions develop their own legal competencies; and
- new ways to educate lawyers and other legal professionals, as law schools provide better-prepared graduates more able to understand and serve client needs using new patterns and technologies.

Exercise. Develop, write, and save answers to the following questions about billing methods, both to help you identify your preferred job and to respond appropriately in interviews:

➢ How would you respond to a hiring partner who asked whether you can meet the firm's target of 2,000 annual billable hours?
➢ How would you respond to a hiring partner who asked what skills you have that would show that you can efficiently produce the firm's set-fee legal products?
➢ How would you respond to a hiring partner who asked you to identify the characteristics that you have that would make you successful in handling contingency-fee cases?

Mark Rysberg, J.D. 2010
"Being an owner of a construction and development business before law school, I already knew how important the business side of practicing law would be to my professional success. What I didn't know was the business aspects specific to the legal profession. My externship while in law school gave me that opportunity. The externship experience helped me transition from law school into an associate-attorney position at a premier construction-litigation law firm right after graduation. I know not only what clients need, but also what the firm needs from me."

Skills

Skills are the way in which a lawyer's knowledge becomes valuable legal service. Without skills, a lawyer can do little to use knowledge of law's concepts and rules to serve a client. A lawyer's knowledge is action logic, of no use until applied to the specific circumstances of a specific client. **Law firms want to retain and employ skilled lawyers,** just as much as they want lawyers who have abundant law knowledge. Whether or not you know a great deal of law, the more skill you possess, the better you are able to serve clients. A lot of law knowledge in the hands of an unskilled lawyer does little for a client. A small bit of law knowledge in the hands of a skilled lawyer can go a long way toward helping a client. **Clients want skilled lawyers.** This part of the book shows you how law school's curriculum teaches the skills that you must have for law practice. It then shows you the professional-development tools that you can use to connect your skills with career transitions.

Law School Curriculum

Law school curricula offer a variety of options for skills instruction to prepare you for law practice, just as they offer a variety of doctrinal courses. Some schools require six credits of research-and-writing courses, while other schools require none. Some schools permit you to take several different clinical or skills courses, perhaps offering a variety of clinics. The law school curriculum may require that you complete a clinical component or offer clinical-course options. Your law school may also have a wide variety of externships that serve the same purpose as clinics although through a different form of program. Law school competitions draw your skills together in forums that highlight your competence. Your faculty advisor can help you shape the skills part of your law-school curriculum by advising on clinical opportunities and skills electives and concentrations, and by showing how lawyers self-evaluate to improve their skills. Your legal education will also encourage you to develop technology skills necessary or helpful for law practice. This chapter explores how you can connect your clinical experience, externship, faculty advising, and technology skills to your career and professional development. **Keep this skills list in mind as you read this section:**

- clinics;
- externships;
- competitions;
- faculty advising; and
- technology skills.

Clinics—*Integrating*

Standard 301 of the American Bar Association Section of Legal Education and Admissions to the Bar's Standards for Approval of Law Schools requires that your law school offer substantial opportunities for

> live-client or other real-life practice experiences, appropriately supervised and designed to encourage reflection by students on their experiences and on the values and responsibilities of the legal profession, and the development of one's ability to assess his or her performance and level of competence.

Law schools fulfill their obligation to you to provide genuine practice opportunities either by maintaining one or more law-school clinics, maintaining a blended clinic operated jointly by the law school and a legal-service provider or other off-campus organization, or offering externships where you work for a legal-service provider under the supervision of law-school faculty. Law schools typically make clinic and externship opportunities available to you after you complete research-and-writing and professional-responsibility courses, in other words, later in your curriculum. Consider each clinical opportunity in turn.

> "Take as many skills courses as you can. You have to understand the basics, but nothing else prepares you as well for the real practice of law."
>
> ***Former State Court Judge Jeff Martlew***

You may find that **a law-school clinic experience is the perfect way to demonstrate your capability to prospective employers and to prepare yourself for solo practice.** A law-school clinic, also known as an in-house clinic, gives you the opportunity to act as a licensed lawyer would, in a law office located within the school. In-house clinics accept clients for representation, assigning you the responsibility to act as the client's lawyer under the supervision of law-school faculty and law-school staff attorneys. The state in which your law school is located may have a student-practice rule that permits you to appear in court and otherwise act as the clinic client's attorney, subject to faculty and staff-attorney supervision. Your law school may also offer a blended clinic that gives you more opportunity to work alongside practicing lawyers outside of the school but still within a law-school program. **Students and graduates often identify their clinic experience as the pinnacle of their law-school experience.** In a clinic, you may learn to:

- interview prospective clients;
- evaluate whether they meet intake criteria;
- open and maintain client files;
- counsel clients;
- communicate with judges and opposing lawyers;
- draft, file, and serve pleadings and other court papers;
- draft and argue motions and responses;
- obtain interim orders;
- conduct evidentiary hearings and trials;
- negotiate settlements;
- enter and enforce judgments; and
- work with secretarial staff and possibly also paralegal staff.

In addition to instructing you in specific skills, clinics can help focus your studies on a specific field. You may find that a clinic gives you specific experience within a field most attractive to specific prospective employers or most capable of preparing you for solo practice in those fields. You may also find that although you do not plan on practicing in a certain field, you would like to participate in it at least once in your law career, supporting the clients and public interests it represents while you also learn more about it. Clinics at different schools focus on the following practice areas, public interests, or specialty niches, among others:

- family law;
- elder law;
- estate planning;
- poverty law;
- criminal defense;
- exoneration from conviction;
- municipal law;
- community reclamation and development;
- immigrant law;
- migrant-worker legal services;
- human rights and civil rights; and
- inter-disciplinary work with other professionals.

As you can see from the variety of clinic options and variety of skills in which they instruct, choosing whether to participate in a clinic and then choosing the right clinic option can involve several considerations. The number of credits you must devote to the clinic can vary from as few as two or three credits (as little as one other course) to as many as six or eight credits (as much as two or three other courses). **Consider how many credits you must devote to the clinic** and what other courses you might have to forgo. Many clinics require that you keep specific hours in the clinic. **Determine whether your schedule has the flexibility to meet the clinic's hours requirements.** Some clinics require that you participate over the course of two terms, pairing you the first term with a second-term clinic student and then allowing you to lead a first-term student in your second term. In those instances, **consider whether you have two terms to devote to the clinic.** Consider the skills that the clinic teaches and the clinic's subject field, and whether they are most valuable to you. Confirm whether you have the credits available to participate in more than one clinical experience, and compare your clinic options to externship choices at your law school, addressed in the next section.

As indicated above, your clinic experience can be the best part of your legal education. It can also require or encourage you to work with an intensity and devotion unlike any other experience in law school. Real matters matter. Your clinic may not require you to devote extraordinary hours to your client's matter, but you may choose or wish to do so. Speak with the clinic director and other clinic students about their experiences to help you evaluate the clinic's rewards and requirements. Consider your other courseload and your outside work, family, and other commitments. **Choosing how to satisfy your clinical requirement is one area where you can shape your learning experience and professional skills and identity more than in other areas of the law-school curriculum.** Do you want to interview and counsel clients, and learn law-office management? Do you want to explore a specific field that has always attracted you, before you make a career commitment to it? Above all, **consult your faculty advisor and career staff as to your clinic decision.** Your clinical experience can be a once-in-a-career opportunity to explore a special field.

Exercise. Research, write, and save answers to the following questions to help you identify whether a clinic is your best clinical-course option and, if so, which clinic to choose:

- ➤ Do you have any experience doing legal work?
    - ○ If so, has your experience prepared you for law practice?
    - ○ Does your experience enable you to choose a practice field?
    - ○ Would you benefit from the experience a clinic offers?
- ➤ What clinics does your law school offer?
- ➤ How many credits and terms do those clinics require?
- ➤ How many credits will you have available for a clinic experience?
- ➤ What days and times do the clinics require you to be available?
- ➤ How many hours of client service do the clinics require?
- ➤ How many hours of client service do students tend to devote?
- ➤ Who directs the clinic in which you are most interested?
- ➤ What other options does your school offer for clinical experience?

Traci Schenkel, J.D. 2009

"I completed three terms in one of my law school's clinics, doing mostly family-law work. It was an amazing experience to get to represent clients in court while still in law school. The clinic director was incredibly effective at supervising and guiding me while still letting me be responsible and learn. After graduation, I joined a law firm where I could continue to represent clients in family-law matters, having confirmed in the clinic that it was the work that I loved."

Externships—*Mastering*

An externship can also be an excellent way to gain clinical experience in law school for academic credit, while developing career opportunities. An externship places you at an office location off of the law-school campus to do legal work under the supervision of a lawyer. A faculty member simultaneously supervises you in classes, by telephone, by remote e-journals, or through other appropriate communications. You register for the externship as you would for other courses, completing the externship within a term while devoting from 3 to 10 credits to the externship depending on the school's program and the number of hours that you work. Some law schools offer only specific externships with certain public offices or private firms with which they have an established relationship, perhaps near the law school or at a special program location. Other law schools offer unlimited opportunities to establish your own externship site meeting the school's externship-program requirements. **In the broadest externship programs, you can work anywhere in the world where there is a qualified lawyer doing legal work willing to supervise you.**

The value of an externship is much like the value of a clinic, that you can learn a wide variety of skills around a wide variety of law subjects, practice areas, and specialty niches of your choice. What is different is that **an externship places you in a professional relationship doing legal work with and for a sitting judge or practicing lawyer.** In a clinic, your primary relationship is with the client, other students in the clinic, and the clinic's director and staff attorney. In an externship, your primary relationship is with the lawyer or judge who gives you work assignments and supervises you. In a law-firm externship, you work much like an associate in the law firm would work, taking assignments from one of the firm's partners, except that you are not an employee of the firm and receive no compensation. You work for academic credit rather than pay. Under Interpretation 305-3 of American Bar Association Section of Legal Education and Admissions to the Bar Standards and Rules of Procedure for Approval of Law Schools Standard 305, your law school must not grant you academic credit for compensated work.

> "In the area of prosecution, and I suppose it applies to other areas as well, I cannot stress enough that when we look to fill a position, we look to someone who wants to be a prosecutor. With staffs trimmed down to the bone now, we cannot afford to train someone and develop their skills when, after a year or two, they decide this is not what they want. Perhaps they decide the pay is too low, the pressure in court is to high, or the nature of the activity is undesirable. Externships demonstrate that a candidate is committed to this area of the law. They have been tested with experiencing the stress of court, using the rules of evidence to make their case, dealing with difficult witnesses, and they still want to be a prosecutor."
>
> **Chief Assistant Prosecutor Michael Sepic**

One difference between a clinic and an externship is that the clinic only simulates the financial side of law practice, while in an externship it is real. Clinics do not charge and bill for your services. Services are instead free. In a law-firm externship, the law firm is not paying you, and in that sense you do not have the pressure to bill, but the lawyers with and under whom you work do. Even if the responsibility is not yet yours, **an externship introduces you to the billing requirements, client-development responsibilities, and other marketing and financial expectations within a law firm.** That environment is what makes practice authentic and exciting for many lawyers, drawing fully on a lawyer's relationship, legal, service, and technological skills.

Another value of a law-school externship program is the variety that it offers you to try different legal fields and worksites. You may extern in a foreign country or other special geographic location where you hope to live and work permanently but want to visit to determine its suitability for permanent residence. Or you may just want to enjoy a distant location for the temporary duration of your externship. Legal work in an unusual place has its own professional-development benefits. You might also extern in a large firm to determine whether you prefer it to a small firm, or a firm that specializes in one field rather than another field that you are also considering. Although you may prefer a law-firm externship because law firms are where most lawyers work, **your law school may also offer you a once-in-a-career opportunity to complete an externship in:**

- judicial chambers;
- corporate counsel's offices;

- administrative agency offices;
- legislative bureaus;
- prosecutor's offices;
- public defender's offices; and
- nongovernmental (nonprofit) organization offices.

The workplace relationship you establish through a law-firm externship can give you a distinct advantage in developing employment opportunities. A law-firm externship gives you an opportunity to establish strong positive relationships with lawyers and staff within the firm. It also gives you the opportunity to prove your knowledge, skills, and ethics on the matters on which you work for the firm and its lawyers. It also gives the lawyers of the firm a substantial basis on which to evaluate your relationships and work. You are no longer unknown but proven, doing the specific work for which the firm would hire you if it had arranged your interview. In short, **your externship may convince the law firm to make you a job offer.** You may want to apply for an externship at an office where there is a job opening posted. Your externship may make you a leading candidate for that position. An externship also gives you the opportunity to learn what it would be like to accept that job offer, meaning whether you really do want to work at that law firm. As an extern, you have already learned the basic expectations for the work.

Some externships hold no prospect for future employment, particularly with judicial externships but also with many government and corporate-counsel offices that employ career staff on fixed budgets. **You can still improve your employment opportunities** externing for a judge, in a government office or corporate-counsel office, or even a law firm where the firm has already indicated that it has no job openings at the end of your externship. Lawyers and judges for whom you do quality work will often write strong positive recommendation letters based on their substantial personal knowledge of your conduct and work. They may also give you specific job leads and even make job inquiries on your behalf. Lawyers and judges who supervise externs understand that an externship is not only a skill builder but a career step. Ask for and expect their help in these and other job-related respects, even when they have no opening to offer you. **Work with your law school's career staff both to evaluate and select an externship, and to help you develop career opportunities while there.**

Exercise. Research, write, and save answers to the following questions to help you identify whether an externship is your best clinical-course option and, if so, which externship to choose:

- ➢ Do you have any experience doing legal work?
  - ○ If so, has your experience prepared you for law practice?
  - ○ Does your experience enable you to choose a practice field?
  - ○ Would your skills improve with an externship?
  - ○ Would an externship help you choose a job location?
- ➢ What externships does your law school offer?
  - ○ Are they in your desired field of law?
  - ○ Are they in your desired location?
- ➢ Does your law school permit you to establish your own externship?
  - ○ If so, what externship site would you choose?
- ➢ Will your externship site have job openings after you graduate?
  - ○ If so, will your externship help you qualify for those openings?
- ➢ What number or range of credits does the externship require?
- ➢ How many credits will you have available for the externship?
- ➢ What days and times does the externship require you to be available?
- ➢ Who would supervise your externship at the field site?
  - ○ Will your field supervisor provide you with substantial feedback?
  - ○ Will your field supervisor help you network for job opportunities?
- ➢ Would the state's student-practice rules support your externship?
- ➢ What professor would you choose to supervise your externship?
- ➢ What other options does your school offer for clinical experience?

> **Melanie Glover, J.D. 2010**
>
> "During law school, I served an externship at a law firm in Madrid, Spain. My externship helped broaden my knowledge of the legal principles I learned in law school, while I polished my researching, writing, and counseling skills through participating in the firm's legal services. Working overseas not only gave me an international perspective on law, but it also improved my foreign-language skills and appreciation for clients from all over the world with unique issues to solve. I enjoyed the experience so much that after graduation, I joined a national nonprofit organization where I could use those same legal, language, and cultural skills to continue helping others from diverse backgrounds."

Competitions—*Challenging*

Competitions can play a significant role in the development of your professional skills in law school. In some ways, **competitions stand at a pinnacle of the skills curriculum** within the law school, where you can test your integrated lawyer skills. At the base of the skills pyramid are your professors' demonstrations of discrete skills spread across the curriculum including in doctrinal courses. You then have the opportunity to take several skills courses in which you may practice aspects of specific skills. Those skills courses may include:

- Interviewing and Counseling,
- Pre-Trial Skills,
- Negotiation and Confrontation,
- Alternative Dispute Resolution,
- Advanced Mediation,
- Trial Skills,
- Trial Technology,
- Mock Trial, and
- Moot Court.

As valuable as these skills courses can be (some of the favorites in law school), competitions can raise the skills art to an even higher level. Competitions often pair you with another student who shares or complements your interest and skill. Lawyers often work in pairs and teams. Team competitions give you an opportunity to learn and practice those collaboration and teamwork skills. Teammates can spur one another on to greater work. The challenge and reward of competitions can also make your teammate a lifelong professional acquaintance and friend. Also, **competitions introduce you to a problem like those problems that you will encounter in law practice.** In that respect, competitions can mimic practice better than many other courses and programs. Also, because competitions typically deal with a single problem, you have the opportunity to work on the problem in much greater depth than most other problems or subjects in law school. Although the spirit of a competition can be very supportive, law students and lawyers like to win. Competition can spur your growth.

Another potential advantage to competitions is the opportunity for constructive criticism. Competitions are judged. Judging means feedback. The judges are often faculty members, adjunct professors, practitioners, and even sitting judges. **Competitions can provide a rare opportunity for you to have a highly skilled practicing lawyer or judge give you detailed critique of your work.** If you qualify for a regional or national competition, then you will also have extensive advising from, practice with, and constructive feedback from a faculty advisor. Your competition relationship with a full-time faculty-member coach can lead to a mentor relationship, career advice, and job recommendations and references. You may also get to travel to a competition site where you can meet and observe competitors and judges from across the country. There are few experiences that can more quickly acclimate you into the professional mystique than to attend and compete in national competitions. Win or lose (and it is hard to call competition losing), **many graduates point back to their competition days as the crowning achievement of their legal education.**

> "The skills and ethics that competitions teach are perhaps the most important lessons. Competitors sharpen their written advocacy skills through the brief-editing process. Word choice, paragraph structure, and even sentence structure affect the emphasis facts and law receive. Competitors also sharpen their oral advocacy skills by responding clearly to questions from the bench. Editing the brief and practicing oral argument also help competitors learn how to work as a team, which is a most sought-after skill in the workplace."
>
> *Professor Evelyn Calogero*

Competitions come in all types at all points in the curriculum, some for credit and others co-curricular. There are first-year, second-year, and third-year competitions. Your law school will offer several of its own school competitions for various skills. It will also offer competitions that lead to fielding school teams for regional and national competitions, where your school pays for your travel. Your school may or may not permit you to enter a regional or national competition on your own without school support, depending on the competition rules and on your school's policies. You may also have the opportunity to serve on a competition board. Students run many school competitions. There are also national and international competitions in different fields. Some common intra-school competitions include:

- Moot Court Competition;
- Mock Trial Competition;
- Criminal Law Moot Court Competition;
- Constitutional Law Competition;
- Environmental Law Competition;
- Negotiation Competition;
- Client-Counseling Competition; and
- International Law Competition.

Competitions often focus on oral and performance skills that go well beyond classroom learning. Competitions can simulate trial-court or appellate-court settings, or in the case of a Negotiation or Client-Counseling Competition, an office setting. Participants thus gain experience that the classroom seldom if ever offers. Employers value that experience because it can more closely resemble practice than the knowledge-based learning that goes on in the classroom. Winners gain the advantage of advertising their success to potential employers. Winning a competition can make your resume stand out from among others. It can also be a great discussion point in an interview. Employers value performance skills, which can be hard for an employer to measure based on traditional measures like class standing and grade-point average. **A competition win is a clear mark of your ability to win the respect of others for your oral presentation and performance skills.** While the greatest benefits of winning a competition are these intangibles, some competitions also make monetary awards, and all provide some form of certificate, plaque, or trophy in recognition.

Competitions also frequently include writing components, meaning that judges score participants on both oral performance skills and written work product. One participant or team may win Best Brief, while another participant or team wins Best Oralist, and the overall winner has the highest total score in both areas. Some competitions involve solely written work products. Law school journals, specialty bars, bar sections, and other organizations sponsor specialty writing competitions. Some of those writing competitions involve advocacy, while other writing competitions involve scholarly papers on policy issues. There are dozens of writing competitions, many offering cash prizes and all offering the challenge and recognition that goes with submitting a competitive writing. **Consider consulting with your school's writing department for the best writing-competition opportunities.** If your schedule does not permit the kind of travel and teamwork that oral performance competitions commonly involve, but you want to challenge yourself in a competition setting, then **consider one of the many writing competitions, examples of which include:**

- American Bar Association Section of Business Law Student Writing Contest;
- American Bar Association Section of Real Property, Probate, and Trust Law Writing Contest;
- Federal Bar Association Section of Taxation Writing Competition;
- National Law Review Law Student Writing Competition;
- American Constitution Society for Law and Policy National Student Writing Competition;
- American College of Trust and Estate Counsel Student Writing Competition;
- American Intellectual Property Law Association Award Competition;
- College of Labor and Employment Lawyers Law Student Writing Competition;
- College of Workers' Compensation Lawyers Writing Competition;
- Grammy Foundation Entertainment Law Initiative Writing Competition;

- Stanford Technology Law Review Paper Contest;
- Davis Wright Tremaine International Law Writing Award; and
- American College of Legal Medicine Student Writing Competition.

> "Ethics and professionalism are also important lessons in any competition. Competitors learn how to follow the letter and spirit of the rules. They learn that not everyone wins a ribbon just for participation. They learn what they can control (preparation, what they cannot control (judges' decisions), and how to gracefully handle disappointment when it occurs. What employer would not want that level of maturity in a new attorney?"
>
> *Professor Evelyn Calogero*

Whether participating in a competition is right for you to build your skills can depend on several factors. Investigate the following questions with your faculty advisor. **Think first of your career and professional goals.** Do they require certain skills that you will not learn in another course or program? Is there a competition available to you that focuses on those skills? What other courses and co- or extra-curricular professional-development activities would you have to pass up in order to participate in the competition? With whom would you like to work as a competition partner? Then consult with competition board members, faculty coaches, and student participants to learn more about the competition in which you are most interested. **Consider entering at least one competition.** You may be surprised how invigorating, exciting, and valuable the experience is. You may also produce a special appellate brief, video-recorded argument, or other work product to represent your skill to prospective employers.

Exercise. Choose one of the above competitions that sounds most interesting to you, and determine the following information for it from school sources including especially the faculty advisor or student board members of the competition:

> ➢ When does the competition take place?
> ➢ Do you qualify to enter the competition?
> ➢ Does it require a teammate?
> ➢ How much time does the competition take?
> ➢ Can you advance to a regional or national competition by winning?

➢ What work product will result (a brief, videotaped argument, etc.)?

John Zevalking, J.D. 2007

"In law school, I competed in a national environmental-law competition, where I won the best-oralist award. It was definitely a high point of my legal education. I most appreciated working closely with the competition team's faculty advisor who had been an outstanding trial lawyer in practice. I later clerked for the state supreme court and then joined a large firm's litigation practice group. I still feel that it was the competition win that focused my interest on litigation."

Advisors—*Reflecting*

Your professors in general, and especially your faculty advisor, can play significant roles in the development of your professional skills within the law-school curriculum. Certainly in the classroom but also outside of it, **the professors with whom you interact shape your professional development.** Do not overlook that they can also help guide you into your law career. Law professors at some law schools have substantial practice experience. They know how law firms, prosecutor's and public-defender offices, corporate counsel offices, and other law-practice settings work. They know how lawyers evaluate, hire, and retain other lawyers. You are likely to find on your law school faculty an advisor who has practiced in the specific field and setting in which you would most like to practice. **Use your faculty advisor for your career and professional development.**

Ask your faculty advisor about the personal and professional rewards and challenges of the kind of practice in which you think you would like to engage. Meet your faculty advisor early to get a better sense of how the law-school curriculum prepares you best for your preferred field. List your questions in advance of the meeting as if you were a journalist who needed to describe the job in which you have an interest. Your purpose in meeting your advisor should not be to simply listen. Instead, **encourage your advisor to help you shape specific plans.** Empirical study shows that career plans, especially written plans, work. *See* George W. Kaufman, The Lawyer's Guide to Balancing Life & Work—Taking the Stress out of Success 224 (ABA Law Practice Management Section 2006). An effective career plan should include your vision, potential expressions of your vision, strategies to further your vision, obstacles to your vision, steps for implementation, and a practice to assess plan progress.

Consider asking your faculty advisor to help you develop your career and professional-development plan around the lawyer skills and value identified by the American Bar Association's MacCrate Report. *See* ABA Section on Legal Education & Admission to the Bar, *Legal Education and Professional Development—An Educational Continuum, Report of the Task Force on Law Schools and the Profession: Narrowing the Gap* (ABA 1992). The MacCrate Report has long been the most widely cited effort to identify the skills and values that law students should learn to effectively practice law. Many employers know about the MacCrate skills and values. You will impress those who do not with your professional-development research and knowledge. Here are the MacCrate skills (see the MacCrate values in the Ethics section of this book):

Skill 1: Problem Solving
In order to develop and evaluate strategies for solving a problem or accomplishing an objective, a lawyer should be familiar with the skills and concepts involved in:
1. Identifying and Diagnosing the Problem.
2. Generating Alternative Solutions and Strategies.
3. Developing a Plan of Action.
4. Implementing the Plan.
5. Keeping the Planning Process Open to New Information and Ideas.
6. Evaluating the Problem Solving Process.

Skill 2: Legal Analysis and Reasoning
In order to analyze and apply legal rules and principles, a lawyer should be familiar with the skills and concepts involved in:
1. Identifying and Formulating Legal Issues.
2. Formulating Relevant Legal Theories.
3. Elaborating Legal Theory.
4. Evaluating the Persuasiveness of a Legal Theory.
5. Criticizing and Synthesizing Legal Argumentation.

Skill 3: Legal Research
In order to identify legal issues and to research them thoroughly and efficiently, a lawyer should have:
1. Knowing the Nature of Legal Rules and Institutions.
2. Knowing and Competently Using the Most Fundamental Tools of Legal Research.
3. Understanding the Process of Devising and Implementing a Coherent and Effective Research Design.
4. Evaluating and Revising the Research Design.

Skill 4: Factual Investigation
In order to plan, direct, and (where applicable) participate in factual investigation, a lawyer should be familiar with the skills and concepts involved in:
1. Gathering Factual Information from the Client.
2. Determining the Need for Further Factual Investigation.
3. Planning a Factual Investigation.
4. Implementing the Investigative Strategy, Memorializing and Organizing Information Obtained.
5. Deciding When to Conclude the Process of Fact Gathering.
6. Evaluating the Information That Has Been Gathered.

Skill 5: Communication
In order to communicate effectively, whether orally or in writing, a lawyer should be familiar with the skills and concepts involved in:
1. Understanding the Need for Communication.
2. Assessing the Recipient of the Communication.
3. Understanding and Using Effective Methods of Communication.
4. Using Effective Methods of Oral Communication.
5. Using Effective Methods of Written Communication.

Skill 6: Counseling
In order to counsel clients about decisions or courses of action, a lawyer should be familiar with the skills and concepts involved in:
1. Understanding the Proper Nature and Bounds of the Lawyer's Role in a Counseling Relationship.
2. Gathering Information Relevant to the Decision to Be Made.
3. Analyzing the Range of Options Available.
4. Counseling the Client about the Decision to be Made.
5. Ascertaining and Implementing the Client's Decision.

Skill 7: Negotiation
In order to negotiate in either a dispute-resolution or transactional context, a lawyer should be familiar with the skills and concepts involved in:
1. Choosing Negotiation as a Method of Dispute Resolution.
2. Preparing for Negotiation Effectively.
3. Conducting a Negotiation Session Effectively.
4. Counseling the Client Regarding the Terms Obtained from the Other Side in the Negotiation and Implementing the Client's Decision.

Skill 8 and 9: Litigation and Alternative Dispute-Resolution Procedures
In order to employ—or to advise a client about—the options of litigation and alternative dispute resolution, a lawyer should understand the potential functions and consequences of these processes and should have a working knowledge of the fundamentals of:
ALTERNATIVE DISPUTE RESOLUTION
Choosing Alternative Dispute Resolution with the Client.

1. Understanding the Fundamentals of Proceedings in Other Dispute-Resolution Forums.

LITIGATION

1. Understanding and Competently Using the Fundamentals of Litigation at the Trial-Court Level.
2. Understanding and Competently Using the Fundamentals of Litigation at the Appellate Level.
3. Understanding and Competently Using the Fundamentals of Advocacy in Administrative and Executive Forums.

Skill 10: Organization and Management of Legal Work

In order to practice effectively, a lawyer should be familiar with the skills and concepts required for efficient management, including:

1. Formulating Goals and Principles for Effective Practice Management.
2. Developing Systems and Procedures to Ensure that Time, Effort and Resources are Allocated Efficiently.
3. Developing Systems and Procedures to Ensure that Work is Performed and Completed at the Appropriate Time.
4. Developing Systems and Procedures for Effectively Working with Other People.
5. Developing Systems and Procedures for Efficiently Administering a Law Office.
6. Ensuring Consistent Contact with the Client and Documenting that Contact.

Skill 11: Recognizing and Resolving Ethical Dilemmas

In order to represent a client consistently with applicable ethical standards, a lawyer should be familiar with:

1. Understanding the Nature and Sources of Ethical Standards.
2. Understanding the Means by which Ethical Standards are Enforced.
3. Understanding the Processes for Recognizing and Resolving Ethical Dilemmas.

> "A frequently untapped resources within a law school are the faculty advisor and other professional staff advisors. So much of being successful in law school is about timing and access to information. With law school being so intense, having trusted advisors to prod, challenge, and support, and with whom to celebrate, can make all the difference in having a satisfying experience contributing to success in the future."
>
> *Dean Paul Zelenski*

Ask your faculty advisor to help you identify the curriculum choices and co-curricular activities through which you can improve on your MacCrate skills. **Then take action, implementing your plan while recording what you did to improve your skill.** The simple fact of making and updating a plan keeps you aware of necessary skills in a way that helps you build them. Planning and implementing plans, and assessing your plan progress, also makes you able to tell others, particularly prospective employers, what are your skills and how you developed and improved them. When you discuss your skills-improvement plan with a prospective employer, you demonstrate an assessment skill that is critical to professional performance.

Exercise. Self assess your MacCrate Report skills. Then, use your self assessment to clarify your plan to develop and improve on your skills to the point that you have mastered or have at least exercised the skills in all areas. Re-read the list of MacCrate skills immediately above, giving yourself one of these five grades in each area:

> - **A,** mastered, meaning that you readily use the skill effectively meeting all applicable practice standards;
> - **B,** exercising, meaning that although you have used the skill, you cannot yet meet all applicable practice standards with it;
> - **C,** observant, meaning that you have seen a practitioner make effective use of the skill but have not tried it;
> - **D,** aware, meaning that although you have heard of the skill, you have not seen or exercised it;
> - **E,** deficient, meaning that you do not know what the skill means and have never seen or exercised it.

Emily Bruski, J.D. 2010

"I realized pretty early on in law school that my career success would depend on more than success in my academic studies. I recognized that I needed to make connections outside of the school in the professional community, both to aid my professional development and to help me find the law-firm job that suited my career goals. My first step was to meet with faculty advisors at my school, all of whom had substantial practice experience and connections. It was one of the best things that I did. They encouraged me to do both a judicial internship and an externship in a prosecutor's office for the trial experience it would give me, which then helped me land an associate-attorney position with a great mid-size law firm."

Technology—*Leveraging*

Your technology skills and use of technology can promote your career and professional development. **You should be making the**

most of your law school's curriculum to identify and use technology-based resources and develop technology skills. Law firms operate in an increasingly sophisticated and technology-rich legal environment. The matters on which lawyers work involve technology issues like employer computer-use and social-media policies, litigation holds on and discovery of electronically stored information, electronic surveillance, intellectual property in software, licensing of software and electronic systems, and privacy in and right of access to electronically stored financial information and medical records. As the business, professional, and social worlds increase their technology use, lawyers increasingly encounter technology issues. **Clients value technology-savvy lawyers.** Indeed, an increasing number of courts accept only electronic filings from lawyers. There are even special courts that hear only technology issues.

> "New lawyers are uniquely positioned to provide expertise on technology-related matters right out of law school. Having spent most of their lives with computers, most law school graduates are naturally at ease with law practice technology. What's more, they are often better suited to learning quickly new technology-driven legal tasks, such as e-discovery management and electronic trial presentation, than are many experienced attorneys. In a strange turnaround, courts and clients are more likely to turn to the new lawyers, rather than their experienced colleagues, for guidance on legal issues posed by email, texting, social media, and other emerging technologies. For these reasons, new lawyers who have taken it upon themselves to master technology-driven areas of law, such as Internet privacy and e-commerce, will be attractive candidates to law firms that have failed to keep up with rapid technological change or believe they need someone to keep them abreast of future changes."
>
> *Professor Derek Witte*

While increasingly dealing with technology issues, **lawyers also increasingly employ technology to improve their own productivity and efficiency, and the quality of their work product.** Desktop-computer, Internet, and email use among lawyers is ubiquitous, while laptop computers and other mobile electronic devices like personal-digital assistants are becoming so. *See* DAVID I.C. THOMSON, LAW SCHOOL 2.0: LEGAL EDUCATION FOR THE DIGITAL AGE 44-45 (LexisNexis 2009). More than nine out of ten lawyers access the Internet at home for work purposes. *Id.* at 46. Law firms and corporate clients increasingly outsource work electronically to contract lawyers. Lawyers working in law firms will commonly choose, access, evaluate, and use the following electronic technologies:

- word-processing software;
- meta-data-scrubbing conversion programs;
- electronic spreadsheets and database software;
- presentation, illustration, animation, and publication software;
- email and other electronic communications;
- websites, blogs, e-journals, and other information sources;
- social and professional media;
- case-management software;
- time-and-billing software;
- electronic calendars;
- personal digital assistants and smartphones;
- network, desktop, and laptop computers; and
- dictation devices and voice-recognition software.

As law firms adopt new technologies and respond to new technology requirements of their clients and client matters, technology plays an ever greater role within the law school curriculum. **Technology permeates legal education.** In the classroom, students use clickers or laptop computers to answer electronic polls that the professor projects on a large screen using an Internet-accessible computer at the lectern, while professors use presentation software for everything and show YouTube clips to illustrate legal concepts. Outside the classroom, professors communicate constantly with students by email while supporting courses with electronic course pages offering electronic quizzes with instant electronic feedback, web-based collaborative wikis, and computer-aided legal instruction. Downloadable podcasts of live courses are ubiquitous, while increasingly, law schools offer videoconferenced or online courses that substitute virtual interaction for personal interaction.

Law school is not only a technology-rich environment. **Law school also instructs students in the legal issues that technology raises.** For example, look for the following technology instruction in the following courses:

- research-and-writing courses teaching electronic research and document assembly;
- civil-procedure courses addressing preservation, discovery, and disclosure of electronically stored information and electronic-filing requirements;
- criminal-law and criminal-procedure courses addressing high-technology forensic science and electronic-surveillance issues;
- contracts and sales courses teaching about e-commerce disputes and the validity of clauses confirmed by click boxes;
- law-practice management courses addressing electronic accounting, management, and law-office systems;
- tort-law courses addressing the defamation liability of bloggers and immunity of Internet service providers; and
- advanced trial-skills courses showing you how to use electronic courtroom presentation and transcription technology.

Technology is not only a legal environment, practice skill, and part of the law school curriculum. **Technology also gives you tools to investigate and pursue your career opportunities.** Internet searches and resources can teach you about potential employers and their needs and interests. Website biographies can prepare you for an interview, giving you background about the lawyers who will interview you and the firm where you hope to be employed. You can also use e-portfolios with hyperlinked executive summaries, web-based slide shows and video clips, and electronic writing samples to demonstrate the depth, breadth, and quality of your knowledge and skill. When you use technology to demonstrate your law-practice skills, you are at the same time demonstrating your technology skills. Technology skills increase your value to prospective clients and law-firm employers, while also conveying to opposing counsel and the court your professional competence. Law firms will hire new lawyers for the technology skills they bring to the firm. **Develop and demonstrate your technology skills.**

Finally, if you really want to stand out in your technology skills, then appreciate and explore what some law firms are beginning to recognize. The cutting edge of law-office technology is no longer simply storing and moving information through word processing and electronic transmission. **Technologies are now emerging that apply and process information in ways that create new knowledge.** Technology is fast creating substantive knowledge sources rather than simply remaining a knowledge-transmission tool. Examples include interactive questionnaires for new-client evaluation and intake, forms that propose appropriate alternative entries, checklists and evaluation tools that serve as decision trees, document-assembly programs that link to alternative texts, and case-management systems that analyze and report on patterns and trends. These smart systems can help lawyers reuse former work, find work that uses former work, and prepare to reuse current work. They also help lawyers plan work, delegate work, prepare for work, do several tasks at once, increase productivity, collaborate with others, and systematize routines. *See* MICHAEL LAURITSEN, THE LAWYER'S GUIDE TO WORKING SMARTER WITH KNOWLEDGE TOOLS 17-21 (ABA Law Practice Management Section 2010).

Exercise. Self assess your technology skills, giving yourself a score of 0 for none, 1 for weak, 2 for minimal, 3 for moderate, 4 for strong, and 5 for excellent in each of the following areas. Then, use your self assessment in consultation with your faculty advisor to develop a plan to improve on your technology skills until you rank at least a 3 and preferably a 4 in every one of the following areas:

➢ word processing, document assembly, and document management;
➢ information management through spreadsheets and databases;
➢ presentations through visualizers and presentation software;
➢ calendaring, time-keeping, accounting, and billing software;
➢ case-management, file-management, and case-filing systems;
➢ email and other electronic communication systems;
➢ personal-digital assistants, cell phones, and other mobile technology;
➢ electronic legal research and investigation of non-legal sources; and
➢ website use, evaluation, and management.

Professional-Development Tools

What you do in law school should not only increase your skills but also create and preserve evidence of those skills. To enter law practice and thrive, you need not only the skills to provide meaningful legal services but proof that you are skilled. If you cannot show your skill, then you may never get that opportunity. Having the skills is not enough. You must also be able to readily demonstrate them in an attractive manner. Law school should help you create useable evidence of your skill, so that you can demonstrate your skill in ways that promote your career and professional development. Your organization of your job search into a portfolio (addressed in the first part of this book) is a prime example. Prospective employers notice how organized you are when they interact with you over your job interest. Organization is a tool that reflects skill, even while it promotes your job search. Financial planning during your legal education is another tool reflecting your professional skill, while at the same time it increases your job options. The research skills that you employ in your job search are another tool to reflect your professional skill to prospective employers. So, too, are your communication practices and interview skills. Finally, how you conduct yourself in the course of job offers and negotiation over terms of employment are another tool to reflect your professional skill. As this section addresses these tools to demonstrate your skill, **keep these connections in mind:**

- planning your finances during your legal education;
- research on job opportunities showing professional skill;
- communication skills showing professional comportment;
- interview skills meeting employer expectations; and
- skill in negotiating and accepting employment terms.

Financial Planning—*Providing*

Financial planning is a fundamental tool in successful career and professional development. You probably had to finance your legal education, meaning that you had to think clearly and responsibly about how to pay for your legal education, plan a course of action, and then implement and evaluate your financial plan as you progressed through law school. You should take the same approach to your career transition. Developing a financial plan for your career transition may make the difference between having to take a job you would rather not and getting to choose the job you really want. Having a clear understanding of your financial position, flexibility, and needs can also help you communicate and negotiate with prospective employers. Clarity in your financial picture may even make the difference between getting a job offer or not. In interviews, you intentionally and unintentionally communicate your confidence, organization, and responsibility, each of which can depend on your financial knowledge and position. **Sound finances make for peace of mind and sound plans.**

> "Personal finance is not something with which people are born. It is a skill that students need to develop. Education is an investment into one's future. Students come to school with a variety of financial needs. Financing education can sometimes be confusing or feel like a burden. The Financial Aid Department is there to assist students in developing the skills and plan to reach their educational goals. Contact your financial aid office to have them assist you in developing your personal financial plan."
>
> *Director of Financial Aid Rich Boruszewski*

To prepare for your career transition, first **assess where your finances stand, and modify your spending until you are acting responsibly.** Review your check register and reconcile it with your account statements. Draft a simple monthly budget of income and expenses using your check register. Also, develop a simple personal balance sheet showing your current assets and obligations. Do not hesitate to get help. Your law school may have student-services or career staff who know basic budgeting, or you may find help from a trusted law school friend. Better yet, use your library privileges and research skills to teach yourself basic personal finances. If you are at all uncertain of any past due obligations, then obtain and review your credit report. There is no better time to live for tomorrow than when you are in law school and studying. Be sure that you answer each of these questions from Steven R. Sedberry, Law School Labyrinth—A Guide to Making the Most of Your Legal Education 21 (Kaplan Pub. 2009), as frankly as possible:

- Is my spending within my means, meaning that I avoid incurring credit-card debt for living expenses?;
- Am I able to pay my credit-card debt in full each month or to pay at a rate that responsibly decreases the balance?;
- Am I current in all other obligations including student loans and mortgage payments?;
- Am I avoiding major purchases like car, furniture, and travel for pleasure that increase my debt on graduation?;

- Do I have at least some discretionary income at the end of each month to save or devote to unplanned contingencies?

If your answers to the above questions discourage you regarding your current financial situation, then act now. **Do not wait for graduation to address unsatisfactory personal finances.** You need to demonstrate to the state bar your character and fitness including your ability to manage your personal finances. Explore responsible ways to increase your income and decrease your expenses. Your law school's career office may help you locate paid work-study or teaching- and research-assistant positions, or part-time jobs in law offices or law-related fields. You law school's financial-aid office may be able to direct you to federal, state, or local grants and private scholarships. You may also find help from family members. On the expense side, you may be able to find alternative less-expensive housing, or you may find or move in with a roommate. Budget a reasonable amount for food, and then stick to the budget. If you do not plan and set aside in advance what you expect to spend for food each month, then you are probably spending more than you would if you did. You may be able to exchange services for expenses, like house-, dog-, or child-sitting in exchange for room and board, or transportation. Live within your means now so that you can live beyond your present means later.

Act responsibly as to student loans. **Borrowing for a professional education can be a wise plan when well managed, but do not borrow simply because you qualify to do so.** The key is to evaluate the cost, risk, and return of each loan in view of your overall circumstances. There are too many variables in loan plans and terms, and personal situations, to provide a sensible outline here. Your law school's financial-aid office has loan guides, financial-comparison forms, and other resources to help you evaluate and plan for loans. Also, look to other sources like the *Law School Labyrinth* text cited above (at pages 42–56) for more detail. In general, follow these steps and principles:

- determine your education costs, choosing sensibly;
- estimate conservatively your ability to cover those costs;
- determine accurately any resulting financial need;
- get complete and accurate loan-offer information;
- determine whether you qualify;

- compare loan offers for which you qualify;
- borrow responsibly only for reasonable need;
- do not borrow more than you need; and
- do not spend borrowed money for anything other than needs.

Next, plan your finances for your career transition. If you are unskilled in budgets and other financial matters, then get help and learn. **Consult your financial plan frequently and modify it as your financial knowledge and circumstances change.** Find out how part-time, interim employment affects your loan-deferment status. Part-time work can extend the period that you have for a job search, although it can also distract you from your job search. If you determine that you should or must work while looking for your law-career job, then look for a job that allows you time and flexibility for your law-career search. Better yet, look for a job that allows you to develop contacts within the legal community and expertise within your legal field, even if it is not law practice representing clients. Investigate loan-consolidation programs that reduce interest rates or extend payment periods so as to reduce monthly payments during an extended job search. If you cannot make loan payments, then immediately seek the lender's voluntary forbearance. Do not dodge loan responsibilities. Above all, **pay attention to your finances.** Ignoring your finances can lead not only to limited career options, poor financial decisions, and bad credit. Financial irresponsibility can also affect your character and fitness for bar licensure.

> "There is nothing wrong with wanting to make a decent living, but keep your priorities straight. Helping people is more important than making money. Develop a reputation for doing things right and the money will take care of itself."
>
> *Former State Court Judge Jeff Martlew*

Although debt levels can affect career choices, **substantial loan obligations need not be an impediment to lower-compensation law careers in public service.** Many states have loan-assistance programs for which law graduates can qualify if they take public-service jobs. The programs can provide several thousands of dollars of loan assistance annually if the public-service job provides an income under a capped amount. Many law schools offer loan-assistance programs or help graduates qualify for a state program.

Congress also recently created several Equal Justice Works loan-forgiveness programs for which law graduates can qualify by taking public-interest jobs. Another federal Income Based Repayment program reduces federal loan payments for law graduates taking public-interest jobs, based on income and family size. If you are interested in public service but expect to graduate with substantial loan obligations, then investigate these programs now.

Exercise. Take each of these steps in order, preserving what you find or develop in a single place such as a paper file or electronic folder:

> ➤ gather your bank statements and other financial records;
> ➤ investigate any unknown financial liabilities including
>> o what loans you have,
>> o when loan payments will begin,
>> o how much the payments will be, and
>> o what opportunities exist to suspend or reduce payments;
> ➤ document your current financial condition in a balance sheet;
> ➤ make conservative estimates of your anticipated income;
> ➤ make generous estimates of your anticipated expenses;
>> o use your check register for realistic expenditure estimates;
> ➤ develop two monthly budgets for the first year out of school using
>> o the job you reasonably expect to receive and
>> o your worst-case scenario of job and income;
> ➤ estimate how many months you have for full-time job search while
>> o planning for at least six months to search and
>> o understanding that some job searches can take a year.

> **Holly Jackson, J.D. 2007**
> "My undergraduate degree is in accounting, and I was working full-time and raising a child when starting law school, so I knew the value and necessity of financial planning. I committed to making wise financial choices while balancing work, study, and family throughout law school. I found a full-time job in a law firm while taking evening law school classes. Doing so enabled me to start a small-firm transactional practice in my hometown with a classmate after graduation. Everything worked out, thanks to financial planning."

Research—*Investigating*

Your research into career and professional-development options is another important career and professional-development tool. Do not leave your career options unexplored. **Use your research skills not only to learn law and prepare to serve clients but also to learn about law careers.** You have already seen a few of the many legal fields in which lawyers work. Your coursework exposes you to those fields. Yet lawyers work using those law subjects in a wide variety of practice settings. Each setting has its own challenges and rewards, and its own opportunities and character. You may love a particular law subject or field but find that you can enjoy and succeed in it only in a certain practice setting. Your research into those settings and alternative fields may lead you to a new career option or, on the other hand, confirm your current career goals. Several publications and resources can help you learn more about your practice-setting options including:

- URSULA FURI-PERRY, FIFTY UNIQUE LEGAL PATHS: HOW TO FIND THE RIGHT JOB (ABA 2008);
- GARY A. MUNNEKE, NONLEGAL CAREERS FOR LAWYERS (American Bar Association 2006);
- DEBORAH ARRON, WHAT CAN YOU DO WITH A LAW DEGREE? A LAWYER'S GUIDE TO CAREER ALTERNATIVES INSIDE, OUTSIDE, & AROUND THE LAW (LawyerAvenue Press 2003);
- GARY A. MUNNEKE, CAREERS IN LAW (McGraw-Hill 2003);
- KIMM ALAYNE WALTON, AMERICA'S GREATEST PLACES TO WORK WITH A LAW DEGREE & HOW TO MAKE THE MOST OF ANY JOB, NO MATTER WHERE IT IS (Harcourt Legal & Prof. Pubs. 1998);

- HINDI GREENBERG, THE LAWYER'S CAREER CHANGE HANDBOOK: MORE THAN 300 THINGS YOU CAN DO WITH A LAW DEGREE (HarperCollins 1998); and
- HILLARY MANTIS, ALTERNATIVE CAREERS FOR LAWYERS (Princeton Review 1997).

As you research practice settings, appreciate that it can make a difference to your career whether you are employed in a firm, as are the great majority of lawyers, or in a corporate counsel's office or other non-law firm position, as about one quarter of lawyers are. Lawyers working within firms generally have more independence than lawyers in non-law firm institutional settings. Lawyer independence brings its own set of rewards and challenges. The challenges can include longer hours and more uncertainty in everything. By contrast, corporate-counsel offices can involve relatively structured hours and predictable compensation, benefits, and workloads. They can also involve more interdependence in roles and responsibilities, meaning more teamwork, budgeting, and planning, less opportunity to advance, and the possibility of personality and political conflicts. There is stress in either setting, law firm or non-law firm. The stresses, challenges, and rewards are simply different. *See* AMIRAM ELWORK, STRESS MANAGEMENT FOR LAWYERS—HOW TO INCREASE PERSONAL & PROFESSIONAL SATISFACTION IN THE LAW 40–42 (Vorkell Group 3d ed. 2007). Do what you love, and you will find it less stressful and more valuable. **Survey the following list of common settings where lawyers work to determine which ones you might research:**

- law firms of varying size including
  - solo practice,
  - small firms (2 to 10 lawyers),
  - medium firms (11 to 50 lawyers),
  - large firms (51 to 100 lawyers), and
  - very large firms (101 to 1,000 lawyers;
- law-office management and administration;
- legal-aid offices and agencies;
- public-defender offices;
- prosecutor offices;
- public-interest organizations and firms;
- federal, state, and local government;
- Judge Advocate General corps and other military law;

- career judicial clerks and court staff attorneys;
- corporations (corporate counsel offices);
- financial institutions and organizations including
    o accounting firms,
    o banks,
    o securities firms, and
    o foundations;
- insurance companies including
    o corporate and compliance counsel and
    o in-house counsel for representation of insureds;
- labor unions and trade associations;
- arbitration, mediation, and other alternative-dispute-resolution services.

If none of the above settings attract you, then know that you have alternatives. Many lawyers begin practice in one of the above settings before discovering an alternative field that they prefer. Not all lawyers practice law in the above settings. Lawyers also use their law degrees and training in alternative fields. There are so many alternative careers for a lawyer in part because law is so prevalent in modern society. It is also true that the skills we learn as lawyers work well in other fields. The kind of critical thinking, problem solving, planning, rulemaking, advocacy, and strategic thinking for which law school trains lawyers are all highly valuable skills in general. These alternative fields, each depending on legal training but not the practice of law, each have their challenges and rewards, and opportunities and character. They are not necessarily any easier than law practice. The compensation may be lower, there may be more reporting and supervision, and there may be less flexibility and standing. On the other hand, they do avoid the billable hour and may minimize stress and provide for greater balance, civility, and security. **Review the following list to determine which alternative field you might investigate further:**

- court staff and administration;
- law school teaching and administration;
- law librarians;
- legal staffing;
- political office;
- legal writing and publication;

- trust administration;
- risk management;
- ethics officer;
- benefits administration;
- human-resources management;
- financial services and planning;
- business management and administration;
- foreign trade;
- nonprofit administration;
- healthcare compliance and administration;
- real-estate and other investment property management;
- homeland security;
- education administration;
- grant administration;
- management consulting and systems.

Your research skills can also help you find specific employers. Your challenge is not simply to choose a field. It includes finding employers within that field who may have an opportunity for your employment. Your research should begin with contacting your law school's career office for its information and resources. It will have job bulletins, postings, and classified advertisements from law firms and law schools across the nation. Also, contact the state and local bar associations where you hope to practice, for their law-firm and lawyer directories. Many bar associations publish job notices, postings, and advertisements online and in journals and newsletters. Law school libraries and public libraries also maintain lawyer and law-firm directories. Telephone directories list lawyers and firms. As you read trade journals in the field of your interest, look for lawyers whom they mention and law firms that advertise in those journals. **You can also research specific employers across the nation through these organizations and their websites:**

- The National Association for Law Placement and its Directory of Legal Employers;
- LexisNexis and its Career Center;
- West and its Legal Directory; and
- Martindale-Hubbell with its compendium of law firms and lawyers.

> "Two fundamental skills that are essential for competent representation in most areas of legal practice—legal research and factual investigation—are also essential for your job search. Investigate fields of practice through the wide variety of resources available online. If you prefer print sources, then a good starting reference is the National Association for Law Placement's *The Official Guide to Legal Specialties* by Lisa Abrams. Research employers through the employer's website, with search-engine inquiries, and by networking, with informational interviews, and through state bar records."
>
> ***Dean Charles Toy***

Your job research can prove even more valuable when economic times are uncertain, unemployment is higher, and employers are hesitating to post open positions. One author urges that you **treat your job research in these times as an effort to uncover the *hidden* job market.** *See* RICHARD L. HERMANN, MANAGING YOUR LEGAL CAREER—BEST PRACTICES FOR CREATING THE CAREER YOU WANT 63–92 (ABA 2010). The author recommends that in these times, when there are few job postings to pursue, you should research expanding and changing practice areas like health care law, telecommunications law, and banking law, and new specialty niches like tribal finance, carbon transactions, and art recovery. **Look for the hot practice areas, industries, and geographic areas.** The same author identifies networking, support groups, industry contacts, and trends analyses as particularly helpful during these times, recommending that you read legal news, trade publications, websites, investment news, government plans, and technology news. Here are additional research suggestions by the same author:

- read all job advertisements, not merely those for law positions, because hiring in one field may mean openings in law;
- look for companies and firms embarking on new ventures, making increasing profits, and expanding into new facilities;
- look for firms that recently hired or promoted lawyers as indication that there may be related openings;
- read press releases for new program initiatives in your area of skill and interest, where new positions may exist;
- read professional-membership organization announcements to see what firms are making new plans.

Your research into prospective employers does not have to be solely online and journal research. **Your law school's alumni network can be an excellent source for information** on law jobs in your chosen geographic area, practice setting, and subject field. Search your law school's alumni database using its geographic-area and subject-area fields. Contact alumni in the area, setting, and field for information about the hiring needs and practices of prospective employers. Use your contacts within the local bar association if you have joined it as a student member. **Do not overlook your family, friends, former employers, and other acquaintances outside of the law field, as potential sources for information on lawyers and law firms.** Job leads through the contacts provided by family and friends can be particularly useful when those family members and friends already have an established relationship with a lawyer in whose law firm you have an interest. When it comes to job searches, it never hurts to know someone who knows someone, especially when the person you know is your family member or friend. Your law school classmates and other law students who are conducting job searches can also help you focus your job search and supplement your research into prospective employers.

Your research skills can also help you find out more about specific employers. Once you locate a specific firm in which you have an interest, then **focus your research on that firm** using the informational interviews discussed in the prior section, Internet research sources, and your law school's alumni network. **Law firms maintain elaborate websites.** They often describe their practice fields, indicate their organizational structure into practice groups, publish detailed biographical information on each of their lawyers, and list their major clients. Medium and large firms also occasionally publish online their hiring information including their application process. You may, in other words, be able to learn much of what you need to know about whether, when, and how to apply for a job with a specific firm simply by reading carefully the law firm's website.

Once you have identified the targets of your job search and researched material information on them, use your research in several ways. First, ensure that you would want to work with and for them. Then, use your research to identify persons within the firm with whom you should be communicating about job prospects, that is, to earn an interview. Then, use the information to prepare for your interview and to conduct the interview in the way most beneficial to your job prospects. Your research should teach you enough about the lawyers who interview you to engage them in conversation in a way that reflects positively on your knowledge and interest, and even your research skill. You may also learn enough to avoid offending their school, institutional, and political loyalties and affinities. Do not snoop into your interviewers' private and social matters but know their professional biographies. Establish mutual trust, interest, and respect using your research. Finally, use your research to understand the probable terms of your employment, especially those terms that you should hesitate to ask in a first interview. That information may include compensation, benefits, partner and associate tiers, partnership track, billable-hours goals, and job security. As you can see, **your research can be the key to your career and professional development.**

Exercise. Reflect on and complete each of the following exercises, writing down and saving your research and reflections for future reference:

> ➤ assuming that you could have your pick of law-practice settings (solo, small firm, corporate counsel, etc.) from the list nearer the beginning of this section, rank your top two and then do preliminary research as to their particulars;
> ➤ assuming that you could have your pick of non-law-practice, law-related jobs (court staff, law teaching, etc.) listed above in the middle of this section, rank your top two and then do preliminary research as to their particulars;
> ➤ for each of the two law-practice settings and two law-related jobs you just selected, identify through further research one such specific employer in the geographic area where you would like to live after law school; and
> ➤ for each such employer, research information on its mission, organization, lawyers, clients, and hiring process.

Jessica DesNoyers, J.D. 2010

"I decided early on in law school that I would enjoy working for a large and stable law firm in a small midwestern town. I began researching firms on the Internet, using my school's career office, and speaking with professors, lawyers, and career-office staff. I was able to develop a list of potential firms to approach. To my delight, I am now an associate at the firm that was at the top of my list, in its branch office in a small town on the shore of Lake Michigan."

Communication—*Respecting*

Your communication skill is another tool to link your law school studies to your career. Clear, constructive, and professional communication may be the single most important skill that you exercise as you develop the contacts and relationships necessary to your further your job search. To some degree, **it may not matter how smart or accomplished you are, if your communications are inarticulate, insensitive, rude, abrupt, or otherwise inappropriate.** Your every communication with judges and lawyers with whom you network, managing and hiring partners of prospective employers, law-firm search-committee members, and their secretaries, staff, and other administrative support should be professional, positive, and supportive.

Rules for professional communication apply not only to resume cover letters and other correspondence but also **to email and other electronic communications.** Email is as appropriate a form of communication for a job search as it is for other professional communications. Email is appropriate for networking, initial contacts with prospective employers, initial inquiries about job postings, thanking those who provide you with references or other assistance in your job search, and negotiating, accepting, or declining job offers. Email is not appropriate for your formal application for a job (unless the employer indicates a requirement or preference for email submissions), thanking those who interview you for a job, or where the person or entity with whom you are communicating has expressly stated some other form of communication than email. **Follow these rules for email:**

- before sending email, reflect on and review it to the same extent as other written communications, assuming its same impact and permanency;
- expect anyone to whom your email refers or whom it involves to read it, even if you intend it as confidential to the recipient—email forwards easily;
- use correct grammar, spelling, capitalization, and punctuation, while eschewing abbreviations, shouting (all capitalization), and emoticons;
- use an appropriately conventional and formal email address, like your school address, rather than something personal and unconventional;

- do not send mass emails;
- do not use a current employer's email address when you are searching for other employment—loyalty matters;
- provide alternative contact information including telephone number and street address;
- convert email attachments to portable document format (pdf) or another stable format that discourages alterations and mining of metadata;
- save every email communication relating to your job search; and
- reply to emails within 24 hours.

> "I have been involved in hiring prosecutors for the U.S. Attorney's Office for more than a decade. The cover letter to a resume is critically important; it is usually the first impression a prospective employer gets of an applicant. In my experience, rarely, if ever, will a candidate get an interview who has grammatical or typographical mistakes in his or her cover letter. It may seem overly harsh and picayune, but my view is that, if a candidate cannot get a simple letter right – particularly one of such importance – why should I expect more of their everyday work? Also, be succinct. If you cannot get a prospective employer's interest in two paragraphs, all is lost."
> **Assistant United States Attorney Phil Green**

Although many of your job-search and networking communications are likely to be in person and by telephone and email, some communications will be by correspondence. **The most significant communication that you are likely to make in connection with your job search is the cover letter accompanying your resume.** Prospective employers may require or prefer that you submit job-application materials by email rather than by regular mail. Even when they do so, you should include a formal cover letter as a separate email attachment or as part of the email attachment that is your resume. Lawyers still print resumes for review and distribution, especially to carry into a hiring-committee meeting or your interview. You want prospective employers to have a formal cover letter introducing yourself and highlighting features of your application and resume. No matter how carefully crafted, an email introduction will not appear as professional as a formal cover letter attachment.

Think of your cover letter as reflecting your professional identity. Prospective employers may make more judgments about who you are and how you conduct yourself based on your cover letter than they do your resume. Cover letters highlight exceptional achievements, unique qualities, and unusual experience. They also convey a sense of how you balance your representation of yourself with your interest in your prospective employer. Write your cover letter recognizing that prospective employers who read it are thinking primarily of their own needs. You should link your qualifications with the employer's needs in a manner that compels its most earnest consideration. **Follow these guidelines when developing your cover letter:**

- Try to keep your cover letter to one page in length. Prospective employers who review dozens of resumes may not look beyond the first page of your cover letter;
- Ensure that your cover letter has no errors whatsoever. Some reviewers may disqualify you on the basis of a single minor grammatical or typographical error;
- Choose high-quality bond white or off-white paper and a matching envelope;
- Print your cover letter with a laser printer using a conventional font like Times New Roman in 12-point typeface for legibility, and format your letter as you would a standard business letter;
- Write a personal cover letter to the specific person indicated for receipt by the prospective employer rather than using a form letter, even if identifying that person requires multiple inquiries to the employer. Include the recipient's full and correctly spelled name, with correct title;
- Keep your writing concise and to the point, avoiding adjectives, adverbs, long sentences, idioms, and unconventional punctuation and sentence structure. Stay positive and enthusiastic;
- Describe yourself by your actions, activities, and accomplishments while avoiding opinions, comparisons, and unsupportable assertions;
- Include information about the prospective employer when you are sure that your research on that information is reliable.

Organize your cover letter in the following manner. If your cover letter is to be no more than one page, then organize it into three or four paragraphs. Begin in the first paragraph by telling the reader why you are writing. Identify yourself by indicating how far along in law school you are and when you expect to graduate and take the bar exam. Name the position you seek with the employer and how you learned about it. If you learned about the position from someone already working for the employer, the employer's client, or another person who may have some influence with the employer, then identify that person clearly. Include in the first paragraph something significant to your application that you know about the employer. A sample first paragraph would be:

> Managing partner John Doe of your La Jolla office recommended that I contact you about the open associate position in the tax group of your Miramar office. I am in my third year at Cooley Law School graduating in April and taking the July bar exam. I read in the state bar's tax section newsletter about the conference your Miramar office tax group just conducted. My IRS externship and undergraduate accounting degree make me a prime candidate for your open position.

Then, in the middle of the letter, tell why the prospective employer should consider hiring you. First make sure to show that you meet any special requirements for the position. Then choose three significant accomplishments that distinguish you from what you believe to be the minimum qualifications for the position. Avoid reciting your resume. Instead, connect each of the three accomplishments you select to the employer's needs. The middle of the letter should show by example (rather than by assertion) how your skills will meet the employer's needs and how you can exceed the employer's minimum expectations. For example:

> I know from Mr. Doe that your Miramar tax group needs an associate skilled in accounting principles and with knowledge of IRS practices. In my full-time externship with the IRS, I worked for several weeks with three IRS supervisors on dozens of files. Those supervisors developed such confidence in me that for the final two months of my externship, they assigned many more files solely to me. My undergraduate accounting degree also enabled me to use the IRS financial

software to make case-file calculations on my own, unlike other externs in the same program.

In the last paragraph, indicate the action you wish the prospective employer to take, usually to discuss the position with you in person, meaning to offer you an interview. Indicate that you will follow the letter with a telephone call on a specific date within about one week after the date of mailing. Calendar that date and make the call on that date. If the employer was impressed with your cover letter and resume, then the employer will appreciate your initiative and take your telephone call. End the letter by thanking the employer. Use a formal salutation like *Sincerely*, and sign your name in black or blue ink. For example:

I would like to meet with you about the associate position. Please expect my telephone call on Tuesday one week from today, to arrange a convenient meeting date. Please also know how much I appreciate your consideration. Thank you, and I look forward to speaking with you next week.

Write a draft of the letter several weeks or days before you need it. Set it aside, and then return to it for revision and editing at least twice before you finalize and send it. These practices should give you a cover letter that gives you the greatest chance of catching the attention of prospective employers, encouraging them to more closely examine your resume and offer you a job interview.

Exercise. For one of the preferred jobs and specific employers that you chose for the previous exercise, select your three accomplishments that you would feature in a cover letter requesting an interview for that job, and then draft the cover letter following the above instructions. Then evaluate your cover letter against these parameters:

- Is it error free?
- Is it one page long?
- Are the paragraphs each of approximately equal length?
- Are the sentences simple in structure?
- Did you avoid adjectives and adverbs?
- Did you use examples rather than assertions?
- Did you show that you knew the employer?

> ➤ Did you show how you could meet the employer's needs?
> ➤ Would the employer think you could exceed their needs?
> ➤ Would you hire the person who wrote it?

Lisa Hall, J.D., 2006

"One thing that I learned in law school while on Law Review and in my externship at a law firm is that there are few things more important to professional success than the quality of one's written communications. I received and accepted an offer from a major statewide law firm after graduation. I represent financial institutions in the areas of banking law and creditor's rights. I am sure that my job offer depended, and my success continues to depend, on the quality of my written communications."

Interviews—*Impressing*

The good interviewer often gets the job. There are good reasons why **the interview is the primary tool for students and graduates to perfect a job search and transition into a career.** Think of it. Most organizations will involve in some aspect of the interview the people for whom and with whom you will work. Cover letters, resumes, and telephone and email communications are no substitute for personal encounters when evaluating a job candidate's personality, interpersonal skills, character, attitudes, and fit to join a specific group of individuals performing complex work as a team. The value of interviews lies in the open interaction between candidate and interview team. The evaluations are no longer on the accomplishments reflected on the resume. Rather, they are in the gaps between the accomplishments, filled in by the myriad of factors that make up a person's character and personality. Most of us want to be liked, especially as a job candidate. **The intangible factors on which interviews turn can include:**

- life experience, balance, and maturity;
- knowledge of commerce and history;
- worldview, ideology, or perspective;
- articulation, sensitivity, and intellect;
- demeanor, attitude, energy, or spirit;
- humor, awareness, and timing; and
- humility, kindness, and thoughtfulness.

Being good at interviewing is like anything else: **it can simply take preparation and practice.** You should not attempt in an interview to change or disguise who you are. Rather, your challenge in an interview is to ensure that your interviewers see you in the best light rather than under the strained and artificial conditions of the interview. If you are overly nervous or unprepared, then your interview will not show you in a favorable light. One strategy to avoid being nervous and unprepared is to prepare for interviewing before you have your first significant interview scheduled. **Do not wait until you find and apply for your dream job to begin preparing for an interview.** You may get a call for an interview on short notice, without time to practice and prepare.

> "Be on time. Be convinced of what you bring to the table. Be prepared to convince the interviewer of that."
>
> **Assistant United States Attorney Phil Green**

Because interview skills involve sustained close personal interaction, you should **exhibit good personal habits and communication skills throughout the interview.** Listen attentively to those whom you meet in and around an interview. Empathize, treating everyone as important. Avoid interrupting. Never criticize or gossip. Yet in-person communication involves more than these basic communication skills. It also involves how you move and position yourself relative to the interviewer and others, to demonstrate courtesy and respect. One technique is to match and mirror the interviewer's posture, expression, and level of rapport. *See* Barbara Miller and Martin Camp, The Law Firm Associate's Guide to Connecting with Your Colleagues 72-74 (ABA Law Practice Management Section 2009). Basic practices include:

- an initial greeting in which you step forward confidently, look the person whom you are greeting in the eye, smile, and extend your right hand forward for a confident but respectful handshake;
- remembering names of persons to whom you are introduced. If you have trouble remembering names, then repeat the person's name aloud as you shake hands while looking the person in the eye, and then immediately say the person's name again twice to yourself;

- when shown to an office to be seated, letting the interviewer show you where to sit. Place your folder on the desk or table in front of you;
- sitting respectfully and attentively. Sit slightly forward in the chair with your hands naturally together in front of you, not slouching in the chair leaning heavily on or gripping its armrests. Keep both feet on the ground if you are at a table or desk, but cross your ankles or legs if you are seated in an open area or at a coffee table. You may respectfully mimic your interviewer's posture unless your interviewer takes a substantially more relaxed posture, in which case you should remain in an attentive posture; and
- speaking at a measured pace without uhs or ums, while maintaining respectful eye contact.

> "Be yourself in interviews. Interviewing is like a first date—why on earth would you try to be something that you are not if you hope to have a long-term relationship?"
>
> **Dean Amy Timmer**

Some employers will have several lawyers interview you at once. Other employers will have a smaller number of lawyers conduct your primary interview and then have you spend a few minutes with several other lawyers one at a time in each of their offices, each of whom will then share their impressions with one another and the interview team. Treat each meeting with each lawyer as its own interview. Also, do not underestimate the challenge of entering a full board room around the conference table of which sit half a dozen distinguished lawyers ready to hear you talk about yourself. Your mind may be perfectly at ease in such a situation, but your body can still play strange tricks on you, like a shaky and breathless voice, sweaty palms, ringing ears, and pounding heart. **Prepare now, when you have the time to practice and learn about interviewing.** Let your body grow accustomed to the challenge, as much as your mind.

One reliable way to prepare is to **participate in mock interviews through your law school's career office.** Mock interviews help you learn about and adjust to interview norms and settings. Interviews have unspoken behavioral rules, just as do other social settings. Mock interviews make the hidden rules evident. Your career office may conduct mock interviews in the same manner as a real interview, although it may also offer speed interviewing (having a few minutes with several different interviewers one after another in line) or other methods that can be equally effective. You should dress for the interview and conduct it as if it were real. Your mock interviewers should be lawyers, judges, and career professionals experienced with interviewing, willing to give you prompt and specific feedback on your interview performance. Your career office should video-record your mock interview for you to review with career-office personnel. Expect to be disappointed with your first mock interview, but also expect your subsequent mock interviews to improve dramatically. Make written note of all constructive feedback for your review before your real interviews.

Before your interview, think carefully about your strengths, and be ready to discuss them. Examples can include your research and writing, organization and administration, speaking and communication, negotiation and confrontation, finances and management, and public and professional service. **Identify and describe your particular skills.** There is a fine line between discussing your strengths and sounding like you are over-confident or (worse) arrogant. One way to avoid sounding like you are bragging is to reveal your strengths through examples rather than assertions, opinions, and comparisons. If your interviewer asks whether you have done much legal writing, rather than say simply that you have written a lot and are a great writer, give your interviewer an example of something significant that you wrote and how it was received by its audience. For instance, if your supervising judge in your judicial internship asked you to draft a proposed opinion granting summary judgment in a significant case, and you produced a ten-page opinion that the judge adopted with few edits, then consider giving that example. Before the interview, **identify your strengths and be ready to give an example for each.**

> "People generally project what they believe, so have confidence in yourself. You won't be able to convince others if you don't believe in yourself."
>
> **Former State Court Judge Jeff Martlew**

Some things are easier to do in an interview than in written communications. Admitting your weak areas is one of them. Many interviewers include among their standard questions where you feel that you most need to improve. What makes the question difficult is that you must say something that is, in a sense, negative about yourself. You cannot answer, "Nothing." To do so would be arrogance and demonstrate an inability to frankly self evaluate and improve. **Before your interview, think about your weaknesses, and be ready to admit one.** Choose carefully. There are some weaknesses that no employer can accept, like embezzlement. Another key is to make your admission in the context of your plan to improve, like:

> Tough question, although I understand and appreciate why you would ask because I do evaluate my weaknesses so that I know where to improve. I am not as familiar with law-office systems (time-keeping, billing, conflict-checking) as I know that I will need to be. I have obviously heard about these things in law school but not yet practiced them. I am hoping that your firm has training on your timekeeping and case-management system, and that I can quickly find a mentor to whom I can turn when it comes down to a judgment call on being responsible to those systems.

One way to be sure that you answer all questions and the employer has all of the information it needs during your interview is to **bring extra copies of your cover letter, resume, references, and writing sample.** Consider the case in which you carry your papers to be part of your professional dress. Prefer a simple, dark grey or black, slim zippered leather folder that you can carry easily like a small notebook in one hand over anything bulky, brightly colored, and distracting. You can then place the folder on a conference table or desk in front of you or on your lap, and open it readily when needed. You can also carry inside it, on the top above your copies, a lined blank 8 ½" x 11" paper pad on which to take any notes, if the need should arise. You should not take notes during your interview unless someone offers information that they specifically expect you to record, like a helpful title or resource. Lawyers carry their papers in zippered folders or clasped cases for confidentiality. Allowing papers to spill out of a dropped folder is unprofessional. No one should be able to see any labels, notes, or other part of your papers unless you want them to.

Anticipate difficult questions. Interviewers ask difficult questions not solely for the content of your answer but to evaluate your ability to control your words and emotions, and to recover and continue to show confidence throughout the rest of the interview.

Most interviewers are highly skilled. They will not be rude or prying. Yet at least once during many interviews, the interviewer will intentionally approach or perhaps even cross a subtle line, using a hint of rudeness or disrespect. For instance, the interviewer may question your choice of undergraduate institution or major, or even your law school. **Never take offense.** The interviewer probably highly values exactly that which the interviewer challenges but wants to see whether you do, too, and to judge how you react. A good approach can be to assume that the interviewer is doing exactly that, waiting for you to speak what you know to be true and then to agree with you in relief that you did not take the question as condemnation and disrespect. Stand politely but firmly by your experience, choices, and convictions, while respecting the interviewer no matter what the interviewer asks.

Interviewers also frequently ask **why the employer should hire you over the many other candidates who applied.** Prepare and practice an answer. Your first practice attempt at an answer will likely not be the one that you ultimately use. For instance, that you are excited at the opportunity would not be unique. Presumably, so would be every other candidate. You need to have a short, clear, and compelling answer that connects your qualifications and character to the employer's needs, for example:

> Well, I do not know the other candidates, although I can presume that you have many fine applicants given the attractiveness of this job. Yet I doubt that many of them combine my engineering degree and background with the externship that I did in the Patent Office. And I doubt that any of them have the recommendation of the Patent Office's chief. I gave my all to that externship with this very moment in mind, that it would show you better than anything I can say that I am your best candidate.

You can and should **anticipate and prepare standard questions that interviewers ask.** Interviewers deliberately develop open-ended questions that force you to think creatively and speak in an unguarded fashion. Do not be taken aback by how little information is in the questions and how much information that they elicit. Open-ended questioning is the art of interviewing. Keep in mind that there are no single correct answers. The best answer can change depending on other questions already asked and the answers you have already given. Your answers can also depend to some extent on the apparent interest and experience of the interviewer. Also, keep in mind that the content of your answer is often less important than your manner of answering. **It is not always what you say but how you say it.** Do not memorize answers. Rather, reflect on each of the common questions and prompts below to the point that they would not surprise you and that you would feel comfortable and conversant in answering:

- What would you like us to know about you?
- What are some of your best qualities?
- What will make you a skilled lawyer?
- What is the accomplishment that you most value?
- What would your previous employers say about you?
- How do you take constructive criticism? Can you give an example?
- How do you respond when unfairly criticized?
- What do you want to see from your supervisor?
- Give an example of a successful workplace collaboration.
- What do you do to adapt and respond to stress?
- What was your favorite course in law school?
- What was your worst law school grade, and why?
- Why did you choose your law school?
- Where do you want to be in five years? Ten years?
- How effective are you at handling multiple responsibilities at once?
- What do you want to see in an employer?
- Why do you want to work for us?
- What do you most bring to the table?
- Tell me about the work you did for your last employer.

Remember to **review your research on the prospective employer** with whom you are interviewing and on each interviewer before the interview. Before the interview, contact members of your professional network such as those professionals with whom you conducted an informational interview. Tell them with whom you are interviewing, to learn anything from them that may help you in the interview. They may make a telephone call on your behalf to an interviewer whom they know. Here is a checklist for what you should review and know before your interview:

- your commitment to the employer's geographical area;

- your ability to serve the employer's clients;
- your ability to bring new clients to the employer;
- why you are interested in working for this employer;
- the employer including its
  - mission;
  - organizational structure (practice groups, departments, etc.);
  - major clients and general clientele;
- the interviewer including
  - title and role (managing partner, hiring-committee chair, etc.),
  - law school and memberships,
  - practice specialty,
  - publications; and
- anything you have in common with the interviewer (alma mater, associations, contacts) about which to converse.

Keep in mind during your interview that you are responding to the interviewer's questions, not conducting a monologue about your life. Your purpose is not to fill the interview's every moment with the sound of your voice. A good basic rule is not to volunteer substantial information about yourself on multiple subjects that the interviewer has not approached. You can and for the most part should **only answer the questions asked** and answer them somewhat concisely. Elaboration using examples is certainly appropriate. Five-minute soliloquies are not. If the interviewer wants additional information, then the interviewer will ask. It is appropriate and even desirable at times during an interview to allow it to become a conversation. Yet avoid carrying the conversation beyond short interludes. Your interviewer has a job to accomplish. Your willingness to let the interviewer control the interview shows your ability to accept supervision and respect the task at hand.

On the other hand, even though a job interview is not an informational interview, do still **prepare questions about the employer.** Your research will have answered basic questions like those above. You should not ask questions that make it appear that you are unprepared for the interview. Yet at some point during the interview, usually near its end, most interviewers will ask if you have any questions. The point of that interview tactic is not solely to be sure that you know what you feel you need to know. It is instead another measure of your skill and attitude. An interviewer may misconstrue your reluctance to ask one or two questions as a lack of confidence or interest. Some questions that are more difficult to answer with research, that suggest good things about you, and that may be appropriate for you to ask during your interview include:

- what qualities the employer wants in a new hire and for promotion;
- how the employer manages assignment of work and supervision of associates;
- more specific duties the employer expects you to fulfill than those disclosed in the job posting;
- specific clients or types of clients whom the employer expects you to serve;
- training programs, conferences, and continuing legal education that the employer will offer you;
- mentors or types of mentors whom the employer may assign or make available to you;
- the employer's evaluation system including how often, by whom, and how the employer communicates feedback;
- practice areas where the employer expects the greatest growth to be in the near and long term;
- new projects the employer expects to undertake in the near future, and innovations or improvements the employer wishes to make;
- professional organizations that the employer expects you to join;
- industry, labor, or trade associations whose members the employer expects you to court; and
- pro-bono and community service that the employer encourages.

Some interviewers welcome questions about the interviewer. You should not try too much to make the interview about the interviewer, especially if the interviewer's work has little relationship to the job for which you are interviewing. You could do an excellent job of learning about and engaging the interviewer but leave the interviewer relatively clueless about who you are, and not get the job offer. Yet interviewers are often as readily pleased and impressed when you take an interest in them as are others with whom you converse. **Asking questions about the interviewer can be a good way to learn more about the employer's goals and practices, and about the workplace, while maintaining rapport.** If the interviewer seems amenable to a personal inquiry, then consider asking about the matters on which the interviewer is working, the interviewer's most interesting work, the interviewer's typical day, and how long the interviewer has been with the employer.

As you can see, there are many considerations surrounding interviews. As with so many things, when you look closely at what preparation and practice an interview takes for you to succeed, there is much to consider and do. **Have a clear picture in your mind of how you want the interview to go.** Consider these outcomes for the successful interview, that you will have:

- arrived on time, prepared, relaxed, and comfortable, greeting the staff and interviewer cordially;
- been professional in your dress and demeanor, consistent with employer norms;
- been engaged and attentive throughout the interview, maintaining consistent energy and interest;
- been reasonably comfortable and relaxed throughout the interview, able to enjoy the process;
- answered all questions without asking the interviewer to let you get back to them with an answer;
- not been surprised by any question that the interviewer asked or at a loss for words;
- had on hand what the employer needed to complete its interview process, including copies of your submissions;
- spoken audibly, articulately, and concisely in response to interview questions, without being dominating or verbose;
- asked the interviewer one or two questions when invited to do so, reflecting responsible interest in the employer;
- were cordial and considerate with every person with whom you came into contact including not only interviewers but staff;
- avoided any misstatements that disrespected the law, legal profession, employer, its clients, its work, and its lawyers and staff;
- responded to all difficult questions in a positive and respectful manner, maintaining your confidence;

- concluded the interview on an upbeat, friendly, and interested tone, ready to send a thank-you note; and
- ensured that the employer had your contact information including a reliable telephone number at which you can be reached.

It may also help you to **have a clear picture in mind of how you do *not* want the interview to go.** Consider these outcomes to avoid:

- arrived late;
- mumbled greetings;
- overlooked offering to shake extended hands;
- forgot the names of introduced interviewers and staff;
- took the interviewer's seat;
- was unenthusiastic and distant;
- slouched listlessly when seated;
- fidgeted inattentively;
- was unprepared;
- was surprised by questions;
- was at a loss for words;
- answered evasively;
- forgot to mention your key accomplishments and strengths;
- refused to admit a weakness;
- admitted a weakness that put you in a bad light;
- was over-confident to the point of arrogance;
- acted defensively;
- took offense and then sulked through the interview;
- blamed others for your own shortcomings; and
- assumed that the job was already yours.

The above guidelines are for in-person interviews. Employers make increasing use of videoconference interviews. A video-conference interview is not a sign of a lack of commitment to the interview process or to you. It may be a screening mechanism for a later in-person interview, or it may be the primary or sole interview. **Take a videoconference interview just as you would an in-person interview, as a sign of strong interest in and commitment to you.** Employers increasingly have lawyers working in multiple far-flung offices on integrated tasks. They make regular use of videoconferencing capability. An employer's willingness to draw into your interview lawyers from distant offices signals the significance of your interview. Prepare for and conduct a videoconference interview as you would an in-person interview.

Then consider these special guidelines for videoconference interviews. Expect an introduction from each participant so that you know who is at the remote site observing your interview. If there are several persons present at the remote site, then consider making quick notes of their names and roles. It can be hard to recall persons you cannot see or can see only partly at the remote site. Be even more patient than usual. You may need to wait for a slight transmission delay. If you speak too quickly, then you may speak over the interviewer due to the transmission delay. If you do so, then stop and ask your interviewer's pardon. Speak in a slightly more measured pace, and end clearly so that remote interviewers know that you are finished even with the transmission delay. Lean slightly in and be sure that your facial expressions are clear for the video transmission. Follow these other guidelines:

- although you should wear professional dress, avoid stripes, plaids, and other patterns that can look distracting and distorted on camera;
- avoid shiny clothing, jewelry, hair, lipstick, and other adornment that may reflect light and be distracting on camera;
- do not substantially alter your voice, demeanor, or interview style simply for the camera, making yourself seem unnatural;
- focus on the interviewer and questions to the point that you forget that you are on camera;
- let the microphones pick up your voice, allowing the technicians to adjust volumes;
- limit head, hand, and body motion somewhat so that the camera can follow you, while avoiding stiffness;
- maintain eye contact even across the video feed, focusing on the interviewer as you would in an in-person interview;
- use the same level of energy, interest, and enthusiasm as you would for an in-person interview;
- end the interview by thanking the remote interviewers each by name, while expressing your continuing interest in the job; and

• leave the interview room before making any comments to anyone at your location regarding how the interview went for you.

Exercise. Choose three of the following activities, completing them within the next term:

➢ schedule and complete at least one mock interview;
➢ write down your strengths, pick three, and write an example of each;
➢ write down your weaknesses, pick one, and write how to improve it;
➢ write answers to five of the standard questions listed above;
➢ answer to a mirror three of the difficult questions from above;
➢ practice greetings until you can remember at least three names; and
➢ video record yourself telling an employer why it should hire you.

Samuel Pratcher, J.D. 2009

"My goal as a law student was to prepare for a career in public service. I knew that I had to have good interviewing skills not just to get opportunities but to advance in them. Winning election as a Student Bar Association representative, president of the Federal Bar Association, and treasurer of the Black Law Students Association in law school helped sharpen my professional identity. I also served as a federal district court extern and state attorney general's office clerk, and then in a post-graduate trial-court clerkship, meaning that I interviewed successfully for each of those competitive positions. I am now an associate at a large law firm where, in a sense, every day is a new interview, and I love the work."

Negotiation—*Agreeing*

Negotiation over job terms is another important tool for your transition from law school to law career. Negotiation occurs at the time of a job offer, not during a job interview. You may wonder what there is to negotiate when you have been offered your dream job or when you simply need any job. Yet your principled and considered communications with an employer who is offering you specific job terms can set the right tone for the beginning of your employment and for future advancement with the employer. The message that "I'll take anything" is not necessarily the message that your future employer wants to hear. Any employer making a job offer wants to believe that they are hiring a professional of value. **You should know the terms of your employment before agreeing to it.** Even in those cases where you know that you will take virtually any terms from an employer who is offering you a job, there are still important options that it can be wise to discuss even if not (strictly speaking) to negotiate, like which of two or more offices or practice groups to join.

Be sure that you know that the compensation you are receiving is fair. There are several sources of information for lawyer compensation. Your law school should publish median salary information. The National Association for Law Placement publishes annual associate-salary surveys. Several state bars perform and publish periodic compensation surveys. Those surveys can show you what lawyers earn based on geographic region, practice area, law-firm size, and years of experience. Government jobs publish specific salary information. There are any number of online services publishing lawyer-compensation information. **Prepare for your negotiation by researching the probable compensation range.** Know that ranges vary by practice type. National Association for Law Placement data for 2007 graduates nine months after graduation indicates median salaries of $108,500 for private practice, $69,100 for business, $50,000 for government, $48,000 for academic and judicial-clerkship positions, and $68,500 for all graduates in all occupations. Know, too, though, that in study of lawyer happiness, lawyers rank income level below their work's public value, ability to make decisions independently, creative challenges, and interpersonal interaction with others. Nancy Levit & Douglas O. Linder, The Happy Lawyer: Making a Good Life in the Law 8–11, 52 (Oxford Univ. Press 2010).

Expect the employer to make an offer by telephone. Some employers will write first, but others prefer to make the first notice of an offer by telephone. Be sure that you are available to take the call. Return any message swiftly. **Expect an offer or a call back for further interviews when you receive an employer's call.** Your surprise is neither necessary nor helpful. It might show that you do not think that you are worth an offer. On the other hand, do not hesitate to show the offering employer that you are pleased at the offer. A job offer is not a conventional negotiation in which you hope to conceal your satisfaction with the first offer made. If you feel it, then show your joy. Yet maintain a reserve that enables you to reflect and communicate sensibly about important job terms. Giddiness benefits neither you nor your future employer.

Do not accept an offer instantly. The employer is hiring a lawyer whom the employer reasonably expects to either negotiate terms or to at least know them before accepting. The employer will give you a time period within which to think about the employer's offer. Listen carefully to what the employer expects in the way of your response, especially how long you have to think about the offer. You may indicate in the initial telephone call that you plan to accept, but if you do so, make it a preliminary acceptance until you learn the details and confirm acceptable terms. If your initial telephone discussion does not include sufficient detail and opportunity for you to negotiate and agree to clear terms, then ask the employer when you should expect a detailed letter with that information. Give the employer an estimate for when you will make a firm reply to the offer, making your estimate well within the time period that the employer indicates.

> "Negotiations are open discussions intended to produce an agreement. An open discussion is not demanding, confrontational, unyielding, nor marked by impatience. Keep in mind that you are never off-the-record or off camera. Always focus the employer on your qualities and how those qualities will have an immediate positive impact on the employer's business. The result of a successful negotiation is that both parties are satisfied. Act wisely. Always remember that the employer has the ultimate choice of not offering you a position or rescinding an offer."
>
> *Dean Charles Toy*

Use the initial offer as an opportunity to clarify job terms especially as to base compensation and benefits, and employment security such as contract status or partnership track. Here is where your research can pay dividends, if you have a sense of the salary ranges and common benefits packages offered associates in your field, firm size, and geographic region. Also, have an idea of what compensation you need. The employer's offer will include a starting salary. Some firms compensate associates at set salaries with lockstep increases each year. Other firms provide a base salary plus bonuses or other merit pay based on billed hours, client recruitment, or similar measures of productivity. If your research did not reveal those terms, then an offer is an appropriate time to inquire. The employer should take your inquiry as an indication of your confidence in your productivity. If the employer does not make it clear, then be sure to **confirm whether the offered position is on the employer's partnership or other long-term track,** or whether the offer is for a contract position that the employer expects to treat as temporary.

In addition to base salary, it is acceptable to **inquire at the time of an offer as to what benefits the firm provides** and what benefits it makes available at your cost. Learn the basic terms of the firm's retirement plan. Federal law requires standardization in benefits offered under employee plans. Do not expect to negotiate health insurance, dental insurance, and contributions to retirement plans, for instance. Yet there may among certain employers of lawyers (particularly small to medium-size law firms) be greater variety in other benefits than you might find or expect in other employment. For example, law firms may offer or negotiate over company vehicles, cell telephones, mobile computing, performance bonuses, professional-development expenses, association and club memberships, moving expenses, and temporary housing expenses. Hesitate to negotiate over vacation, personal days, and other terms that make it appear that you hope to limit or avoid work. Instead, **negotiate over terms that would improve your professional development and productivity.**

If you want terms other than those that the employer offers, then avoid making a simple rejection of the offer, even if you are willing to risk losing the offer. Instead, indicate why you deserve other terms. If the offer does not meet the compensation provided to others in comparable employment, then explain so. Your research may help inform the employer in a way that will justify its making a higher offer. If your request has to do with your skill and alternatives, then indicate so. It may help the employer value you more than it otherwise would have. On the other hand, do not attempt to force an employer to negotiate against other employers. Present information. Do not leverage other opportunities. Doing so may suggest lack of loyalty and interest, and can either cause the employer to withdraw the offer or give you a reputation within the firm that will not be conducive to your advancement. If the employer will not negotiate base compensation to your satisfaction, then **negotiate benefits** that increase the overall value of your employment. Do not evaluate offers solely on base compensation. Include the value of all benefits.

Know when and how to accept and reject. **Get the help of your faculty advisor, mentor, and career staff.** Many counselors make for wise decisions. Reject an offer when the total value of the offer is not within what you determine from research and the counsel of reliable advisors to be a fair range. Also, reject an offer when you firmly believe the employment to be a bad fit, even if the compensation meets your expectations. Accept when compensation is fair and doing so will further your career. Not every job seems at first to be a perfect fit. Often, those jobs that did not at first seem to be the best fit end up being just what you would later choose. Jobs can gradually change to fit the gifts of their occupants. Do not force or expect an employer to change for you, but do expect the role and your skills to gradually change and the job to become a better fit over time. Ordinary jobs can become dream jobs in time, as you and the job both grow.

Accept and reject in person or by telephone, not by telephone message, email, or correspondence. If you call to accept or reject and do not reach the responsible lawyer at the employer, then leave a message indicating that you wish to speak to them in reply to their offer, without disclosing your decision. If there are any unusual delays, then follow up through another appropriate channel such as a secretary who supports the responsible lawyer. Wait to disclose your decision until you can do so in a live communication, either by telephone or in person, when you can express your gratitude and excitement with an acceptance or your appreciation and regrets with a rejection. Immediately after accepting, send the employer your written letter thanking the employer and confirming your acceptance. Expect and if necessary request the employer's letter confirming the employment, compensation, benefits, and start date. Then notify your law school's career office for its statistical purposes. Be sure to handwrite individual thank-you notes to each person who helped you in the job-search process. Although you expect to remain for a long time in the job you just won, there are few guarantees. Your law school's career staff is your resource throughout your career, not just for your first job.

Exercise. Before your first interview, confirm that you are ready to respond to a job offer in each of these respects, that you know:

> ➤ the compensation range for comparable jobs;
> ➤ the available benefits you might negotiate;
> ➤ what office or practice-group assignment you would accept;

> ➤ what start date you can meet (soonest and latest); and
> ➤ anything that would delay your decision, and for how long.

Kevin Keenan, J.D. 2008

"I worked in Manufacturing Management for many years before going to law school. In that role, I was involved in numerous negotiations dealing with labor issues, so the thought of negotiating my own law job intrigued me. I also had extensive contacts in my community. During law school, my externship at a large firm taught me some of the differences between law-firm employment and other employment. While volunteering as a mediator, I was introduced to a managing partner from a small 125-year-old firm comprised of a few very distinguished lawyers who were not in the habit of hiring new associates. My ability to appreciate the firm's interests while helping them to value my negotiation skills and community contacts led to an associate position and great relationships. I have a dream job largely due to skilled negotiation on both sides."

Career Transitions

As you should have just seen, identifying and developing your skills while using tools to capture and reflect them are important steps in your career and professional development. Yet you must then use those tools to connect your skills with specific career opportunities. One way that you connect your skills to careers is to identify the specific community in which you expect to practice. Another way is to identify your preferred environment, whether formal or informal, and preferred level of teamwork or independence. You may also connect your skills to career choices through your preferred population for interaction, whether primarily with other lawyers and professionals or with clients. This chapter helps you begin to reflect on these connections between your skills and your career choices and preferences. As we go through them one by one, **keep these connections in mind:**

- the community of which you should be a member;
- the formality or informality of your preferred work environment;
- the level of teamwork or independence your skills best match;

and

- the population with which you prefer to interact, whether lay or professional.

Communities—*Flourishing*

Lawyers practice in specific communities, not just in the state of their licensure and within their law firms or other organizations and practice fields. Many factors may influence your choice of community in which to practice including climate, culture, recreation, affordability and finances, family, faith, friends, and other social interests and personal preferences and relationships. Your lawyer skills and law career also have something to do with the community in which you should practice. The skills that you exercise depend in part on the community in which you practice. **Every community has its own culture and conventions of practice.** Skills that work excellently in one community may hardly work at all in another. Skills that you find comfortable and natural may work well in one community, while another community may require that you practice in ways that hardly seem to fit you at all. The best in one community is the bully in another.

Although there are many variables along which communities of practice differ, **practices differ especially between communities of different population sizes.** Because of the larger numbers of lawyers in larger metropolitan areas, practice there tends to be relatively more anonymous. Your new matters often involve lawyers and clients whom you have never met before and may not again. The relative anonymity of practice makes for constantly fresh encounters and new relationships, which you may or may not prefer. It also makes encounters less predictable. Each matter depends on your performance in that matter, meaning that you must prove yourself each time rather than relying on your reputation and relationships. In small-town practice, you tend to know and have significant professional experience with most or all of the lawyers and judges, and perhaps also the clients. Relationships from matter to matter may be as or more important than performance in any one case. Consider your skills, whether suited to big city or small town.

"I was amazed at the rather profound differences in practice culture as I moved from New York City, where I began my practice, to smaller cities like Buffalo and Pittsburgh, where I spent my later practice years. While this is certainly a generalization, it is safe to say that on balance practice in New York City placed more of a premium on aggressiveness and results, while in the smaller cities it was first important to establish good working relationships with your opposing counsel in the practicing bar. Indeed, in the smaller communities it was a prerequisite to success to 'get along' with opposing counsel, whereas in New York City that was rarely mentioned as a core value. That difference informed much of how I conducted myself as a professional, from my relationships to other attorneys to, surprisingly, support staff at my respective firms. It took some time for me to adjust as I made the move from large to smaller city. Lawyers frequently note this cultural difference as they compare cities, but it is not until one experiences it that it actually resonates. It certainly is something about which all law school graduates should be aware. Location and geography make a huge difference to how you will experience your career."

Dean Charles Cercone

Communities of professionals differ in other ways. **The proximity of your professional community to other professional communities can influence either the unity of your professional community on one hand or its openness and fluidity on the other hand.** If there is no other local bar for many miles as may be true in Western states, then you may have a relatively more stable, closed, and connected community. The lawyers may know much of what is going on with one another. Professional relationships may be slower to develop and change, and reputations harder to earn and easier to lose. If there are other large population centers nearby with substantial local bars as may be true along the metropolitan East or West Coast, then your professional community may be less stable, closed, and connected. Professional relationships may form and dissolve more quickly, and reputations may be easier to earn and harder to lose because the lawyers are less able to know as much of what is going on with the more loosely connected lawyers. Consider your skills, whether suited to stable or fluid bars.

Regions can affect the character of a professional community and the skills you should possess and exercise. The Northeast, Southeast, Midwest, Deep South, Plains States, Northwest, Southwest, and West Coast each have their professional culture, just as they do their own popular history and culture. What passes for character in one region lawyers may see as buffoonery in another. What is high art in one region judges may see as recklessness in another. What is appropriate restraint in one region clients may see as insultingly cold and aloof in another. In civil litigation, styles and methods can vary widely from region to region in oral advocacy, pleading, discovery, alternative dispute resolution, brief writing, and other procedure, as can the conduct of criminal cases. Dockets may be crowded and case schedules fast paced in one region, rewarding those who can balance multiple changing responsibilities, while other regions may have slow dockets and longer case schedules, rewarding those who plan assiduously. **Consider how your skills will fit in the region in which you are most interested.**

Communities also differ widely in their industries, employment base, and economies, affecting the skills you should have for practice. Some communities have sophisticated economies involving technology, advanced manufacturing, green energy, and finance, where you would benefit from having corporate and technical skills. Other communities have economies based on agriculture, mining, fishing, timber, and related services, where you might benefit from having a mix of labor and industry-related skills. Other communities have economies based on healthcare, education, and social services, where a lawyer's organizational, communication, and collaboration skills may be at a premium. **Consider the economy of the community in which you wish to practice and how your skills may match it.**

Seeking a job in a community at some distance from your law school presents specific challenges. Be prepared for those challenges. Law graduates go all over the country for their jobs. You need not graduate from a local law school to get a job in the firm or with the employer you most desire. Simply address the distance concerns. Be ready to pay for or negotiate travel expense to an interview, if the firm or employer is not sending a representative to your school. Consider combining interviews with other travel, either for housing searches, sightseeing, or visiting family and friends. Determine whether the employer will conduct an initial interview by videoconference or teleconference. When you do arrange an interview with an out-of-town employer, be ready to demonstrate your commitment to relocating. Have a plan and timetable for applying for bar admission and taking the bar exam in the employer's location, to demonstrate your willingness to relocate. Follow this list of do's and don'ts suggested in RICHARD L. HERMANN, MANAGING YOUR LEGAL CAREER—BEST PRACTICES FOR CREATING THE CAREER YOU WANT 250 (ABA 2010):

- do research the location thoroughly;
- do learn the housing and other living costs;
- do emphasize your ties to the area when interviewing;
- do not assume the employer will pay for your relocation; and
- do not assume that the employer will help your spouse.

Exercise. Choose a community in which you have an interest in practicing. Then, research the following conditions as to that community, recording and saving your notes. Then, reflect on how these conditions might affect whether your skills are a good fit for the community. Also, consider whom you might ask about that fit, especially a lawyer, judge, or other leader in the community who knows you:

- ➤ the population of the community's metropolitan area;
- ➤ the proximity of other large metropolitan areas;
- ➤ the number of lawyers in the local bar association;
- ➤ the size of any nearby local bar associations;
- ➤ the community's social and legal services;
- ➤ the community's history and philanthropy;
- ➤ the lawyers' professional culture and prevalent style;
- ➤ the community's services or industries;
- ➤ the number of courts and judges;
- ➤ the court docket sizes and average time to trial;

Kara Rozin, J.D. 2008

"I did an externship downtown in a major Midwest city and loved the fast pace of my law firm. Yet although the firm offered me a job after the externship, I decided that big city life was not for me. I took a job in a smaller Midwest city and am so glad that I made that choice. Things have worked out well for me."

Environments—*Adapting*

The work environments in which lawyers practice also vary in ways that can fit, more or less effectively, your individual skills. Founders tend to establish a law firm's culture both deliberately and without intention. Your hiring and eventual promotion may depend on recognizing and ascribing to the founder's conventions and firm's culture. Renegades, rebels, and nonconformists tend not to make partner. Even when the firm's founders are no longer alive or with the firm, their influence often lasts, either through the deliberate plans and programs of the firm's managing partners or simply through the firm's established practices, protocols, and culture. Managing partners also influence the culture of a law firm, as they manage the firm's personnel and articulate the firm's protocols. So do the clients whom the firm's lawyers serve. Clients tend to pick law firms whose culture suits them and lawyers whose style suits them.

You can learn much about a firm's work environment by studying what the firm publishes about its founders, managing partners, and clients. Work environment and culture matter. **Do not expect to join a firm and change its culture.** You should expect instead to adapt your skills and preferences to the firm's expectations. For example, law firms and other organizations employing lawyers vary in their degree of formality. Some firms are highly structured, hierarchical, conservative, and restrained or relatively more entrepreneurial, flexible, individual, and even free-wheeling. Some lawyers work best in a relaxed work environment in which they can exercise their skills according to their individual style. Other lawyers prefer a structured environment in which the firm's leadership communicates clear expectations and assigns clear responsibilities, and the lawyers know when they have met those expectations. Some organizations adapt well to different employee skills and preferences, as part of their fluid culture. Yet for the most part, **if you join a firm that has the opposite work environment than that in which you prosper, then expect to change or soon find a new employer.**

"When considering a career path, think about how your choice of legal career will affect your lifestyle choices at least as much, if not more, than thinking about a substantive area of law. So, rather than focusing on, 'Do I like family law, estates and trusts, or criminal law?' ask yourself, 'Do I want to have set hours where I know I can be home at a certain time?' or, 'Do I want a lot of contact with clients?' or, 'Do I want to be in court a lot?' or, 'Would I prefer most of time to be quiet in the library or my office?' If you can answer those questions, then certain careers will emerge as possibilities while you eliminate others."

Professor Kim O'Leary

Some firms have less structure, encouraging or at least allowing their lawyers to work how they think best. Some firms, particularly smaller firms, tend to recognize and more quickly reward personal initiative. Those firms may also tend to more quickly identify and address the absence of personal initiative, by warning and other corrective action right up to firing. Those firms may have fewer resources and less time to nurture the late bloomer whose skills do not yet earn their own keep. They expect and require the new hire to "hit the ground running." Other firms expect and require the opposite, that a new hire would not venture forth alone until after a suitable gestation in the firm's culture. Those firms may have management systems, protocols, and lines of supervision that are important to the timing and integrity of the complex work required by their corporate clients. Freestyling could disrupt the work, embarrassing firm and client.

Firms and other employers of lawyers also differ in their political leanings, religious understandings, philanthropic activities, and artistic and cultural involvements. One firm sponsors the symphony where partners sip wine with clients during intermission, while another firm sponsors an entry in the river-raft race where partners and associates drink beer in cutoffs. One firm displays modern art, another the classics, and another no art at all. The point again is not that you must find and fit within your affinity group. As a matter of law and policy, employers of lawyers do not discriminate based on protected characteristics. Firms seek, value, and maintain substantial diversity. The question of work environment has more to do with how well your skills will work within the relationships and protocols that certain affinities may represent. The firm that sponsors the river-raft-race entry just may offer you more flexibility in professional matters when you need it.

> "A lawyer's job satisfaction relates closely to whether he or she feels that the work environment reflects mutual respect and good personal relationships among colleagues. We just enjoy our work more when we like and respect those we work with, and they like and respect us. Even outstanding lawyers cannot thrive in an atmosphere of apathy, animosity, or distrust."
>
> *Professor Paul Sorensen*

The influence of work environment can extend beyond staffing and work structure to more personal matters like your daily professional attire. It is not always about conformity. Just because some lawyers dress more formally does not in every firm mean that others must also do so. Yet **many firms do set expectations for professional attire.** If everyone whom you meet in a firm is dressed relatively alike, then the firm may have established and to some degree enforced those expectations, whether by explicit dress code or implicit messages. You may wish to consider whether you can and are willing to dress like your interviewers dress. Whether the firm has a dress code or expectation is a fair interview question. Some firms also have expectations not only about the number of hours that you work but the time of your arrival and departure. In some firms, the unspoken expectation may be that associates arrive before and leave after the partners. Other firms just want you to get the work done and so permit broader latitude to arrive and leave early, or arrive and leave late. (Few employers encourage arriving late and leaving early.) **Investigate prospective employers' expectations if your daily schedule is important to your work habits or family situation.**

Some law practices and legal fields frequently take you out of these office environments. In some practice areas, lawyers spend considerable time at the place of their clients' business, or in hospitals, prisons, or schools. Defending products-liability cases may take you to manufacturing plants and engineering firms, wearing hard hats and safety glasses. Litigating construction-defect cases may take you to construction sites, wearing mud boots and work clothes. Prosecution work may take you to grisly crime scenes and morgues. Public-defender positions, private criminal-defense work, and prisoner civil-rights cases may frequently take you to prisons, which as sad and dangerous as they seem are also places that hold their own alluring stories and stark beauty. Representing utilities may take you on power-plant inspections, climbing the outside of a smokestack. Representing nursing homes may take you among the elderly. **There is no end to where you find lawyers going in their work.** Your challenge is to discern where you want to go.

In sum, as you develop your skills in law school, **think about the type of environment in which your skills would prosper.** Some work environments encourage social interaction outside work, recognize outside achievements, celebrate birthdays, births, and weddings, and permit part-time or other flexible employment. Having an occasional beer with co-workers after work might be expected. Other work environments that discourage each of those activities may to some seem less humane but to others more focused, productive, and professional. The point is not to judge one employer culture right and another wrong. It is instead to find what suits your skills so that your work and career prosper. Ultimately, the healthier environments tend to be those in which there is a culture of trust, respect, courtesy, community, dialogue, responsibility, responsiveness, and commitment to high standards. *See* Preston K. Munter, *Law Firm Policies and Procedures to Reduce Stress*, in Julie M. Tamminen, ed., Living with the Law—Strategies to Avoid Burnout and Create Balance 69–70 (ABA Law Practice Management Section 1997).

Exercise. Reflect on, identify, and record in a saved writing your thoughts on your ideal work environment in each of the following areas, giving an example for each:

> ➤ level of formality or informality;
> ➤ level of interaction with the local community;
> ➤ degree of interpersonal interaction among lawyers;
> ➤ degree of interpersonal interaction between lawyers and staff;
> ➤ workplace recognition of significant personal events;
> ➤ place and valuing of diversity and inclusion;
> ➤ significant political or religious commitments;
> ➤ prominence of artistic and other cultural tastes; and
> ➤ openness to flexible working arrangements.

Beth Simonton-Kramer, J.D. 2009

"Before law school, I was a financial analyst and accounting manager for a major school district, working in a highly formal work environment where everything was structured, supervised, reviewed, and audited, as it had to be. One of my goals in attending law school was to develop a practice that had greater independence and informality. While in law school, I served as the Law Review's Editor-in-Chief and clerked for a state appellate court. Both were also formal environments. Yet after graduation, I started a small firm with a law school classmate who had similar career preferences and goals. The practice allows me to teach, volunteer for charitable organizations, and do other worthwhile activities while still drawing on my financial and legal expertise in a professional setting. The practice provides a more flexible and satisfying mix."

Supervision—*Following*

Consider matching the level of supervision in your workplace to your skills and preferences. The previous section already addressed the formality or informality of the work environment, touching on supervision. Yet the subject of supervision is sufficiently important to bear separate treatment. Some of us like to fly alone, others of us in flocks, and still others following a strong lead. Working independently energizes some lawyers. Others feel better about their work when they interact with and depend on others who share in the work. You may be highly skilled at independent work and not particularly skilled at working in collaborative groups and following a clear leader as part of an organized team, or the opposite may be your case. Independent work requires one set of practices and skills, while group work and team work require other sets of skills. **You can probably discern your skills and preference from the activities that you undertook in law school and the way that you managed your legal education.** Lawyers work alone, collaboratively, and in teams. If you have found that you have strong skills and a strong preference for independent work, then you may wish to avoid choosing an employer whose supervisor will closely monitor your every move. If, on the other hand, you flourish under supervision where you have expert guidance and reliable endorsement, then you may wish to choose that very employer.

Law firms and other organizations that employ lawyers supervise new associates in different ways that can work better or less well for you. **Some firms quickly give new associates substantial responsibility with limited supervision.** After the new associate has an appropriate period of training in the firm's protocols, the partners in those firms may do little more than have periodic informal discussions with the new associate, sample the associate's written work for review, and check periodically with judges, court staff, lawyers outside the firm, and clients on whether the associate is performing appropriately. **Other firms supervise new associates more closely.** Those firms may not for weeks, months, or even a year or more permit an associate to do any of the following tasks alone, without the presence, participation, or advance approval of a supervising partner:

- accept a matter;

- meet with a client;
- sign a pleading or other court paper;
- serve a pleading;
- retain an expert or investigator;
- schedule or conduct a deposition;
- travel at firm expense;
- appear in court;
- file an appeal;
- resolve a matter;
- prepare and tender a bill;
- request assistance from other associates;
- terminate a client relationship; or
- close a file.

> "Show up before your boss and leave after she pulls out of the lot. When you're working for someone, don't ever say 'I have always had a hard time getting up in the morning, ask my mom.' Respect the deadlines. If the deadline is Friday, turn it in on Thursday. Don't ever ask on the day the project is due for extension. It doesn't work for judges; it doesn't work for your boss. Since Adam and Eve, people have been complaining that the younger generation is lazy. Take ownership of a project, see the brief (or memo or contract) all the way through and don't dump it on your supervisor on Friday at 4 p.m. so your supervisor gets to work the weekend."
>
> ***Law Firm Founder and Managing Partner Stephen Bough***

The cause or reason for your supervision may also make a difference to you. The form and level of your supervision can depend on the culture of the firm and its established protocols, the individual preference of the partner or other supervisor with whom you work, or the practice area in which you work. You may prefer supervision if the highly specialized nature of your work and its attendant risks warrant close supervisor review. Under those circumstances, you might be uneasy if your firm instead appears lax. On the other hand, you may be equally or more uneasy if the only apparent reason why you are under close supervision is your supervisor's inexplicable predilection. There are also firms in which it is neither the work nor the particular supervisor that requires supervision but instead the firm's culture, which may be more or less meaningful to you. Some of us flourish working in structured environments where we can always get yes-or-no authorization, even down to whether we can order lunch in for a client meeting. Others of us flourish when it all depends on, and is all up to, us alone.

> "As you consider appropriate work environments, it is important to know yourself. Do you have the confidence and flexibility to be comfortable in a 'sink-or-swim' environment? Would you prefer more structured training and feedback from an experienced supervisor? There are no right or wrong answers to these questions. You are not better or worse, stronger or weaker, because you prefer more or less supervision as you launch your career. Don't choose a 'minimal supervision' environment because you think this choice makes you appear more competent or more confident. Choose the environment that fits your personality, as then you will be happiest and will learn best."
>
> *Dean Lauren Rousseau*

Although supervision tends to depend on the individual employer, and there are certainly exceptions in any category, **here are some employment patterns that may help guide your investigation and promote your skill fit:**

- Lawyers working for government agencies may find more supervision in those settings than in private practice;
- Judges will supervise judicial clerks closely, as will court administrators supervise court staff;
- Corporate-counsel offices may involve more supervision than law firms in general;
- Large law firms may involve more supervision than smaller firms in general;
- Highly specialized legal fields may involve more supervision than common and general practices;
- Legal services for corporate clients may require more supervision than services for individuals;
- The prosecution side of criminal cases may involve more supervision than the defense side;
- The insurance defense side of personal-injury cases may involve more supervision than the plaintiff's side; and
- Larger cases of all kinds may involve more supervision than smaller cases.

Exercise. Complete each of the following requests about your experience with supervision, recording and saving your answers for future review as you evaluate job opportunities:

> ➢ Identify any disputes you have had with work supervisors. How did you and the supervisor resolve them?
> ➢ Identify any team of which you were a member. How appreciative and supportive were you of its leader?
> ➢ When you and family or friends do something that requires some degree of leadership, do you lead, follow, or mediate?
> ➢ Evaluate your experience working within any group in law school where you took direction from another.

Kara Sova, J.D. 2007

"I had paralegal skills and experience before going to law school, and so I knew how law offices operated. During law school, I decided to look for a position with a small firm where the lawyers acted with greater independence and I could rely more on my confidence and experience. The small firm that I joined right after law school fit my skills and preferences just right. The independence and schedule flexibility also helped me balance my new family responsibilities when I had a baby."

Relationship—*Caring*

Your skills may also affect whether you work better with clients and other lay persons, or with lawyers and judges. Some lawyers work solely or primarily with judges and other lawyers rather than with clients. The skills for working with judges and lawyers are different from the skills for working with clients. You may have excellent skills for working with lawyers but only rudimentary or awkward skills for working with clients, or vice versa. Other lawyers deal solely or primarily with lay clients, meaning clients who have no particular expertise in law or any other field, rather than expert clients or client representatives, meaning individuals who have substantial knowledge, skill, and experience in a particular field. The skills for working with expert clients or client representatives are different from working with lay clients. You may have the skills to work with experts more so than non-experts, or vice versa. **Evaluate**

job opportunities based on how well your skills fit the needs and interests of the persons with whom you will work.

> "There are three key factors to job satisfaction: (1) the culture of the organization you are working for; (2) the character of the people you are working with; and (3) the nature of the work you are doing. Truly satisfied workers are engaged in positions where their fulfillment is because of, not in spite of, the operation of these factors in their workplace."
>
> *Associate Counsel Jeremy Brieve, Priority Health*

Take estate-planning practice as an example. Lawyers drafting smaller estate plans often work solely or primarily with lay clients. Those lawyers are typically the only expert present in their day-to-day practice. Most or all of their meetings and other communications are with clients whose wishes are critical but whose expertise is irrelevant. Lawyers in transactional practices serving real-estate and small-business clients may also work solely or primarily with non-expert individuals, while rarely encountering other lawyers. They may help lay individuals start and manage small businesses or help lay individuals buy and sell homes and other real property, in each instance being the only or primary expert involved in the transaction. If your skills require or encourage that you control the form (if not the objective) of your work, free of the influence of other experts including your clients, then estate planning or small-firm transactional practice may be your preference.

Consider a prosecutor's job as a contrary example. Prosecutors do not deal with lay clients. Their client (so to speak) is the state. Prosecutors instead deal constantly with judges, defense lawyers, detectives, investigators, and other law-enforcement officers. Insurance-defense practice and business litigation can be similar, where the lawyers work primarily or solely with medical, engineering, accounting, and other experts, and judges, opposing lawyers, and court staff. If your skills require or encourage that you deal solely or primarily with other experts, sharing control over the work while advocating with similarly skilled professionals, then prosecution or insurance defense may be your preference. Working with other lawyers and developing a reputation within a vibrant professional community energizes some lawyers. Also, some lawyers are so effective at working with judges and other lawyers and professionals, while so ineffective at working with clients, that they rely on non-lawyer staff to make sensitive client communications. As you evaluate job opportunities, consider your skills and preference for professional relationship and interaction.

> "Do not be too familiar. Be personable, but respectful. Be confident, but not over confident. An intern who turns things in saying 'I'm sure this isn't right but here is what I've found' is so unbelievably frustrating. With that introduction, I briefly look at the work and just do the research myself, wasting my time and the intern's time. Never, ever, ever trash-talk the attorneys or staff in the office or your fellow interns. You may be tempted to, especially if everyone else does it, but don't do it. It will be noticed and frowned upon."
> **Former Federal Law Clerk Christin Masimore, MFY Legal Services**

Exercise. Consider the following questions about your preferences for professional relationships, writing and saving your answers for later review:

> ➢ While in law school, have you cultivated and maintained substantial interaction with persons who are not law students or lawyers? Why or why not?
> ➢ While in law school, have you cultivated and maintained substantial interaction with persons who are law students or lawyers? Why or why not?
> ➢ Where do you think your skills are, in interacting with other professionals to resolve matters or in interacting with lay persons who depend solely on your expertise? Why?
> ➢ Which would you prefer, a practice in which most of your interaction was with persons who know nothing about law or a practice in which most of your interaction was with persons who are lawyers, judges, or other legal professionals? Why?

> **Beth Swagman, J.D. 2009**
> "Before deciding to earn a law degree, I already had a substantial professional career that enabled me to travel the world for an organization where relationships meant everything. As I studied law and learned about its practice, it became clear to me that estate planning involved similar long-term relationships of clients trusting my expertise. Even as my former work continues, I am enjoying a solo estate-planning practice. It was a natural and welcome fit for me."

Ethics

Ethics involve the embodiment of a lawyer's knowledge and skills. Without professional identity, there can be no legal service. Knowledge is knowing, skills doing, and ethics becoming. Without a professional identity, a lawyer cannot use law knowledge and legal skills to serve a client. A lawyer applies law knowledge and skill to a client's specific circumstances through the lawyer's professional identity. **Law firms want to retain and employ ethical lawyers,** just as much as they want lawyers who have abundant law knowledge and abundant skill. Whether or not you know a great deal of law or possess substantial legal skill, if you develop and maintain a strong professional identity, then you are able to serve clients. A lot of law knowledge and legal skill in the hands of an uncaring, uncommitted, and unethical lawyer does little for a client. A small bit of law knowledge and legal skill in the hands of a compassionate, committed, and principled lawyer can go a long way toward helping a client. **Clients want ethical lawyers.** This part of the book shows you how law school's curriculum teaches the ethics that you must have for law practice. It then shows you the professional-development tools that you can use to connect your ethics and professional identity with career transitions.

Law School Curriculum

The law school curriculum instructs in ethics in several ways. The Professional Responsibility course teaches the rules of ethics and the system through which the profession enforces those rules. Less apparently, the curriculum also introduces you to model professionals including professors, deans, staff attorneys and other staff members, alumni, speakers, and practitioners. You may find a mentor among them along the way. Law schools offer you mentors just as intentionally. As part of the curriculum, law schools also help you identify your professional values and vision, recognize your personality and the personalities of others, and develop and demonstrate your character and fitness. Each of these curriculum objectives help to build your professional ethics and identity so that you can then connect them with your career. As you read this section, **keep these ethics objectives in mind:**

- rules;
- models and mentors;
- values and vision;
- personality; and
- character and fitness.

Conduct Rules—*Complying*

Your law school's Professional Responsibility course should prepare you to take and pass the Multistate Professional Responsibility Exam. **Licensure in nearly every state requires it.** Currently, in 47 of 50 states, you cannot obtain a license and practice law until you have passed the Multistate Professional Responsibility exam. Check the National Conference of Bar Examiners website for the few jurisdictions that do not require it. The 125-minute Multistate Professional Responsibility Exam is comprised of 60 multiple-choice questions testing your knowledge and application of the ABA Model Rules of Professional Conduct and ABA Model Code of Judicial Conduct. State bars require different scores, some states higher than others. The National Conference of Bar Examiners administers the exam in early March, August, and November each year at many sites throughout the country including many law schools. You must register approximately one month before the exam. **Do not rely on word from others for your state bar's Multistate Professional Responsibility Exam requirements.** State bars change their exam requirements from time to time, making unreliable the experience of others. Check with the National Conference of Bar Examiners and your state bar.

As to your timing for taking the Multistate Professional Responsibility Exam, many states permit you to take the exam while in law school. You may want to take the exam shortly after your Professional Responsibility course in law school, well before you graduate and focus on the bar exam. **Research your state bar's requirements.** Some state bars require that you take the exam within a certain time of when you take that state's bar exam, meaning that your Multistate Professional Responsibility Exam score will not count and you will have to retake it if you took it too early. Find out your state bar's exam-timing requirements now. Register now for the exam date that makes the most sense.

Also, find out what Multistate Professional Responsibility Exam score your state requires. **Plan to study for the exam before taking it.** Some commercial bar-review courses offer special classes for the Multistate Professional Responsibility Exam as part of your fee for bar-exam review. You may retake the Multistate Professional Responsibility Exam if you fail to achieve your state bar's required score, but retaking the exam may delay your bar licensure if you waited too long to take the Multistate Professional Responsibility Exam. Take the Multistate Professional Responsibility Exam early enough to allow for a retake, if necessary. The National Conference of Bar Examiners does not release the names of individuals who fail the Multistate Professional Responsibility Exam. You can take it as many times as required for you to pass.

Your knowledge of ethics rules influences your career and job opportunities. Ignorance of the rules can end a career when it leads to ethics violations. It can also cause you to miss a job opportunity. Lawyers who interview job candidates can be highly sensitive to a candidate's inadvertent indication, by the candidate's uninformed question or answer, that the candidate has poor knowledge of ethics rules and ethical practices. Ethical lawyers want to practice with other ethical lawyers. A serious or even relatively minor ethics violation can cause quick, deep, and lasting damage to a law firm's reputation. On the other hand, lawyers who develop a reputation within the bar for knowing ethics rules and procedures can develop a practice of advising and representing other lawyers in grievance matters, while earning status and respect within the bar. Be careful in interviewing, networking, and other professional interaction how you reflect your knowledge of ethics rules and your ethical commitment. Law firms do not hire candidates who inadvertently reveal character issues.

Interviewers also occasionally ask directly about ethics with questions like, "What would you do if a partner in a rush told you to sign and file an attested court paper without reading it?" You should know that doing what the partner asked could lead to license discipline, court sanction, criminal perjury charge, and civil malpractice action. Rule 5.2 of the ABA Model Rules of Professional Conduct provides that the rules bind subordinate lawyers notwithstanding a supervising lawyer's direction, creating a safe harbor only for "reasonable resolution of an arguable question of professional duty." You would properly decline the partner's instruction, explain why, and consult your mentor within the firm or a managing partner if the partner persists. Your interviewer likely asked you the question knowing and expecting that correct answer. You need not memorize every word of every conduct rule, but you should know the rules and, above all, care about doing the right thing.

Exercise. Research the following information by contacting the state bar of the state in which you intend to practice and searching the National Conference of Bar Examiners' website, recording and saving your answers:

> ➢ Does your state bar require that you pass the Multistate Professional Responsibility Exam?
> ➢ If so, then what passing score does your state bar require? How does that score compare to other jurisdictions?
> ➢ Does your bar-review course offer a class to help you study for the Multistate Professional Responsibility Exam?
> ➢ When, relative to your application for the state bar and your taking its bar exam, must you pass the Multistate Professional Responsibility Exam?
> ➢ What is the ideal date for you to take Multistate Professional Responsibility Exam so that you have enough time to retake it if necessary without delaying your bar application and licensure?
> ➢ What is the last registration date available for you to register for your preferred date for taking the Multistate Professional Responsibility Exam? Calendar that date, or register now.

Models and Mentors—*Inspiring*

Learning ethics rules through your studies in Professional Responsibility is only one part of developing a complete professional identity. **Law school also provides you with professional models and mentors** to help you develop appropriate professional ethics and personality. We learn not simply by instruction but also by observation. Law schools hire full-time and adjunct faculty, recruit competition judges, hold speaker events, and recruit judges and practitioners to campus for other student activities specifically to give you examples of model professionals. Law schools introduce you to lawyers intentionally in order that you can see how they think, act, and conduct themselves, and learn from those observations. You do not have to behave exactly as any other particular lawyer would. You and every other person have unique personality. Every lawyer develops professional identity unique to that lawyer. Yet **models and mentors can help you develop an identity within the broad standards and norms of the profession.**

Your professional identity can have a substantial impact on your career opportunities. **Law firms and other employers hire lawyers based as much on who they are as what they know or do.** Employers evaluating candidates will say that you can correct performance, but you cannot correct character. When clients describe lawyers, they tend to describe general attributes more so than specific skills or knowledge. You hear clients and lawyers say that a certain lawyer is a "go-getter," "the nicest," "great," "solid," "upstanding," and "all about integrity," or on the other hand "a loose cannon" and "a little shady," and to "watch out for him." People remember character, including especially how a lawyer makes them feel ("you can trust him," "she'll get you on the right path") more than they remember details of performance. **Models and mentors help a law student and new lawyer discern and claim that character.** Law firms or disciplinary officials will sometimes even assign a "big brother" or "big sister" lawyer of strong positive character to an experienced lawyer who has strayed from the path, to influence the straying lawyer by character as much as rule knowledge.

> "Good examples and mentors are critical to the growth of a young professional. While you must ultimately be true to yourself, finding strong models and emulating good behavior is important to self-development. One way to become a very good lawyer is to seek out a great lawyer who is willing to invest time in you and then soak up all she can offer."
>
> *Former State Bar President Jon Muth,*
> *Miller, Johnson, Snell & Cummiskey*

If you came to law school with a lawyer for a model, then be sure to preserve that inspiration. You can find model lawyers throughout history, like Cicero, Francis Lieber, Abraham Lincoln, Belva Lockwood, and Thurgood Marshall. You can also find model lawyers among family and professional acquaintances, and in the national, state, and local bar. **An Internet search of law firms can give you as many examples of model lawyers as you have time to explore.** They are real lawyers doing important work within fascinating law practices. Ask successful lawyers including those who interview you, and they are likely to be able to identify other lawyers to whom they looked as their models. Be ready to identify in your interview whom you hope to model. Identity is unique but not without ancestry. The sum of our identity is ours alone, but we all observe and borrow. **Be sure that you are borrowing deliberately rather than inadvertently.** The company that we keep has its effects. The more intentionally that you identify model lawyers, the greater will be your positive professional development. Let your research and reflection on lawyer models, made possible throughout your law school's curriculum, help you imitate and borrow most productively. Compare and contrast your model lawyer's qualities with your own until you have a deeper sense of your desired professional identity.

With so many recorded and visible examples, you need not meet your model lawyer. You can learn much from afar. Yet you can also seek out, meet, and spend time with model professionals. **Judges and lawyers recognize their responsibility to mentor law students and new lawyers.** A mentor is someone who guides you through counsel, helping you to form a strong, positive professional identity of your own. Judges and lawyers will take time to meet and speak with you, telling you stories of their own professional development, giving you career advice, and giving you an opportunity to observe how they conduct themselves. In most professional communities, there are outstanding mentors whose time, care, and counsel have shaped the professional identity and careers of many new lawyers. A mentor can save a law student or new lawyer from developing bad practices, forming poor relationships, and making bad decisions. Mentors can also give you job tips, write recommendations, and give references. Yet seek a mentor not so much for advice but to observe the authenticity of their professional actions. George W. Kaufman, The Lawyer's Guide to Balancing Life & Work—Taking the Stress out of Success 42 (ABA Law Practice Management Section 2006).

Law schools, law firms, and bar associations develop and maintain mentor programs to ensure that you have the best opportunity for a strong mentor just when you most need one. Law schools have lawyer and judge mentors for first-year students adjusting to law school, second- and third-year students making career choices, and new graduates making the adjustment to law practice. Those mentors may invite law students to the law office for coffee and introductions, share study and placement tips and resources, or invite a law student to accompany the mentor to court or a speaking engagement for observation. Law firms appoint mentors to new associates, encouraging or requiring that the mentor meet with the associate to engage in specific professional-development activities. Those activities may include introductions to judges at the courthouse, introductions to other lawyers at bar meetings, and observation of the associate's client meetings and court appearances followed by formative feedback. Bar associations offer mentors to ensure that new lawyers who are looking for a job or have solo practices find guidance from experienced lawyers and adopt the bar's norms of professionalism and civility. **Seek out and expect to have a strong mentor throughout law school and your first years of practice.**

> "You are entirely responsible for your own happiness. Surround yourself with positive people. See the blessings in life. Believe that good things happen. Do good to others. Mentors are everywhere—sitting next to you on the bus, working beside you, living with you. You simply need to open your mind to what you can learn from others and then listen to them."
>
> *Dean Amy Timmer*

In the better relationships, mentors and protégés share some attributes and responsibilities while also having different attributes and responsibilities of their own. **Both mentor and protégé should care about and commit to the relationship, communicate timely and appropriately, and maintain a high level of confidence and trust.** What defines a mentor, then, is the mentor's leadership in modeling, counseling, teaching, guiding, and encouraging. The protégé's role is different. Perhaps surprising, it is the protégé who should determine the relationship goals and provide the initiative. The protégé knows generally what the protégé needs and should provide the impetus for to obtain. It is not up to the mentor to determine the purpose for the relationship and then make the relationship work. Those functions belong to the protégé. The protégé should also be open to the mentor's guidance and appreciative for it. Appreciation is not the mentor's role.

There are also different forms of mentor programs and relationships. *See* IDA O. ABBOTT, THE LAWYER'S GUIDE TO MENTORING 22-23 (National Association for Law Placement 2000). Formal mentor programs are appropriate, helping you and the mentor make the relationship more effective. Traditional mentor programs and relationships depend on finding affinities between the mentor lawyer and protégé law student or new lawyer, that give them something in common to share or develop over time. An affinity relationship can last years, if the mentor and protégé wish it to. Mentor and protégé can see one another once a week, once a month, or once a year, depending on need and availability. In the traditional model, the mentor teaches the protégé in a one-on-one relationship within an organization. In a traditional affinity relationship, **mentors and protégés may have in common that they:**

- are of the same heritage, culture, or ethnicity;
- attended the same undergraduate institution;
- attended the same law school;
- share the same recreation or hobby;
- shared military or other public service;
- faced poverty or been raised by a single parent;
- overcome substance abuse;
- faced domestic violence;
- like the same restaurant;
- share political views; or
- simply enjoy one another's company.

Yet **do not limit your mentors to those who are like you.** Not all mentor relationships are affinity based. Newer models for mentoring value differences between mentor and protégé. It can be especially rewarding to find an experienced lawyer who is so different from you that you must learn something every time you encounter them. Choosing a mentor who holds a distinctly different worldview, has distinctly different personality, and maintains a distinctly different range of interests can teach you more than you would learn from someone much like you. Newer models also encourage multiple mentors outside one's own school or employer affiliations. In non-traditional mentor relationships, mentor may learn as much from protégé as protégé from mentor. Rather than addressing development of general identity, non-traditional mentor relationships may also focus on more specific issues like skill development or overcoming a character issue like substance abuse or financial problems. They may also involve peer relationships rather than relationships with senior lawyers. You can learn a lot from a classmate who has already faced your particular issue. Here, from above-cited *Lawyer's Guide to Mentoring*, is a list of possible mentor roles:

- **host** for you or a group in a mixed professional and social setting;
- **bridge** to other helpful professionals and institutions;
- **protection** against undermining persons or agendas;
- **guide** to unwritten and hidden norms and rules;
- **champion** advocating your qualities to influential others;
- **teacher** of law knowledge and legal skills;
- **model** demonstrating appropriate behaviors;
- **coach** providing feedback on your performance;
- **counselor** suggesting alternative career paths;
- **troubleshooter** helping you solve specific problems;
- **confidante** hearing and helping assess your proposals;
- **sponsor** for membership in exclusive groups;
- **publicist** promoting you to outside groups;
- **friend** giving you personal social support; and
- **catalyst** making things happen for you.

Ultimately, **base your mentor relationship on its ability to help you assess your career and professional development** rather than on having a good time or impressing one another. Ask your mentor what makes a good lawyer. Record what your mentor says, and reflect on it. Mentors are fundamental to a lawyer's development. **Consider these ways to find mentor opportunities:**

- specific law school mentor programs for prospective, first-year, second-year, and third-year students. Some of these programs offer as mentors upper-term students or recent graduates who can be especially effective in recalling what you face and helping you to navigate it;
- your faculty advisor and other faculty members. Law schools train, equip, and devote their faculty members to your

nurturing as a professional. Do not overlook that you may find a faculty member in your field of interest or familiar with your geographic home;

- your law school's alumni office for alumni mentors for students or recent graduates. Use your school's searchable alumni database to find a mentor in the field of your interest or your geographic area. Use email to set up a meeting when you return home over term break;

- your state bar. State bars use mentor programs to introduce law students and new lawyers to the professional responsibilities of a lawyer, reduce grievances, and recruit new lawyers for service to the profession. Check your state bar's Young Lawyers Division;

- your local bar association. Local bars are returning to mentor programs to increase membership, provide service opportunities for senior members, help with employment, and ensure civility and professionalism;

- Your local American Inns of Court chapter. Your law school may sponsor or support a local Inns chapter. The Inns are among the finest of formal mentor programs, often drawing on leaders of the local bar;

- law fraternities like Phi Delta Phi and Phi Alpha Delta. Law fraternities comprised of both students and graduates devote their members to ethics, professionalism, and service, with mentor opportunities as their express intent; and

- the courthouse coffee shop or local diner or watering hole. Many local bars have an informal place to which judges and lawyers go for fellowship outside of their professional roles. They are natural places for mentor opportunities.

Do not expect or require substantial time or a long-term relationship from every lawyer whom you ask to be your mentor. **Mentor relationships do not have to last over a long period or take substantial time.** They also need not be formal. Some of the best mentor relationships can be brief and informal. It can takes years for new lawyers to realize that they have been drawing on specific experienced lawyers as if they were mentors, in effect making them so without even having asked. Informality is fine. Brevity is also fine. A brief conversation or interaction having to do with your career and professional development can mean more at the right time and from the right mentor than hours of deliberate mentor programming. Mentor relationships that constitute nothing more than infrequent, brief, and coincidental conversations in the courthouse hallway, sustained over time, can be the most helpful. **Think of a mentor relationship as learning from another lawyer.** Look for the opportunity to turn a moment's meeting into a mentor episode. Make it a point to be among lawyers where they might have that moment's time. Engage them purposefully in conversation about your development. Then let the relationships take their own form.

Mentor conversations have their own paradigm. **Be prepared to ask specific questions.** Although your mentor may be perfectly willing to do so, do not expect your mentor to carry the conversation forward. You should not question your mentor like you would question a witness in cross-examination. Be conversational, using prompts like, "Tell me about when you ..." or "What usually happens when you ... ?" Also, observe your mentor. The value is not always in what a mentor says but can be in what they do or how they say it. Here are some other suggestions to make your mentor encounters more productive:

- seek guidance on self-assessment and meta-cognitive practices using questions like, "How do you know when to ...?";
- seek feedback on specific actions you are considering using questions like, "I am thinking about .... Is that wise?";
- build relationship around the mentor's experiences using suggestions like, "Tell me about your role in that new waterfront development.";
- ask about the value of specific professional-development activities using questions like, "Does being a member of that section help you?";
- keep the conversations positive and focused on professional development using comments like, "I wanted to meet you because of your great reputation with the social-service agencies.";
- draw on the mentor's network with questions like, "I learned from your secretary that that I should deliver your judge's copy to her. Would you mind if I speak with your bailiff about your preferences for my upcoming trial?"

You can address various professional subjects in a mentor episode and use it for various activities. Avoid turning the mentor relationship into a job hunt. Do not implore your mentor for a job. Your conversations should be about much more than simply getting a job. **Consider these subjects and activities that may be of help to you when meeting with a mentor:**

- how to perform better in general on law school academics;
- how to understand a subject (e.g., perfection of a security interest);
- what law school courses and concentrations to choose;
- what co-curricular activities are most beneficial to practice;
- introduction to judges and lawyers looking for interns or externs;
- critique of specific work that you may use later as examples;
- evaluation and critique of your law school portfolio;
- advice on how to prepare for the bar exam;
- advice on the transition from law school to law practice;
- resume and cover letter review and critique, and mock interview;
- writing a recommendation letter or giving a reference for you;
- how to shape a long-term professional-development plan;
- what the mentor is encountering in practice for which to prepare;
- opportunities to accompany the mentor to observe;
- service projects in which the mentor is involved and might share;
- bar meetings to which the mentor might invite you;
- what specific practice areas are like;
- how to balance work with personal and family life;
- how to act professionally in a specific difficult situation;
- introduction to judges, other lawyers, and other professionals; and
- introduction to individuals using their law degree outside of law.

When you have completed a mentor episode or relationship, consider reflecting on and making a record of what you learned. **Develop an electronic mentor journal, folder, or file in which you**

gather significant experiences, observations, and advice. Small contributions to the file over time can result in an astonishing compendium of useful guides. It might even be something that you would share with your own protégé some day. Make a goal to complete at least one entry in your mentor journal, folder, or file each month or at least each law school term. Return to and review the file when making major decisions like where to seek a job, where to apply, and whether to accept a specific offer on what terms. For each entry in your mentor file, include:

- the date, time, and place of the mentor episode;
- the lawyer's name, law firm, and subject field;
- how you met the lawyer, through what program or personal effort;
- the qualities or experiences that attracted you to the lawyer;
- the lawyer's advice or the observation you made; and
- what you would like to have of the lawyer's qualities or experiences.

Exercise. Choose and complete one of the following exercises. Be sure to save your research:

➤ Identify the lawyers who attracted you to law school. Choose one of them, and research their career to identify the qualities that made them a model for you;

➤ Choose a ground-breaking new case from your law studies, identify the lawyer who won the case, and research the lawyer's website biography until you find a lawyer whom you admire as a model professional;

➤ Identify your law school's mentor programs, apply for a mentor, schedule and complete one mentor episode, and make an entry in a mentor journal, folder, or file; or

➤ Identify your state and local bar associations' mentor programs, contact them to see if mentors are available to law students, and if so, then arrange to meet with a mentor on your next term break.

Juanita Bocanegra, J.D. 2008

"I worked with my immigrant family in the fields when I was young but, since kindergarten, always knew I wanted to be a lawyer. After college, I began working as a legal assistant in a law firm for a lawyer who became my mentor. My mentor has great skill, poise, and character, and a big heart for service. While working full time and caring for my parents, husband, and two small children, I attended law school. I will be forever grateful to my mentor and the rest of my law firm family for their support, guidance, and encouragement, which made it possible for me to pursue my dream. I left my mentor's firm when I began clerking for a large law firm while still in law school. I am now a litigation associate in that large firm where I have other wonderful mentors, but I will always remember and admire my first mentor."

Vision and Values—*Committing*

Law school helps you develop and confirm your individual vision for law practice while embracing shared professional values. Vision in this professional-development context implies a sense of who you are and who you want to become. Some label it your mission or calling. Outstanding law students and lawyers often have a clear sense of personal vision or mission. **Do not underestimate the career and professional-development value of a clear vision.** Law firms and other employers of lawyers like to hire associates whose strong personal vision aligns well with the institution's mission. Appreciate how powerful it can be for you to choose an employer whose mission facilitates your personal vision. There may be few choices in life that contribute more substantially to overall personal satisfaction and success than to spend substantial time daily working within your personal vision.

"My beloved mentor and former law partner Clark Shanahan advised me early on, 'Live your life like an open book. Don't do anything you would be embarrassed about having on the front page of the local newspaper.' I came to believe that any lawyer can be a technician— simply get someone divorced. But the art comes in helping the family reconstitute so that the family is happy and healthy while living under two different roofs. Whatever your practice area, be an artist, not a technician."

Professor Victoria Vuletich

Not all of us are good with the vision thing, but you can **learn to identify, develop, and articulate your vision.** Your first challenge is to understand what your vision is. Visions can include a sense of the legacy you hope to leave, what others might say about you on your retirement or at your passing, what you hope your children or grandchildren would think of you someday, how you hope other lawyers will perceive and appreciate you, how you would like the larger community to know you, how you have changed others' lives for the better, how your career aligns with faith commitments, what institution or work you hope to have created or supported, or what else you hope to have accomplished by your retirement. Recognize that your vision or calling may take the shape of and depend on virtually anything. Keep an electronic journal, folder, or file for your vision where you can easily store the thoughts that you collect. Investigate and reflect on those texts, experiences, intuitions, circumstances, and relationships that seem to inform your vision. Consider including in your vision inventory:

- personal history,
- family relationships,
- religion, spiritual, and faith commitments,
- personal talents and gifts,
- special resources,
- specific inspiration,
- art, music, or cultural influences,
- heritage and legacy influences, and
- social or political ambition.

Do not let convention constrain your vision. Study by the author of law students' personal and professional commitments shows remarkable variety. *See* Nelson P. Miller, *An Empirical Study of Student Ethical Commitments*, in AMY TIMMER & NELSON MILLER, EDS., REFLECTIONS OF A LAWYER'S SOUL—THE INSTITUTIONAL EXPERIENCE OF PROFESSIONALISM AT THOMAS M. COOLEY LAW SCHOOL (William S. Hein & Co. 2008). Law students express literally hundreds of appropriate ethical ambitions. Many ambitions center around the ethical quality of one's own conduct (following rules, not lying or cheating), while other ambitions center around one's personal relationship to others (care for family, loyalty to friends) or anticipated professional relationships (competency, service). Other ambitions involve developing and maintaining a relationship with sources of vision and ethics, including learning, philosophy, and faith. The ten most popular commitments in descending order include:

- honesty,
- ethical behavior,
- pro-bono and public service,
- being the best one can be,
- helping others,
- life-long learning,
- abiding by and upholding rules,
- doing to others as one would have done to oneself,
- not lying or cheating, and
- following personal and professional codes.

Lawyer-career coach Tim Batdorf suggests several ways to help you discern your career vision. One is to recall the most rewarding experience of your life and study it for what made it meaningful. Another is to recall the worst experience of your life and study it for what made it so bad. Another is to consider the possibility of your imminent demise, just as some people make major life changes after a near-death experience. Another is to imagine yourself a superhero and then determine your most challenging quest. *See* TIMOTHY D. BATDORF, THE LAWYER'S GUIDE TO BEING HUMAN—HOW TO BRING WHO YOU ARE TO WHAT YOU DO 72-73 (iUniverse, Inc. 2007). The idea is to develop a vision that is so powerfully audacious that it looks impossible to achieve except by the myriad of small steps that one can take over the course of a career. Mr. Batdorf encourages you to use positive action verbs in your vision statement, like to sustain, serve, restore, respect, value, enhance, connect, integrate, inspire, heal, generate, reform, alleviate, and affirm, and then to connect them to law and the populations it serves. He gives as examples to:

- simplify the law to everyone;
- protect and foster safety for children;
- restore peace within families;
- empower women everywhere;
- equalize opportunity and create possibility;
- make law a healing and respecting profession; and
- bring peace and democracy to the world.

> "If you have a choice to make that will affect your career, always pick the experience that you will enjoy the most. Then, when you put together your resume, you will have a set of experiences you have enjoyed, which will better qualify you for something you will enjoy doing. The alternative is selecting the choice you believe somebody else will find more attractive, which will only leave you with a resume full of experiences other people like, not experiences doing things *you* like. Examples might include choosing an elective, choosing a volunteer position, choosing a student club, choosing an externship or clinic, or choosing a job."
>
> **Professor Kim O'Leary**

Once you identify fundamental commitments you hope to fulfill through your career, your next challenge is to **fit your vision to its new professional context.** Here is where law school helps. Standard 302(a)(5) of the American Bar Association's accreditation standards for law schools requires that your law school provide you with substantial instruction in the profession's values. Law schools provide that instruction through various means and programs. In the classroom, your professors model and instruct in professional values, while assigning texts and other studies that likewise do so. The school's advisors, administrators, and career staff also model and advise about professional values. Every event on campus in some sense is an effort, more or less intentional, to help you recognize, appreciate, and adopt the profession's values. The American Bar Association's MacCrate Report, *see* ABA Section on Legal Education & Admission to the Bar, *Legal Education and Professional Development— An Educational Continuum, Report of the Task Force on Law Schools and the Profession: Narrowing the Gap* (ABA 1992), identified these four general categories of shared lawyer values:

Value § 1:
As a member of a profession dedicated to the service of clients, a lawyer should be committed to the values of:
1.1 Attaining a Level of Competence in One's Own Field of Practice;
1.2 Maintaining a Level of Competence in One's Own Field of Practice;
1.3 Representing Clients in a Competent Manner.

Value § 2:
As a member of a profession that bears special responsibilities for the quality of justice, a lawyer should be committed to the values of:

2.1 Promoting Justice, Fairness, and Morality in One's Own Daily Practice;
2.2 Contributing to the Profession's Fulfillment of its Responsibility to Ensure that Adequate Legal Services Are Provided to Those Who Cannot Afford to Pay for Them;
2.3 Contributing to the Profession's Fulfillment of its Responsibility to Enhance the Capacity of Law and Legal Institutions to Do Justice.

Value § 3:
As a member of a self-governing profession, a lawyer should be committed to the values of:
3.1 Participating in Activities Designed to Improve the Profession;
3.2 Assisting in the Training and Preparation of New Lawyers;
3.3 Striving to Rid the Profession of Bias Based on Race, Religion, Ethnic Origin, Gender, Sexual Orientation, or Disability, and to Rectify the Effects of These Biases.

Value § 4:
As a member of a learned profession, a lawyer should be committed to the values of:
4.1 Seeking Out and Taking Advantage of Opportunities to Increase His or Her Knowledge and Improve His or Her Skills;
4.2 Selecting and Maintaining Employment That Will Allow the Lawyer to Develop As a Professional and to Pursue His or Her Professional and Personal Goals.

Your last challenge is to articulate your vision for your professional career. It may not be as difficult as you think to **connect your vision with specific potential employers.** Study of law-firm associates indicate that they value the following employer qualities in roughly this descending order: support for personal and family commitments; control over work schedule; fewer working hours; fit between personal and firm values; opportunity to advance; intellectual challenge; larger compensation; and variety of legal work. George W. Kaufman, The Lawyer's Guide to Balancing Life & Work—Taking the Stress out of Success 237 (ABA Law Practice Management Section 2006), *citing* Catalyst, *Flexibility in Canadian Law Firms* (2005). Another survey of lawyers showed that they measured quality of work life by these descending measures: opportunity for advancement and growth; interest and challenge of the work; clarity of responsibilities; co-worker relationships; responsibility for clients; control over work; time allowed for work; and compensation and other recognition. *See* Gerald Le Van, Lawyers' Lives out of Control—A Quality of Life Handbook 53–54 (WorldComm Press 1992). Articulate your vision so that when you speak with new networking contacts or interview with potential employers, you are prepared to discuss how your vision connects with employment opportunities. Here are some examples drawn from WILLIAM S. DUFFEY, JR., AND RICHARD A. SCHNEIDER, EDS., A LIFE IN THE LAW—ADVICE FOR YOUNG LAWYERS (ABA 2009);

- grasping the brass ring of judicial service;
- administering responsible justice as a federal prosecutor;
- showing the professional courage to try cases;
- rediscovering a rooted calling to help others;
- remembering why you became a lawyer;
- helping others walk through the life's valleys;
- valuing client relationships through perspectives;
- being able to tell clients what they need to hear; and
- practicing to leave a legacy to the profession.

Your ability to fit your vision and values with your employment can affect not only your mental and physical health but also your willingness to continue practice. *See* JEAN STEFANIC & RICHARD DELGADO, HOW LAWYERS LOSE THEIR WAY—A PROFESSION THAT FAILS ITS CREATIVE MINDS 62–71 (Duke Univ. Press 2005). Veteran lawyers recognize that **law practice must mesh with what you value.** GEORGE W. KAUFMAN, THE LAWYER'S GUIDE TO BALANCING LIFE & WORK— TAKING THE STRESS OUT OF SUCCESS 4 (ABA Law Practice Management Section 2006). Lawyers who value their practice tend to have clear goals, plan to achieve those goals, implement those plans, believe in their competence to achieve those goals, and assess their progress, expecting challenges that they can influence and overcome. AMIRAM ELWORK, STRESS MANAGEMENT FOR LAWYERS—HOW TO INCREASE PERSONAL & PROFESSIONAL SATISFACTION IN THE LAW 170, 191–192 (Vorkell Group 3d ed. 2007). The psychologist just cited, who specializes in working with lawyers, urges that you **choose careers consonant with your values in these seven areas:**

- finances (security, status, wealth),
- work (competence, advancement),
- character (integrity, discipline, courage, loyalty),
- growth (fulfillment, learning, expression, liberty),
- relationship (interaction, affiliation, friendship, family),
- society (causes, rights, justice), and

- faith (worship, study, prayer, observance).

Exercise. Choose and complete one of the following exercises. Be sure to save your work in a vision journal, folder, or file within your electronic professional portfolio:

> ➢ Write your personal and professional story in a few paragraphs including what most influenced your personal development, what brought you to law school, and what you see in your law career;
>
> ➢ Review the MacCrate values identified above. Choose several that trigger for you aspects of your vision, writing those aspects while amplifying them into a professional vision;
>
> ➢ Write your own professional code of conduct, including your guidelines in personal conduct, professional relationships, professional service, and professional commitments; or
>
> ➢ Draft and rehearse your vision statement that you would share with a prospective employer whose institutional mission most closely resembles your individual vision.

Anna Rapa, J.D. 2007

"I had clear vision and values before coming to law school. I also knew that law school would take some exploring to make the right career choices. A school program helped me form a charitable nonprofit while still in law school. That work ultimately helped me connect my vision to law practice. Although I started as a full-time staff attorney with an appellate court after graduation, I soon realized that the work, as valuable as it was, did not fit my mission. I now teach law, practice criminal defense, and direct the work of my nonprofit in a stimulating mix that fits my vision and values."

Personality—*Mediating*

Your personality and how you understand and manage it can be another bridge to your career and professional development. Do not think that lawyers are either smart or not, and that intellectual talent is the only or even the best predictor of success. It is not all about the law school that your LSAT score got you into and your class rank there. **Personality can make more of a difference than you might think.** It is not so much being aware of your personality that matters as knowing what your personality traits are and how to put them to greatest effect. In both a job search and career, attitude can be everything. Attitude and personality are also plastic to some extent. Personality develops subject to influence. Work to conquer bad attitude. As indicated in RICHARD L. HERMANN, MANAGING YOUR LEGAL CAREER—BEST PRACTICES FOR CREATING THE CAREER YOU WANT 13–18 (ABA 2010), you should overcome low self-esteem, self-pity, bitterness, negativity, hubris, and disrespect. If you question how fit your personality is to a law career, then consider focusing on the qualities listed in BARBARA MILLER AND MARTIN CAMP, THE LAW FIRM ASSOCIATE'S GUIDE TO CONNECTING WITH YOUR COLLEAGUES (ABA Law Practice Management Section 2009), that researcher Daniel Goleman associates with career success:

- persistence,
- zeal,
- willingness to defer gratification,
- motivation,
- self awareness,
- empathy, and
- social deftness.

Professional personality is the mediating character through which lawyers work with other lawyers and serve clients. Professional personality traits comprise several dimensions including extroversion, perception and reaction, emotional and intuitive intelligence, and discernment. A lawyer with a great personality can be one who is energized by interacting with others, intuits sensitively and predictively, thinks and articulates clearly, and judges effectively. On the other hand, effective personality traits can involve a large capacity for introspection and immersion, compassion and emotion, feeling rather than thinking through situations, and withholding judgment. **There is no one perfect professional personality type.** Different personality types can make effective professional identity. **The key is to know your personality, recognize other personalities, and have the skill to discern how to make differing personalities interact effectively.**

Law school can help you understand, develop, and manage your personality, while building your skill in recognizing and drawing on the personality of others. Some law schools give the Myers-Briggs Type Indicator® on your entry to law school, in the Professional

Responsibility course, or through special courses. The Myers-Briggs assessment measures personality type in four binary dimensions, producing 16 different potential personality types. Personality exists along many different spectra. There are certainly many more than 16 different personality types. Yet Myers-Briggs typing can help you understand more about features of your personality and the personality of others. Consider taking the Myers-Briggs assessment if you have not already and then having a trained professional provide its interpretation. If it is not available to you, then consider using an online or text resource. Beware, though. **It is not solely in knowing your type but is also in having sound counsel on how to interpret your type and benefit from knowing it.**

As helpful as it can be, the Myers-Briggs Type Indicator is for the general population, not specifically for lawyers. There are various assessments related specifically to law. For example, career coach Angelique Electra created The JurisDoctor Profiles® as a self-assessment instrument specifically for lawyers. Her assessment purports to identify seven lawyer types, each of which she associates with specific career options. The seven types include the warrior, counselor, rainmaker, negotiator, problem solver, activist, and manager. Assessments are tools. Hesitate to take any assessment as a reliable indicator of your actual preferred career. Yet know that **there are archetypal lawyer personality types, some of which do tend to relate well to certain law practices and legal fields.** As you meet, hear about, and read about lawyers, see if you can identify archetypes. Also, see if your personality tends toward one of those archetypes.

"I learned many years ago that 'you only know in others, what you know in yourself.' As professionals, the journey of self-reflection and personality development helps us to grasp what we see and hear in our clients, namely, their inner dynamics and motivations of their personality type. Lifting the veil of our inner self and exposing the framework of our personality type permits us, if we choose it, to divest ourselves of our biases, prejudices, and human wounds. This process frees us to serve our clients with honesty, integrity, and wholeness. Our personal quest drives the process of accepting the clients who come to us even when they struggle with issues of inequity, adversity, bias, and exclusivity. Personal growth and typology fosters understanding, while understanding creates a lens for respecting others."

Director Bob Funaro, Ed. D., LLP

Personality knowledge and skill can help you in your job search and career success. There are exceptions to every assumption, yet **certain personality types probably tend to work better in certain legal fields and law-practice settings than others.** The extrovert may make a better trial lawyer and the introvert a better researcher. Also, family law may serve an extrovert well while intellectual-property law may serve the introvert. The intuiting personality may make a better negotiator and the thinking personality a better drafter. Also, tort law and other common-law subjects may serve the intuiting personality while secured transactions and other code courses serve the thinking personality. The judging personality may make a better arbitrator and the feeling personality a better mediator. Also, criminal law may serve the judging personality while constitutional law serves the feeling personality. A combination of an intuiting, judging, extroverted personality may make an effective sole practitioner, while a combination of a thinking, feeling, introverted personality may make a better associate in a large law firm. Any of these presumptions may be wholly inaccurate in any single case but may, on the other hand, be generally reliable guides. As you meet lawyers, **evaluate and inquire how their personalities fit with their practice fields and settings.**

Once you know something about your personality traits and those of others, **consider how you can draw on your traits and type while mediating the personality of others to improve relationships and performance.** If you recognize an introvert, then moderate your extroverted trait to reduce stimuli that would burden the introvert. If you work with an intuitive trait while yours may be a thinking type, then you do the empirical work and let them do the communication. If you encounter a feeling personality trait, then hesitate to justify an action to that person by your logical analysis. If your dominant type is to judge quickly and take action but you have the opportunity to work for a law partner whose strongly perceiving personality resists any commitment, then either consider another job or be ready to resist your urges to jump into action and even more ready to laugh or work off your frustration. **Develop self-awareness, awareness of the personality of others, and the skill to anticipate and mediate how personalities interact.** You may earn the admiration of others for your richly stable personality and avoid shame, misunderstanding, and confusion. You may also impress an interviewer. Know what law firms prefer in the personality that their lawyers should exhibit including, as indicated in RICHARD L. HERMANN, MANAGING YOUR LEGAL CAREER—BEST PRACTICES FOR CREATING THE CAREER YOU WANT 39–45 (ABA 2010), the following:

- personable demeanor;
- fit with other personalities in the firm;
- a propensity toward intelligent observation;
- willingness to think quickly on one's feet;
- attention to organization and detail;
- interest in broad thinking and skills;
- transparency and accountability to others;
- ambition to proceed in a career; and
- stable emotions.

Exercise. If you have taken the Myers-Briggs assessment recently, then retrieve and review your results for your personality type. If you have not taken it, then do so, having it interpreted by a qualified professional. If it is not available, then use a reliable online or text resource for a personality assessment. Then, drawing on what you learn about your personality type, reflect on and record and save your thoughts as to your ideal:

- ➤ law-practice field;
- ➤ law-practice setting;
- ➤ law-related employment; and
- ➤ non-law employment using your law degree.

Cindy Osman, J.D. 2009

"I was employed with a municipality before deciding to go to law school to help with immigration issues. My career in municipal work matched my personality. I liked the stable environment, co-workers, and public nature of the work. Although I could have pursued private practice after graduation, instead I volunteered for an immigration clinic while continuing in my municipal career, where my law degree gives me more credibility and flexibility."

Character and Fitness—*Proving*

Your character and fitness are other qualities that affect your career and professional development. Character and fitness have special meaning for lawyers. To get a law license, you need more than to pass the bar. You may graduate first in your class and have the highest score on the bar exam but still fail to qualify for licensure. State bars license only those lawyers who have the character and fitness to practice law. **State bars place the burden on you to prove your good moral character by clear and convincing evidence.** State bars screen applications to ensure that they reflect that evidence and then refer for fitness review those applications that indicate questionable character. If your application fails to reflect sufficient evidence of good moral character, then you may find yourself appearing at a hearing before a panel of highly experienced and reputable attorneys, whose decision could deny you a law license. When one bar denies an applicant, others will also do so, and it may take years and multiple applications before a denied applicant can demonstrate the requisite good moral character. Even if you readily establish your good moral character at a panel hearing, the fitness-review process can delay your bar licensure by months or longer, potentially costing you job offers and substantial income. You have every incentive to collect evidence of your good moral character.

> "There is no substitute for honesty and integrity in the practice of law. A good lawyer is a respected and trusted advisor. Those fundamental traits define character and are essential to meaningful success, both in practicing law and in life itself. They are not merely assumed, but must be earned."
>
> *Former State Bar President Scott Brinkmeyer, Mika Meyers Beckett & Jones*

You have several areas through which to demonstrate good moral character. **You must disclose your history, good and bad, in each of these areas**, providing records substantiating particular incidents. Although you must disclose your history in each of these areas, past bad behavior does not prevent you from proving good moral character in any of these areas. The key is your current character and fitness after any appropriate rehabilitation. Even if you have no history of bad behavior, you must take care in preparing your application. Applicants create their own problems by submitting incomplete applications, applications that are inconsistent with other records including particularly law school applications, and applications that are untruthful. State bars investigate and cross-check your application against law school, court, financial, employer, and other records, and may deny an applicant whose representations were misleading or untruthful. **Complete truth and candor is critical.** State bars may require you to provide detailed information in each of the following areas:

- residence history, requiring that you disclose your specific addresses and accurate dates of residence back to age 18 for any residence where you lived for two weeks or more;
- educational history, requiring that you disclose not only the schools you have attended with their addresses but also whether any undergraduate or graduate program disciplined you;
- military history, requiring that you disclose not only your service record but your status, the terms of your discharge, and any discipline the service imposed against you;
- employment history, requiring that you disclose any employer from whom you received income beginning at age 18 (available from the Social Security Administration), including the employer's address, your job duties, the dates of employment, and the reason for its termination;
- professional history, requiring that you disclose not only any professional licenses but also any license applications, denials, or discipline;
- financial history, requiring that you disclose any overdue obligations, checks returned for insufficient funds, bankruptcies, and collection efforts and proceedings against you, with the bar cross-checking that information with credit reports;
- psychological and substance-abuse history, requiring that you disclose any disability or condition that could impair you from representing clients competently including a release of medical, psychiatric, and other mental-health records;
- criminal history, requiring that you disclose not only convictions but also charges including those that the court dismissed, sealed, or expunged, with your explanation of the circumstances and outcomes;

- civil litigation, requiring that you disclose not only those cases in which you were a defendant but also those that you filed as a plaintiff, including an explanation of the claims, defenses, factual circumstances, and outcomes.

Law school helps you establish and prove your character and fitness. Your application to law school is the first step through which your law school fulfills its responsibility to you to help you prepare for admission to the bar. Standard 501(b) of the American Bar Association's accreditation standards prohibits law schools from admitting "applicants who do not appear capable of ... being admitted to the bar." Law school admissions committees judge applicants' character and fitness. Proving to a law school that you have the character and fitness for admission to law school does not guarantee admission to the bar but is a necessary first step in that direction. Law school applications require you to disclose some of the same information that you must disclose for admission to the bar.

> "It is important that law students and new lawyers place as much emphasis on developing and maintaining excellent character as they do on the type of law they wish to practice. After all, character defines a person. Whether we like it or not, we write our own eulogies by the lives that we live. How do you wish your eulogy to read? Decide what legacy you want to leave, then live it.."
>
> **Assistant Dean Martha Moore**

You must disclose to your law school fully and truthfully, just as you must disclose to the bar. **It does far more harm to fail or refuse to disclose or to delay in disclosing misconduct** suggesting bad moral character than it does to promptly and fully disclose. Students who fail to disclose can face dismissal from law school. Graduates can face revocation of their law degree or denial of bar admission, or both. Obtain from your law school registrar a copy of the law school application that you completed, not an earlier or later version but your own completed application. Review your application now to ensure that you have made full and truthful disclosures. If you have not, then immediately correct your application following your law school's procedures. Save a copy of your law school application. **As soon as an event occurs during law school that makes your application incomplete, update your application** following your law school's procedures. It is far better to correct and update your law school application than it is to try to explain discrepancies and omissions to a state bar. **Ensure that your law school application and bar application contain the same information.** If they do not, then expect the bar to hale you before a hearing panel for character-and-fitness review. Keep copies of each correction and update to ensure that you can prove your timely and full disclosure.

> "If you have gotten into trouble, then confess what you did, promise not to do it again, and take your punishment. If you balk at taking your punishment, then you have not really accepted that your actions were wrong."
>
> ***Dean Amy Timmer***

Your law school may also maintain an honor code to ensure that you seek no undue academic advantage through misrepresenting, lying, cheating, or stealing, and that you do not tolerate those who do. **Comply with your law school's honor code** at all times. Your state bar will require you to disclose and explain honor-code sanctions and even honor-code complaints against you. Earning your law degree without sanction or complaint is a big step toward demonstrating character and fitness. **Write, adopt, and follow your personal code of conduct meeting all school and professional rules and norms.** Particularly if your history includes dishonorable conduct, then use the period of your legal education to develop, implement, document, and prove your own code of honor. Commit in writing and action to civility, responsibility, respectfulness, trust, and loyalty. It is not easy, but individuals with histories involving serious misconduct have over the course of time and with deliberate action been able to establish the requisite good moral character for bar admission.

Your law school may also have disciplinary procedures to ensure that you maintain the requisite character and fitness for law practice and that your behavior does not unreasonably interfere with the studies of other law students. **Do nothing to implicate your law school's disciplinary procedures.** Your state bar will require you to disclose and explain disciplinary complaints and actions. **Be aware of and respect the broad scope of disciplinary procedures.** Your law school's disciplinary procedures may permit or require discipline for misconduct that occurs off school premises. If you have overdue debt, then address it responsibly. If you have substance-abuse issues, then get immediate help so that you can demonstrate that you have corrected them. If you have relationship issues, then keep a cool head rather than engaging in behavior that others see as harassing or threatening. If you have a mental or emotional disability that could affect your law practice, then ensure that you are under treatment by a care provider who can attest to your ability to practice reliably. Avoid conduct on and off school premises implicating school disciplinary procedures, including:

- substance abuse affecting your interaction with staff or students;
- drunk-driving and disorderly conduct charges;
- stalking or harassing resulting in personal-protection order;
- threats, fights, assault, battery, and domestic violence;
- repeatedly bouncing checks for tuition, fees, and books;
- stealing from or defrauding other law students;
- using profanity and other abusive language toward staff;
- failing to return library books and pay library fines;
- marking in library books or damaging other school property; and
- depression resulting in aberrant behavior or suicide attempt.

These steps will help prepare you to address or, better yet, avoid having to address, your character and fitness in a job interview. Interviewers tend to rely on bar-admission procedures, background checks, and references for character-and-fitness disclosures rather than to ask you directly. For instance, it is unlikely in an interview that you would volunteer or that an interviewer would ask a question that would require you to disclose that you had a drunk-driving conviction long before attending law school. If, on the other hand, you feel that your past misconduct may arise during an interview, or if you feel that you would better disclose that misconduct in an interview, then **consult your law school's career staff, your faculty advisor, and your mentor.** There are times, places, and reasons to disclose past misconduct, where you have the best opportunity to address why it should not impact your career and professional development. Get counsel in those situations.

> "Every case you touch will deal with human life in one way or another. You have an awesome responsibility to do things right."
> **_Former State Court Judge Jeff Martlew_**

Although *character and fitness* is a term of art for lawyers, "fitness" in its everyday meaning can help your career and professional development. **Law firms and other employers of lawyers value your physical, mental, and emotional health.** Good nutrition, aerobic exercise, rest, and recreation all improve physical and mental health. Controlling one's thinking, developing a healthy internal dialogue, maintaining a supportive social network, and interpreting situations to accentuate opportunity and autonomy can all improve mental and emotional health. *See* Val J. Arnold, *Converting Stress into an Ally*, in JULIE M. TAMMINEN, ED., LIVING WITH THE LAW—STRATEGIES TO AVOID BURNOUT AND CREATE BALANCE 15-19 (ABA Law Practice Management Section 1997). Although interviewers will not in general inquire as to physical and mental disability because of employment-rights laws, interviews can present occasions for casual discussion of those subjects (food and exercise preferences, recreation, etc.) related to health. If the opportunity presents itself and you share those interests with your interviewer, then appreciate the opportunity to discuss them.

Exercise. Review again the above list of character-and-fitness areas (residence, education, finances, employment, military service, etc.) for which state bars require you to disclose information. For each of those areas, determine and record the following, addressing now each issue on which you perceive a potential problem:

> ➢ whether you have or can readily obtain the necessary information and records to complete and substantiate your disclosures;
> ➢ whether there is something in your disclosure that a state bar may construe as an indication of bad moral character;
> ➢ what explanation you have for the behavior that suggests bad moral character, if you have a true and responsible explanation;
> ➢ what accomplishments and behavior demonstrate that you have corrected any bad moral character;
> ➢ whether your law school application reflects the same information that you must disclose to the state bar; and

> who at your law school or the state bar will review with you now the efforts you have made or intend to make to demonstrate that you have rehabilitated bad moral character.

Thomas Smith, J.D. 2006

"After graduating from law school, I won appointment to the United States Air Force Judge Advocates General Corps and became a military lawyer, earning the rank of captain. The JAG Corps recruits competitively. Character and fitness are critical to winning a JAG Corps opportunity. One thing that helped me was that I won my law school's Leadership Achievement Award after having been an editor for the Law Review, president of the Federalist Society, vice-president of the Student Bar Association, and a school ambassador. I have always admired and hoped to demonstrate character."

Professional-Development Tools

What you do in law school should not only strengthen your ethics and professional identity but also create and preserve useful evidence of them. To enter law practice and thrive, you need not only the ethics through which to provide sound legal services but proof that you are ethical. Clients and others need to respect and trust you. If you cannot demonstrate professional character, then you will not have much opportunity to serve because you may have no job or clients. You must also be able to communicate to others that you have professional integrity. Law school should help you create useable evidence of your character, so that you can demonstrate your character in ways that promote your professional opportunities. One way to build evidence of your character is through your law school's alumni. When you need a community of professionals who respect and trust you, a great place to start is your law school's alumni. Alumni are only the first part of a broader network that you can develop to reflect your professional identity. Another tool that you have to connect your ethics and professional identity to career options is the collection of recommendations and references that you earn while in law school. Faculty, deans, externship supervisors, and others with whom you have substantial interaction like to write recommendations and give references when earned. Another tool for connecting your professional identity to your career is your professional dress and demeanor, representative of the cconcern you have for how you appear to others. Finally, your resume is another tool that captures and reflects your professional whole, connecting it to your career opportunities. As this section addresses these tools to demonstrate your ethics and reflect your professional identity, **keep these connections in mind:**

- your law school's alumni;
- your professional network;
- the recommendations and references that you earn;
- your dress and demeanor; and
- your professional resume.

Alumni—*Assisting*

Your law school's alumni are one community within which you can readily demonstrate your professional ethics and identity so as to connect it to career opportunities. It is not that alumni are your job search or professional network. Alumni contacts are different from the professional network described in the next section. **Alumni are your professional family.** Family members know and accept you more readily than strangers, providing an important stage for your social development. The importance of family to social development suggests that acceptance within a similar **professional community can likewise be critical to professional development.** Alumni are like your professional family because they share important aspects of your professional development. Many of them will have had the same professors, programs, courses, and clinics. Alumni also share professional culture, history, and (most importantly) loyalties. **Alumni will give you the benefit of every doubt,** just when you need a place to be comfortable and safe within which to establish your professional identity.

Law schools do several things to help their students draw on their alumni. Law schools invite their students to join in alumni gatherings held all over the country. You may find that your law school is holding an alumni event in your home area or the region where you wish to settle. Make an effort to investigate and attend those gatherings. You will find current deans, faculty, and staff reminiscing with alumni while sharing with you and other students their career insight, lawyer lore, and inspiration. Law schools also bring alumni back to the school for social mixers with current students, to judge student competitions, and to speak about their fields. You need not necessarily travel to locate alumni. **Your school will bring alumni to you for the specific purpose of giving you a professional home and family.**

Law schools also gather, organize, and share alumni information with their students. Using your law school's alumni database, you can **search for alumni who live in the region where you expect to practice, who practice in your desired field, who practice in a law firm of the size you desire, or a combination of these data fields.** Use your school's alumni database to find alumni with whom you would like to meet or have a conversation. Investigate their backgrounds online or through other resources so that you get a clearer idea of the roles graduates of your law school undertake. You may be surprised at the public, judicial, and corporate offices they hold and the breadth, depth, and attraction of their law practices. Your investigation may help you see your own opportunities more clearly. If they can do it, then so can you.

> "Alumni meetings that I host across the nation are often attended by a mix of veteran alumni, who are well established in their practice and legal community, and recent graduates, who have just passed the bar examination and are looking for work in that very community. It warms the heart of even the most traveled alumni relations officer to watch them exchange business cards and share advice while they reminisce about their favorite professors. Do not underestimate he important and strength of the alumni connection."
>
> **Dean and General Counsel Jim Robb**

By meeting and spending time with you at more than one event, **alumni may gradually help you develop the professional identity to reach your career goals.** Your law school's career office can help you determine how to approach alumni and which alumni are most likely to respond. When you encounter a case, subject, problem, or skill in law school that interests you, locate alumni who have experience in those matters. Also, consider locating a recent graduate of your law school to discuss the transition from school to practice in your desired field. The key is to **make your alumni interaction about your professional exploration and development, not getting a job.** Alumni may give you a chance to visit their law offices, learn about their work, and hear about its challenges and rewards. Like a family member, they may just listen to you talk about your career goals, giving you hints about what sounds most professional, authentic, and attainable.

Exercise. Get the help of your law school's career office to find out how to navigate and search the school's alumni database. Then, identify, record, and save the following, until you feel that you are ready to contact and meet with alumni following your career office's advice:

> ➤ an alumni who practices in your hometown;
> ➤ an alumni who works in the town where you want to settle;
> ➤ an alumni who works in the field in which you want to practice;
> ➤ an alumni who graduated recently and works near your law school;
> ➤ an alumni who uses the law degree other than to practice law; and
> ➤ a famous alumni whose career is an inspiration to you.

Sarah Hartman, J.D. 2007

"After graduating with a bachelor's degree in music and moving to a Midwestern city, I decided to attend a nearby law school. Since then, I made the city my home and have joined a leading small law firm there. The firm has outstanding clients, and one of the principals of the firm is an alumnus from my law school. The principal, who serves on an alumni-association board, knew and respected the quality of my legal education. I have found that knowing other alumni from my law school in the community has been helpful in developing professional relationships as well as seeking advice."

Networking—*Conferring*

Networking is a classic career and professional-development tool. The concept behind networking is that **meeting one professional gives you access to many professionals** within the community in which the professional practices. Law practice takes place within a community of professionals who maintain good relationships with one another while depending to varying degrees on one another. When you meet and establish a professional relationship with one lawyer within that community, you have access to a network of practitioners. Even if the lawyer whom you meet does not have the contact or resource that you need, other members of that network likely will. Lawyers tend to know several important things about one another, any one or more of which may help you, including:

- who is currently in practice in the area;
- who currently practices in what legal field;
- who is currently serving what client populations;
- who currently has excess work and who does not;
- how practitioners are bundling or unbundling their services;
- how practitioners are pricing their services;
- how practitioners are marketing their services;
- who is referring to whom on what terms;
- who is accepting referrals on what terms;
- who has hired recently;
- who is hiring now; and
- who may be hiring soon.

Do not overlook the value of networking during a job search. **Employers never post more than half of all available law jobs.** Well more than one half of law graduates find their jobs in the legal field through networking. Employers decline to post jobs for several reasons. They may not be fully committed to hiring anyone but only willing to do so if the right person is available. They may wish to reduce hiring burdens and costs. They may not want clients or competitors to know that they are hiring or may even want to keep it from the associates in the firm until a hire is actually made. Especially during uncertain economic times but also during labor negotiations, employers may not want it known that they have the resources to take on the cost of new employees. In those cases, employers will network to advertise the position's availability and recruit candidates by word of mouth. **Not to network is to miss out on job opportunities.**

> "Networking establishes important connections that foster a lawyer's reputation and credibility. I advise students to get involved in organized bar association activities as soon as possible. One never knows where even an informal connection might lead. I have personally met all the justices of my state supreme court, many appellate judges, and many of the federal and state trial court judges in the counties where I have practiced through a most unlikely activity, my participation in bar association musical talent shows. Now when I go into their courtrooms or encounter them at events, they know me and see me as someone actively involved in the community."
>
> **Dean and General Counsel Jim Robb**

Yet networking is not simply about finding a job or starting a law practice. **Networks remain highly valuable to your professional development and success even when you are not looking for a job or are already in practice.** In addition to the above information, networked lawyers tend to share resources and tips like the names of qualified (and unqualified) expert witnesses, medical examiners, and animators and illustrators. They communicate about local judges' decisions and tendencies in certain cases, new requirements of the court clerk, and specific decisions or general patterns in the appeals courts. They communicate about office systems and equipment, staffing practices, and reliable help available for hire. **Even if you already have a specific job or opportunity in mind, recognize the value of networking to your growth in that job.**

Get to know well-respected practitioners who can connect you with other practitioners either in your geographic area or legal field of interest. **Networks exist both in geographic areas and in subject fields.** A lawyer in practice within a local bar tends to know the other members of that local bar. A lawyer in practice within a specialty field tends to know other lawyers in that specialty field even if those other specialists are widely distributed geographically. Lawyers in some specialties may know most or all of the other lawyers in that specialty within an entire state. A lawyer who practices in a very narrow specialty or industry (airliner-crash liability, oil-spill liability, property rights in genetically altered life, telecommunications antitrust) may network with many of the lawyers across the country or even around the globe in that same specialty or industry. Lawyers develop and maintain networks through local, state, national, or international services, activities, and events like:

- associations and sections of associations,
- bar and committee meetings,
- e-journals and newsletters,
- conferences and workshops,
- administrative hearings,
- bidding and other competition to do legal work,
- pro-bono and public-interest work,
- present and past employers,
- social clubs and philanthropic events,
- political and legislative matters, and
- publications, contacting authors of interesting articles.

Do not limit your networking to lawyers. Career and placement staff, not to mention successful lawyers, can tell you odd stories of how law graduates have gotten their jobs through networking through family, friends, and other acquaintances. For example, it would not be unusual to find a network trail that led to a job offer, in which a law graduate's family member knew of a friend whose spouse heard an acquaintance mention hearing of a company looking quietly to add a new lawyer to their counsel's office. When a job is available but not announced and posted, then recruiting occurs through family relationships, friendships, acquaintances, professional and employment relationships, social clubs, and other connections. Exercise the confidence of a lawyer to communicate with others with whom you do not yet have an established relationship. Your objective is to meet lawyers who know of law-practice opportunities, but you may do so through others who are not lawyers or currently practicing law, including:

- family, friends, and acquaintances;
- current and former employers and co-workers;
- college roommates and friends;
- law school friends, faculty, staff, and alumni;
- bar association staff;
- social and recreational clubs;
- volunteers in service activities;
- real-estate agents, bank employees, and financial advisors;
- schoolteachers, principals, and parent-teacher-association members;

- physicians, therapists, and other medical-care providers; and
- people whom you read or hear about in the local trade news.

Networking is an activity to begin early in your career and professional development. Do not wait until near graduation or when you need a job. As graduation approaches and immediately after you graduate, you may need to focus on other higher-priority tasks like bar application and studying for the bar, and locating and moving into new housing. Networking takes time, and the dividends that it pays can be slow in coming to fruition. Payments on educational loans typically begin six months after graduation. **Have an established network in your target community well before graduation nears.** If you do not have a job offer, then you want to have a network on which to draw for job leads, recommendations, references, and information that will help prepare you for job interviews. As indicated in Richard L. Hermann, Managing Your Legal Career—Best Practices for Creating the Career You Want 21-23 (ABA 2010), pursue multiple avenues at once, working every connection at once while avoiding tunnel vision. When your resume gets you an interview offer, your network may include someone who works in or knows the firm and can put in a good word for you. As the cliché goes, sometimes it is not what you know, but who you know.

Keep in mind that networking is a two-way interaction. You also have knowledge, skills, identity, and information to offer. Keep networking relationships fresh, helpful, and authentic. **Sincerity counts.** Care about the people with whom you network, and they will care about you. If you know of job leads in which you are not interested, then share them with those who are interested. Think about how you can help others in your network, and act on those thoughts. Productive networking entails giving as much or more than receiving. Then, when it comes time to ask for help, you will have people who are committed to you. Reaching out to your network whenever you have something to offer keeps you visible. Communicate who you are by sharing your skills. Make your networking meaningful to others, and you will make yourself memorable. **Follow these guidelines in your networking encounters:**

- approach others rather than avoid them;
- start conversations rather than end them;
- be friendly, outgoing, and at ease with others;

- speak about others more than about yourself;
- offer your help before asking for help;
- ask for a business card before sharing your business card;
- say something positive about the other person's business card;
- write helpful information on the back of business cards;
- do not ask directly for a job or about job opportunities;
- do not hand out resumes when networking;
- do let your career and job interests be known;
- be specific, not vague, about your interests;
- tell others that you are going to be a lawyer;
- go beyond your normal contacts and community;
- follow up with an email or note to those whom you meet;
- follow up on all helpful job and networking leads; and
- store cards and contact information where you can find and use them.

One way to build your skill at networking is to **develop a *job talk* that you can tell on a moment's notice.** Be able in 5 to 10 seconds, meaning a couple of short sentences, to let others know your networking purpose. You should be able to give your job talk on a short elevator ride, for instance. You can always expand on the job talk if you have more time. The idea is to have something clear, short, and compelling to say with confidence about yourself. Rehearse your job talk in the mirror, to family and friends, and with your career staff, until it is a perfectly natural expression of you. A job talk should include not only your interest but something singular and attractive about yourself. Consider which of these examples sounds best to you:

- "I am graduating from law school in May looking to join a litigation practice after winning a national trial-advocacy competition";
- "My mother was the state's first female appeals court judge. I am looking to follow in her footsteps by joining an appellate practice";
- "My hero father was a non-lawyer magistrate in a border town. I plan to serve his Hispanic-Latino community using my law degree";
- "I want to show my three older siblings, all of whom are lawyers, that I can be an even better transactional lawyer than they are";

- "Every other kid in my grade school wanted to be a police officer, but I wanted to be a prosecutor since the first time that I can remember";
- "I advocated for my severely mentally disabled brother until he passed away. I am earning my law degree to help others like him."

Social networking online, especially through forums that are reserved for or preferred by professionals, is acceptable within certain guidelines. With the right timing, content, and distribution, instant messaging and wiki and blog posts can also be helpful. The primary guideline is to **consider everything that you post to be viewable by prospective employers.** Employers check social networking sites. The stories are legion of attractive job candidates who prospects were foiled by an indiscrete social networking photograph or post. Also, do not use social networking sites to contact and offer special (friend) access to supervisors, faculty members, and prospective employers, who might see the offer as too personal. **Keep it professional.** Organizations are still adjusting to the informality and personal nature of social networking sites. Here is a list of social networking guidelines:

- use a professional networking site rather than a social one;
- constantly update your information current to keep it current;
- share successes and accomplishments, not gripes and complaints;
- stay upbeat and positive in all of your posts;
- post only tasteful photographs in appropriate settings;
- do not make posts during work or class;
- do not offer special (friend) access to a work supervisor;
- do not criticize supervisors and others in authority positions; and
- do not rule out or denigrate opportunities you may desire later.

Exercise. Look again at the job-talk examples above, and then try the following:

- ➤ draft your job talk in writing;
- ➤ rehearse your job talk until you can say it flawlessly;

> tell your job talk to your closest family member or friend;
> ask for their evaluation, and listen to them;
> re-draft your job talk in writing incorporating their comments;
> rehearse it again until you can say it flawlessly;
> tell your job talk to your career staff;
> ask for their evaluation, and listen to them;
> re-draft your job talk in writing incorporating their comments;
> rehearse it again until you can say it flawlessly; and
> pick a new networking opportunity to try out your job talk.

LeeAnn Ford, J.D. 2006

"I came to law school with an engineering background, wanting to work in intellectual property. One of my professors helped me locate a law firm that was not advertising any open positions but that did some work in the field of my interest and was pretty busy. I did an externship at the firm to develop a stronger relationship and prove my skill. The firm took me on after graduation, and I continue to love the work."

Recommendations—*Certifying*

You have another excellent tool to connect your ethics and professional identity to career options in the recommendations and references that you earn during law school. **Law school is a great place to earn the respect and recommendation of model professionals,** whether they are full-time or adjunct professors, deans and other administrators, or judges and other speakers who visit the school. Law firms and other employers of lawyers know that law professors and deans can be effective judges of legal talent. They are trained to assess your knowledge, skills, and ethics. A glowing recommendation letter from a prominent judge or lawyer who serves as an adjunct faculty member, or from a full-time faculty member or dean, can carry weight with prospective employers, just as can their willingness to act as your character reference. **Cultivate relationships in and through law school that give you the best opportunity for strong positive recommendation letters and references.** Expect by the time you apply for a job to have gathered recommendation letters and listed professional references.

Employers value recommendations and references. Law firms and other employers of lawyers make substantial investments in their new hires. They may incur, directly and indirectly, tens of thousands or even hundreds of thousands of dollars in developing a new associate to the point that the associate makes an overall positive economic contribution to the employer. **Employers want and need to get hiring decisions right the first time.** Employee turnover is at least as costly and damaging to law firms as it is to other employers. There are few better ways to ascertain the knowledge, skills, and ethics of a job candidate than to communicate with a professional who is skilled in assessing performance and who has observed the candidate perform. Employers make decisions on resumes and interviews, but they also make decisions based on recommendations and references. Employers will check your references. **Do not underestimate the value of a strong recommendation and reference from a leading professional.** There are some positions that are simply not available to you without it.

One key to an effective recommendation is that there be a substantial basis for it. Simply taking a class from a professor is ordinarily not enough to earn you a recommendation. Even if you ask for one on that basis and a professor relents, then there may not be much that the professor can write on your behalf. A good grade alone, even with your classroom demeanor, does not give a professor much to write or say. Judges, lawyers, faculty members, deans, and other professionals are far more likely to write you a meaningful recommendation letter or give you a valuable reference if they have a substantial basis for doing so. **Judges and lawyers for whom you intern or extern, and faculty members for whom you act as a teaching or research assistant, ordinarily have a substantial basis on which to evaluate your character.** They know the time, effort, and skill that you devote to that work. A recommendation letter is not a quid pro quo following an internship, externship, or assistant position. Do not assume it as a right. On the other hand, you may certainly respectfully request a recommendation and reference. It is probable that the judge or lawyer for whom you intern, extern, or clerk, and professor for whom you act as a teaching or research assistant, has written letters for other law students in the past.

In particular, value your reputation and relationships with law school faculty, deans, and staff from your first day on campus. Honor code proceedings, disciplinary complaints, and other events calling your reputation into question can foreclose you from obtaining helpful recommendations and references. Also, **get to know your professors outside of class through volunteer and pro-bono**

service, student organizations, and other service work supporting your law school. These activities can give your professors and deans a basis on which to give you a recommendation and reference. There are few activities that can better demonstrate your ethics and character than to assist a professor with pro-bono or public-interest work. Think intentionally about forming faculty, administration, and staff relationships on which you can draw for recommendations and references.

Another key to an effective recommendation is that the prospective employer respect the recommender. Certain positions, including faculty or dean status, elected office and good reputation within the local bar, and status as a trial or especially an appellate-court judge, carry their own weight with most employers. Yet some employers may depend on specific recommenders. For example, certain professors, lawyers, or judges may be key recommenders for certain judicial clerkships. In some instances, successful past recommendations leading to qualified candidate hires can create a pipeline of sorts from recommender to employer. Before you commit to a teaching- or research-assistant position with a professor, or to an internship or externship with a lawyer or judge, **consider whether that professional's recommendation is likely to facilitate your desired employment opportunities.** Many experiences have their own value, while the greater value of other experiences may be in where they lead. Plan backward from your ultimate job, earning the recommendation and reference of the professionals who are most likely to influence your prospective employer. Consult with your faculty advisor and career staff for advice in this area.

As to the mechanics of obtaining a recommendation or reference, request a recommendation letter or reference in person if able, or if not, then by a respectful email or correspondence to the recommender. Acknowledge the recommender's discretion to write or not to write. In your request, politely **remind the recommender of who you are and what you did** that would give the recommender a substantial basis for complying. Judges, lawyers, and professors interact with many and may momentarily overlook your relationship with and service to them. Spare them that embarrassment. Also, be prepared to **supply a resume and additional details of your activities and successes.** A good recommendation letter melds what the recommender observed of your character and work with other background that the recommender may or may not know or recall about you. Your resume and an email with additional detail can help the recommender write a letter that portrays your current skill as a designed product of your lifelong commitments.

The timing of a recommendation request can be important. You may wish to ask for an open "to whom it may concern" recommendation letter as soon as your service for the recommender is complete, especially if it may prove difficult to get a timely recommendation from the recommender later. On the other hand, if you wait until you identify a specific employer to whom the recommender can direct and craft the letter, then you may get a recommendation that is significantly more specific to the job that you seek and significantly more effective. In other words, **it may be better to wait until you need it before you ask.** If you do wait to ask until you have a specific employer in mind, then provide your recommender with the employer's name and address. Do not rule out doing both, getting an immediate letter but then asking again later for a more specific letter. Recommenders typically save recommendations in electronic form for reproduction or modification later. If you have several specific employers in mind, then consider asking the recommender's secretary or administrative assistant if the recommender would mind having several specific letters prepared.

Routing of the recommendation letter may be important. Most employers accept open "to whom it may concern" recommendation letters written by the recommender but provided by the job applicant. Some recommenders will provide multiple signed originals of an open recommendation letter, so that you can submit an original to several prospective employers. **A few employers, particularly those in government or other positions involving security issues, may prefer or require that your recommender provide the recommendation directly to the employer.** If your prospective employer requires that your recommender route the letter directly to it, then be sure that you provide your recommender with the correct routing information and also that you give your recommender sufficient time. Allowing your recommender sufficient time is always important. Recommenders have other things to do. Be respectful, and make your request weeks or at least several days in advance.

Job candidates treat references differently from recommendation letters. You should be prepared to give to a prospective employer a list of three professional references. Some employers prefer or require that you list references when you first apply with your cover letter and resume. Some candidates include references at the end of the resume. If you have particularly distinguished references, then you may wish to do so. On the other hand, many employers do not request or check references until after a satisfactory job interview. You may wish to wait on providing references. When you do provide references, make sure that they are all professional references (judges, lawyers, professors, deans, etc.) rather than family members, friends, pastors, and other social and personal acquaintances. In general, prefer references within the legal field over references outside of it, although it can be appropriate to list a former non-law employer. A recommendation letter often ends with an invitation to the employer to contact the recommender. You may list these recommenders as references. Consider these additional guidelines for obtaining a reference:

- Do not list a professional as a reference unless you have contacted that professional and received permission. They may not be prepared to give you a positive reference;
- If you list a reference once with permission, ask again before listing the reference again. They will likely approve but will appreciate knowing who may be calling; and
- Always let the professional who offers you a reference know in advance to whom you intend to give their name as a reference. They may not have the relationship with that person that you expect.

Exercise. Reflect on and complete these exercises to help you explore how to acquire appropriate recommendations and references:

➢ identify your three most desired jobs;
➢ determine who are the best recommenders for those jobs;
➢ determine what it takes to earn a recommendation from them; and
➢ determine whether you qualify for that opportunity.

> **Robert Suarez, J.D. 2010**
>
> "Active-duty military service interrupted my legal education, making it especially challenging. Yet after I returned from active duty, I had the opportunity for an externship at a leading law firm near my law school. I learned a lot about civil litigation, did well, and had great relationships there. The strong recommendations and references that I received helped earn me an interview and job offer at another great local firm where I now practice."

Dress and Demeanor—*Looking*

Professional dress and demeanor are other tools through which you reflect your professional ethics and identity. Dress and demeanor convey messages. Every profession and trade has its own uniform and expectations for conduct. Professional dress is not about remaining within a strict dress code as much as it is recognizing and respecting the conventions and why the profession maintains and values them. **Your willingness to dress to meet professional expectations is an indication of your respect for the profession and those who hold positions of authority within it.** Your willingness to conform your demeanor to professional norms does the same. After an organization hires you, you may over time somewhat affect the professional dress and demeanor norms of your employer. There are trendsetters and groundbreakers. It is far less likely that an organization will hire you as a trendsetter or groundbreaker when it comes to dress and demeanor. Save trendsetting for later, and do not expect it to be easy.

> "The best compliment I ever received was a client who told me, 'I have interviewed several attorneys and asked around about you. I chose you because I was told you would fight like hell for me but remain a lady the entire time.' I once had a client hire me after interviewing and rejecting two very smart and talented attorneys up the street because they 'just didn't dress like a lawyer.' In that moment, I realized that if people are going to plunk down their hard-earned money for a lawyer, they want the whole package—not someone who necessarily looks and dresses just like them."
>
> **Professor Victoria Vuletich**

Professional dress involves your clothing, jewelry, and accessories. The key here is to get qualified advice. Professional sales staff and tailors at retailers who serve a lawyer clientele in your area are appropriate, although ensure that their taste meets employer expectations. **Professional dress need not be expensive.** You may overshoot your mark if you attempt to impress with expense. Instead, make sound choices. If you cannot afford professional dress, then check with your law school for a professional clothing ministry or exchange. Identify leading practitioners in the geographic area and subject field with impeccable dress, and ask for their recommendations. Although much of law has a national character, there can be some regional and local variation in acceptable dress. There can also be some variation in dress among practice fields, depending on the forums in which those practitioners work. Transactional lawyers may wear business casual for office work, for instance, whereas dark suits may be the only acceptable dress for federal-court appearances. **Consult your law school's career staff, and examine the career office's guides on professional dress.** You may find guidelines for networking events and interviews that include:

- dark fitted two-piece suit;
- solid white collared shirt or blouse;
- red or other conservatively colored tie;
- black leather-soled shoes (low heels for women);
- black belt with conservative clasp;
- modest silver, gold, or black-leather-banded watch;
- no earrings for men;
- no long dangling earrings for women;
- no lapel pin or tie tack or bar for men;
- no (or very modest) broach or pin for women.

It is not simply what you wear but how you wear it. You may have the perfect outfit but wear it so imperfectly that prospective employers could criticize your professional dress. Shirttails should always be fully tucked in. Men and women should ensure that their coattails and pant cuffs are straight when they stand. If you are a man, then whenever you stand, you should straighten your tie and button your suitcoat leaving the bottom button unbuttoned. Whenever you sit, you should unbutton your suitcoat and center your tie. If you are a woman, then whether you unbutton your suitcoat when you sit will depend on its style. You should not kick off your shoes or push them partway off when you sit. Pull your suitcoat down away from your collar when you sit so that it lies naturally and does not stick up around your neck. By paying modest attention to these and other small details, you can keep your professional dress looking professional.

> "Be on time, dress appropriately, speak well and thoughtfully. What you may think of as old-fashioned values still matter."
>
> **Dean Amy Timmer**

Professional dress includes accessories like purses and briefcases. An outsize, beat-up old briefcase will not help. Avoid large briefcases. You are not a salesperson in need of pulling out samples. **Try to avoid carrying a briefcase on career and professional-development activities.** Doing so can make it more difficult to open and hold doors, shake hands in greeting, and get seated with a convenient place for the briefcase. For interviews or other places where you need to carry a pad, cover letter, and resumes, try carrying a 9" x 12" black leather folder with a zipper around the outside. Always have a zipper or clasp on your bag or folder so that if you drop it, you will not have the embarrassment and breach of confidence that comes with papers falling out. Do not wear a hat. You may wear conservative sunglasses outside, but do not wear sunglasses inside. Avoid tinted eyeglasses if the tint does not dissipate reasonably quickly when moving from outside to inside. They can make it look like you have dark circles around your eyes, as if you were not sleeping or taking good care of yourself. Women carrying a purse should make it a small dark handbag that would look inconspicuous when set on a conference table.. When you get advice on professional dress, include these accessories.

Professional demeanor is different from professional dress. Professionals work within a professional community promoted and maintained by professional norms. Professional norms include respect for professional responsibilities, evaluations, judgments, and opinions. Your demeanor must reflect the ability to separate the professional from the performance and to respect the professional even when you disagree (and especially when you disagree) with the performance. Professional norms also include trust. You must develop a professional demeanor that conveys and elicits trust. Professional demeanor involves carrying yourself, expressing yourself, and interacting with other professionals in ways that promote these and other professional attributes. **Professional demeanor involves not the content of your communication but its embodied form including:**

- volume, quality, and tone of voice,
- eye contact,
- facial expression,
- emotions and energy level,
- attitude and outlook,
- posture when sitting and standing,
- carriage and gait, and
- manner of greeting and handshake.

Your demeanor as to each of these criteria should engender confidence, trust, and respect in every professional interaction. Evaluate and conform your demeanor when greeting another professional, speaking with and listening to another professional, walking or driving with another professional, dining with another professional, and, especially, advocating and disagreeing with another professional. It is not so much a matter of being on your guard—you can and should act naturally—as being aware that others are observing you. **People look up to lawyers. They want to see you behave like a lawyer, even when you are not in court.** In all exchanges, avoid distracting and potentially demeaning reactions and behaviors like:

- frowns, grimaces, and scowls,
- grunted or inaudible communications,
- frequent speaking over another and interrupting,
- failing to acknowledge or answer another,
- fidgeting and looking away in distraction,
- animated hand motions and gestures,
- profanity and crude references,
- slapping on the back and other touching, and
- gum chewing and sucking on candy.

Exercise. Complete one or both of the following exercises on your professional dress and demeanor:
  ➢ Refer again to the list above of the several criteria to consider for professional dress. Dress so as to satisfy those criteria.

Then choose a willing lawyer, faculty advisor, or career staff person of your same sex to evaluate your professional dress with you;

➤ Refer again to the list above of the several things that comprise your professional demeanor. Make a videorecording of yourself doing each of those things. Then choose a willing lawyer, faculty advisor, or career staff person to evaluate the recording of your professional demeanor with you.

Robert Hinojosa, J.D. 2008

"I had a family and military career and was a sports official and firefighter. I started law school seeking to extend my career in public service. I felt that the dress, demeanor, and organizational skills that I learned in the military would translate well to prosecution practice and so completed an externship in a prosecutor's office. After graduation, a service-member classmate and I opened a law practice until he returned to active duty. I then took an assistant prosecutor's job in my family's home area and am loving it. Professional demeanor means so much in public service."

Resumes—*Attracting*

Your professional resume is another tool to connect the ethics and professional identity that you develop in law school to your future law career. Your resume does more than list your activities and achievements. It reflects your professional whole, meaning that it conveys the essence of who you are as a professional. **A resume states your basic qualifications but then highlights what an interested employer would most want to know about you to choose you for its open position.** Your resume conveys who you are not only through its content but also through its form, articulateness, detail, and organization. Do you recall the old adage that "you are what you eat"? A truer adage may be that you are what you *write*, perhaps always but particularly when it comes to your resume. You are also *how* you write. Your resume should have the appearance of an accomplished professional or, at a minimum, a professional prepared to accomplish.

Rely on your law school's career staff for resume forms and information. Use the following information as a helpful guide. A good place to start with your resume is to **think of what *employers need***

to know about you, before you proceed to what *you want* employers to know. There are some basic building blocks that every professional resume must include. Those prerequisites include at a minimum your ontact information, education, and prior relevant employment. They do not include an Objectives section. Your cover letter will communicate your thoughts and information about your career interests and goals. Make your resume satisfy the employer's requirements. Do not make the employer go searching for things about you that the employer must know but that you have failed to reveal. Here are guidelines on **what to include,** in the order in which to include them:

- a heading with your contact information;
- an Education section;
- an Employment section; and
- possibly a Skills section.

For the heading, begin with your current legal name using a middle initial if you have one. If others know you by another name in professional settings, then consider mentioning that other name in your cover letter or signing it in your cover letter. Do not add nicknames to your resume. Include your current address in the heading. **Be sure that you use an address at which mail will reach you from prospective employers** to whom you give your resume, when they are likely to respond. Include your telephone number in the heading with the area code. If you have a home and cell telephone but are seldom home to answer the home telephone, then provide your cell telephone number or both the home and cell telephones. Include your professional email address in the heading. **Avoid frivolous, unprofessional, and unduly revealing email addresses.** Lawyers notice details. Requiring prospective employers to reply to your email address at lawyerwannabe@gmail.com or megadeath@aol.com does not leave the best impression.

For the Education section, begin with your law school, city and state, anticipated degree, and anticipated month and year of graduation. For example: "Thomas M. Cooley Law School, Lansing, Michigan, Juris Doctor expected May 2012." Then list class rank (see the section of this guide on that subject) and grade-point average in the form "Class Rank: 52/231. GPA: 3.11/4.00." Then list school honors like Dean's List and Honor Roll, and activities like Law Review and Moot Court Competition, with your law school education and degree, not in a separate section. Follow your law school information with similar information for any other graduate or undergraduate degrees and education, using reverse chronological order. If you had significant honors and activities in other graduate or undergraduate programs, and they relate in some way to the skills you expect to use in your law career, then include those honors and activities with the graduate or undergraduate program information. Team and individual undergraduate sports participation in structured and competitive programs can convey relevant qualities like organization, leadership, and discipline. Do not list intramural and recreational activities. Do not include colleges and universities that you attended without earning a degree. Do not list high school information. **Here is a summary of these guidelines:**

DO INCLUDE:
- Class rank (see this guide's section on that subject);
- Law Review and other journals;
- Dean's List, Honor Roll, and other awards and recognition;
- Moot Court, Mock Trial, and other competitions;
- teaching and research assistant positions;
- officer positions in student organizations.

PROBABLY INCLUDE:
- student-organization memberships;
- articles, book reviews, and other publications;
- non-law-related school volunteer service (i.e., ambassador role);
- pro-bono service activities.

MAYBE INCLUDE:
- non-law-related student-organization volunteer service.

DO NOT INCLUDE:
- intramural sports;
- social activities or leadership.

For the Employment section, begin with your most recent employment, proceeding in reverse chronological order. As to the form, list your job title first such as "Law Clerk" or "Research

Assistant." Then list the employer's name followed by the city and state. Then briefly describe what you did using phrases beginning with active verbs such as "Researched international-trade issues" and "Drafted consent judgments." Do not use passive phrases like "Duties included ..." or "Responsibility for ... ." If you have legal or law-related work experience and significant non-legal and non-law-related work experience, then divide the Employment section into two sections titled Legal or Law-Related Employment and Other Relevant Employment. Be sure to include the word "relevant" in the other-employment heading if you are omitting non-relevant employment. Do not mislead employers into thinking that you are listing all employment when in fact you are omitting employers. If you have unpaid positions that you wish to include, then identify the headings as Experience rather than Employment. Do not mislead employers into thinking that someone paid you to do work that you actually did for free.

> "Your resume must get past the employer's initial 10-second review for a specific quality or fact, which filters out 90% of the applicants, and make it to the more thorough review where the employer can truly learn about you. To accomplish this feat, your resume must contain relevant and distinctive information that is easy to locate. Your resume must be an honest reflection of you while tailored to the needs of the employer."
>
> *Dean Charles Toy*

Be sure to list all legal experience including clinical experience in law school in which you were actually representing clients. If you have no legal work experience, then consider listing here (instead of under your law school education) any teaching- or research-assistant positions for which you were paid in law school and any pro-bono service. Also, **examine your non-legal work experience closely for transferable skills**, and include any relevant work. You should strongly prefer to show some work over showing none. **Avoid listing controversial work, activities, experience, or interests** unless you are sure that your prospective employer appreciates them or you do not mind losing the opportunity while preserving your beliefs and commitments.

If you decide to include a Skills section, then **list any MacCrate Skills in which you have actual experience,** like drafting discovery requests and conducting interviews. See the Advisors section above identifying the MacCrate Skills. Also, consider listing foreign-language skills. If you do so, then be sure to qualify if your knowledge of the foreign language is only for conversation. Do not mislead an employer into thinking that you can speak, read, and write in a foreign language in professional settings if you do not have those full skills. Employers may value foreign-language skills, but in professional settings, those skills need to be reliable. Also, consider including special technical and computer skills. Do not include skills with basic word-processing and other consumer software. You are not applying for a secretarial position. Instead, list specific case-management, time-and-billing, and other law-office-management software that you are skilled in using. Also, if you are able to use financial, business, accounting, design, animation, and other specialized software, then consider listing those skills while connecting them to your law-career or law-related employment with phrases like "Skilled in using computer-aided design and animation software for trial illustration."

As to the length your resume, many career officers recommend that you **try to keep it to one page** unless you have many years of substantial work experience. Employers can receive dozens or even hundreds of resumes for a single position. Lawyers who review resumes grow skilled at doing so. A quick scan down a resume taking no more than a few seconds can alert a lawyer to a qualified, highly qualified, or unqualified candidate. If you format and condense your information so that it all appears on a single page, then the reviewer will miss nothing of preliminary significance, understanding that every candidate has more information to offer and that initial resume reviews are for winnowing rather than hiring purposes. Do not make your reviewing lawyer flip back and forth between several pages. Especially, do not allow a small number of important lines of information flow over to a second page that a reviewer might skip. Keep important things immediately and highly visible. If you have more information than readily fits on a single page, then career staff and faculty advisors can help you determine which information to include a the single-page resume or whether to provide a longer resume.

As to the overall appearance of your resume, **use a high-quality bond white or off-white paper.** Do not use buff, tan, manila, grey, light blue, or other colored paper. Some employers of lawyers may be less sensitive to convention, but law firms, especially, are traditional institutions. You would not file a pleading on colored paper. Do not submit a resume on it. Use a single standard font like Times New Roman or the font of this text, Cambria. Avoid using multiple different fonts and script-style fonts. To organize and highlight information, use boldface font, italicized font, modest font-size changes, and bullet points, but use them sparingly. Do not make your resume look like a font sampler. **Use a laser or other highest-quality printer,** not ink jet or other lower quality. Use only black ink, not blue, red, or other colors or highlighting. Keep font size between 12-point and 10-point font. Do not use font sizes smaller than 10-point font. Lawyers read a lot. Do not make your resume hard to read. A tired lawyer with strained eyes may overlook it. Except possibly for your name, do not use font sizes larger than 12-point font. If your resume does not fill the page and instead looks spare, then increase the margins to inch-and-a-half or elaborate the content, or both. Take a step back from the resume, and adjust its format until it looks balanced on the page. The aesthetics of the printed page can convey a subtle confidence and sensitivity.

Ensure that your law school's career staff reviews your resume after you have proofread it several times. Meet with your faculty advisor and career staff to review and revise your resume. Treat that session not as a proofreading effort but as an opportunity to explore your activities, qualities, and accomplishments in fresh ways to help you connect them with the open position for which you are applying. Do not distribute a resume that your faculty advisor, law school career staff, or another qualified professional has not reviewed. **Resumes require just as much or more thought, planning, drafting, review, and revising as any other significant writing.** Do not treat your resume as a perfunctory list. Drafting a good resume requires self knowledge. It also requires knowledge of the specific job for which you are applying and the specific employer. Applicants craft resumes to the position for which and employer to whom they apply. So long as every word of every resume is accurate, **there is nothing wrong with having different resumes for different employers who are advertising different positions.** Be prepared to craft your original resume to reflect different activities, qualities, and accomplishments for different employers advertising different positions.

Use a cover letter whenever you submit a resume. See the section above on Communication, describing the form, content, and value of cover letters. **Give the same attention to the cover letter that you give to your resume,** including making multiple drafts of it over time and reviewing it with your faculty advisor and career staff. Use the same paper, printer, and font for your cover letter that you use for your resume. Your cover letter should be one page in a standard letter format. Your name, address, telephone number, and email should be at the cover letter's top. Date your letter near the top in the conventional style for dating, "January 24, 2011." Follow the date with the full name and any title of the person to whom you direct your cover letter. and complete address of the prospective employer. As the section above on Communication recommends, your cover letter should not repeat the information in your resume. Instead, use your cover letter to support and amplify your resume, making your candidacy even more meaningful to the employer than your resume readily reflects. As the Communication section above recommends, organize your cover letter in three short paragraphs as follows:

- briefly introduce yourself in a short first paragraph highlighting your greatest two or three assets;
- connect in a second short paragraph your career objective with the employer's advertised need; and
- end with a short third third paragraph regarding your timing and availability.

Follow-up letters are another excellent tool with which to support your resume. A follow-up letter keeps your name and interest in front of the employer for further consideration. It also documents any file that the employer is maintaining. It also shows your appreciation, diligence, interest, and sensitivity. Each follow-up letter should express your continued interest in the advertised position, while also addressing whatever issue telephone calls, interviews, or other communications or developments have raised. The follow-up letter should also describe any enclosures that it includes and why they are enclosed. That said, make your follow-up letters short, to the point. Consider sending a follow-up letter on the following occasions:

- any time a prospective employer contacts you;
- two weeks after you submit a resume if you have not heard from the employer, confirming that the employer received your resume, although you may substitute a telephone call here;
- immediately after an interview;

- with a list of references, writing sample, or any other information that the employer asks you to provide, even if you have provided that information orally or by email;
- any time that your resume information changes, especially if you discover any inaccuracy but also with updated grades, graduation, bar passage, and other accomplishments; and
- any time that you are no longer interested in the position for which you submitted a resume.

Exercise. Obtain several sample resumes from your law school's career office to complete the following for each resume:

- ➢ determine whether the sample resume complies with the length, font, and other format requirements described in the above text, while identifying your preferred format;
- ➢ order (rank) the sample resumes from the most attractive to the least attractive on their organization, style, and format alone, without reference to content;
- ➢ determine whether the sample resume complies with the content requirements described in the above text, while identifying your preferred content;
- ➢ order (rank) the sample resumes from the most compelling to the least compelling on their content alone, without reference to the attractiveness of the format; and
- ➢ make your first draft of your own resume based on what you learned from this exercise.

Lindsay Davenport, J.D. 2010
"I was doing very well academically in law school but wanted to be sure that I had the best opportunity to work in a leading law firm of some size. So, I worked on my resume with the staff of my school's career office, improving it with each version. I then attended a networking event where I passed out cards with my contact information and collected cards from lawyers at the event. Afterward, I sent each lawyer a thank-you note with my resume. This experience was invaluable and helped me find a job at a private law firm shortly after I graduated."

Career Transitions

You have just seen how developing your ethics and professional identity while using tools to capture and reflect them are important steps in your career and professional development. Yet you must then use those tools to connect your ethics and identity with specific career opportunities. Your ethics and professional identity have a lot to do with the career you should choose. One way that you connect your ethics and identity to careers is to choose the specific side on which you prefer to advocate. Lawyer advocates tend to represent one side or the other side in adversarial matters. Choosing sides wisely can be important to one's career. Another way is to identify your preferred forum. Lawyers speak and work in several different forums, each with their own character. Choose wisely. You may also connect your ethics and identity to law careers through community and pro-bono service. This chapter helps you reflect on these connections between your ethical identity and your career choices and preferences. As we go through them one by one, **keep these connections in mind:**

- the side on which you should advocate in adversarial causes;
- the forums in which you should speak and work;
- the community service you may wish to perform; and
- the pro-bono service that would build your practice and character.

Sides—*Choosing*

Your ethics and professional identity can have a lot to do with the side on which you should practice early in your career. Law often involves advocacy. Lawyers are good at analyzing, evaluating, articulating, and rationalizing toward decisions. Lawyers help others decide. Whenever there is advocacy, there are sides. **Lawyers take sides in many matters in law practice.** Certainly, in criminal and civil matters within the justice system there are clear sides, either prosecution versus defense or plaintiff versus defendant. Conflict rules require that lawyers in those matters either be on one side or the other, not both. Yet also in transactional matters, lawyers take sides anywhere two or more parties have differing interests in a matter to negotiate. Just as in litigation, the parties' transactional relationships may be more or less adversarial. Indeed, transactional negotiations can be just as contentious or more contentious than litigation. In many if not most practice settings, lawyers take sides. **Consider the following sides common in law practices:**

- plaintiff against defendant;
- prosecution against defense;
- buyer against seller;
- insured against insurer;
- lender against borrower;
- individual against corporation;
- creditor against debtor;
- developer against community representative;
- owner against contractor;
- shareholder against management;
- management against labor;
- regulated against regulator;
- employee against employer;
- licensor against licensed.

Recognize for career purposes that it is not just that there are two sides in so many matters. It is also that **sides are different, the differences tend to be the same from matter to matter, and lawyers tend to remain on the same side from matter to matter.** Take criminal matters as an example. Prosecution of criminal charges is starkly different from their defense. Prosecutors have a single government client to represent, even while they owe duties to the public including the criminally charged. They are usually salaried, career employees of a governmental unit where time and cost spent on each matter are muted concerns. Their role requires that they attend to public peace and order, punish wrongdoers, and avenge victim wrongs, balanced by a respect for individual rights. Criminal defense work is almost utterly unlike prosecution. It is intensely personal to the represented defendant, while not at all public. The defender's concern is with the individual client's welfare, not the victim's or public's. Whether it is private or public defense work, time and cost are constant and immediate concerns. Prosecution is cool, while defense is hot. There is no day-to-day mix of prosecution and defense work. You are either one or the other.

> "The practice of law should be more than a job and a paycheck. You should feel passionate, motivated, and enthusiastic about the work you do. Engage in an honest and careful introspection of who you are and what moves you. These considerations should serve as your guideposts. Shortly after leaving the United States Attorney's Office, following almost 30 years of public service, someone asked me if I could turn the clock back would I again make the same career choice. I immediately responded that I would."
> *Former United States Attorney's Office Criminal Division Chief Alan Gershel*

The differences in sides are everywhere. Take collections work as another example. Lawyers who represent creditors must see their work as a matter of economics, both their's and their client's. It is primarily if not solely about the money. To litigate where there is nothing to be gained is to throw good money after bad for both lawyer and client. Those lawyers need to be sound evaluators of economics, chasing the rich scoundrel for hidden assets but not the penniless fool. On the other side, though, the lawyer representing the debtor sees the work as primarily personal rather than economic. Except in the relatively uncommon case where the debtor can genuinely dispute the debt, the economics are obvious enough that the debtor owes money the debtor cannot pay. The lawyer's work for the debtor is strategic and personal, not economic. **In most practice, you see lawyers on either one side or the other, and for the most part playing only one side.**

Sides get even more important when you consider the dynamics within a law firm. Concurrent conflicts of interest, where a lawyer cannot represent one client in one matter because the lawyer is on the other side against that same client in another matter, tend to keep lawyers on the same side case to case. *See* ABA Model Rule of Professional Conduct 1.7. Even more so, ethics rules impute the disqualification of one lawyer to the disqualification of other lawyers in the same firm. *See* ABA Model Rule of Professional Conduct 1.10. What that means in many instances is that you cannot take one side in one matter while another lawyer in your firm takes the other side in another matter that involves one of the same parties. Clients also often do not like it when you play the other side, even if there is no direct conflict. **Reputations and loyalties matter.** In some fields, **law firms deliberately court the representation of only one side or the other.** For example, if an insurer who sends dozens of cases to a law firm to defend hears that lawyers in the firm are taking plaintiffs' cases, then the insurer may just decide to send its defenses cases elsewhere. When a lawyer switches sides in a career change, other lawyers speak jokingly of that lawyer having "gone over to the dark side." For these and other reasons, law firms tend to serve only one side especially in these fields:

- worker's compensation (claimant or employer sides);
- medical malpractice (physician or patient sides);
- motor-vehicle-accident and other personal-injury cases;
- bankruptcy (creditor or debtor sides);
- criminal cases (prosecution or defense);
- labor law (management or labor);
- civil rights (individual or employer);
- consumer rights and safety (consumer or manufacturer).

Choose sides wisely to fit your ethics and professional identity. Sides vary along several different ethical and identity dimensions. The examples given above suggest some of those dimensions. Review the section above on Personality and the Myers-Briggs Personality Test® indicators. The point is to identify your side of the dimension and then connect it to sides in a career. For example, if interpersonal relationships energize you, then consider choosing the more individual rather than corporate side. If you prefer principle over strategy, then choose the principled rather than strategic side. If you are risk averse, then choose the corporate side. Use informational interviews, faculty advisors, mentors, internships, and externships to help you discern your best fit. When you discern a difference in sides, you will probably find yourself attracted to one side or the other. **Listen carefully to your advisors and intuition.** You can change sides later. Plenty of lawyers have started out on one side and found themselves preferring the other. You can promote your professional development by starting on one side and going over to the other, having learned the other side's norms and strategies. Yet switching sides often means switching jobs and starting over. **Consider these potential differences when identifying potential employers and choosing sides:**

- payment models (hourly or contingency);
- financial requirements, risk, and reward;
- time commitments (high or low, regular or varying);

- client relationships (personal or impersonal, individual or corporate);
- adversarial or collaborative nature;
- skill sets;
- authority or independence;
- reporting requirements;
- budget requirements and time and cost constraints.

Exercise. Review the lists in this section again before completing the following exercise:

➤ Use the lists in this section to make two columns, one column for your likes and the other for your dislikes;

➤ After informational interviews, faculty advising, and mentor sessions, review and modify your likes and dislikes;

➤ Review and rely on your likes and dislikes when selecting internships and externships; and

➤ Save your work for when you begin to research and apply for specific job positions.

Anne Whitney Mabbitt, J.D. 2007

"After graduating from law school, I joined a litigation firm with offices in two cities. The firm does almost entirely defense work, receiving cases from several insurance companies and government clients. In law school, I had considered many different paths, including criminal and constitutional practices. But after working for both a defense firm and a plaintiff's firm in law school, I felt that I had a good foundation to work as a civil litigator. I'm really happy that I made the decision to continue in civil practice; I especially like the steady pace of practice and long-term relationships with the lawyers and company representatives with whom I work."

Forums—*Engaging*

Your ethics and professional identity can also influence the forums through which you would best engage in your law career. **Lawyers employ their professional identity in different forums,** each of which has its own characteristics. Courtrooms are obvious examples. Speaking to a jury is the greatest privilege that some lawyers can imagine. For them, everything mundane about the profession disappears in favor of the cause, in a forum where they can speak freely to foundational truths in a way that professional discourse does not usually permit. Other lawyers do not see a jury trial in the same way. They prefer addressing an experienced judge only in bench trials such as in family law or review of administrative proceedings. Other lawyers eschew trials but flourish in pretrial motions and conferences. Other lawyers prefer the appellate courtroom where they can exhibit their mastery of thought, analysis, and precedent. Still others do not see any part of a courtroom as their preferred forum.

The courtroom is not a lawyer's only forum. A forum can be anywhere that a lawyer makes an influence felt. Hearing rooms, boardrooms, corporate offices, workplaces, schools, government agencies, and of course law-firm offices are other forums in which lawyers commonly work. Do not overlook that many lawyers work entirely or primarily through documents and other written communications rather than with a personal or even a telephone presence. Indeed, some of the most influential forums in which lawyers work today are entirely virtual, through exchanges of email and other forms of telecommunication. **Consider the following forums in which lawyers frequently work:**

- jury trials in courtrooms;
- bench trials in courtrooms;
- motion hearings in courtrooms;
- pretrial conferences in courtrooms and chambers;
- mediations and other settlement proceedings at neutral sites;
- arbitrations before expert panels at neutral sites;
- public meetings and legislative hearings at government sites;
- professional conferences and workshops at conference sites;
- inspections and meetings at client locations;
- meetings at other lawyers' firms;
- meetings and individual work within the lawyer's own firm;
- teleconferences and other voice communications; and
- electronic and other written communications.

In some practices, you can choose or influence the forum. Some lawyers are very good at getting matters into court where their skills flourish, while others are good at keeping matters out of court. Some lawyers are great in telephone calls and relaxed meetings, while others are too quick to put their proverbial foot in their mouth and instead flourish through the exchange of correspondence and documents or electronic communications. Some practices permit you to select or shape the forum to suit your preferences and skills. **In other practices, the forum chooses you.** You may have no choice but to appear in person or not to appear but to respond only by telephone or in writing. Just what will define the forum can depend on several factors including:

- client and client preferences;
- type of client matter;
- law firm or other employer;
- level of the lawyer's responsibility;
- quality of the lawyer's skills and experience;
- subject field;
- side on which the lawyer works;
- geographic location and travel restrictions;
- time zone and other considerations of distance; and
- language barriers and cultural influences.

Use internships, externships, clinics, speaker events, mentor sessions, and other opportunities to watch how effective different lawyers are in different forums. **It is special to see a lawyer in the forum for which they were made.** It is more than merely personality that enters into this forum equation. Your best choice of forum depends not on your personality but on your whole professional makeup. For example, some lawyers who are relatively or even acutely introverted actually make wonderful trial lawyers. Interpersonal relationships are relatively unimportant at trial. What is important at trial is the ability to know and speak frankly to fundamental truths, something with which an overly blunt and withdrawn introvert may be quite comfortable and familiar. The wrong extrovert can seem too light and frivolous for the gravity of trial. **Do not choose your forum based on single characteristics and preferences.** It is instead a matter of matching your forum to your professional identity as a whole. You will know it and feel it when you do. You will also know it and feel it when you do not. Your challenge is to make discerning choices that lead you to your best forum.

Exercise. Review again the above list of forums in which lawyers commonly work. Visualize yourself in each of those forums.

Then write and save your answers to the following questions for review at a later date when you investigate job opportunities:

> How hard or easy is it to see yourself in that forum?;
> How well do you see yourself performing in that forum?;
> How does seeing yourself in that forum make you feel?;
> What aspect of your ethics and identity resonates in that forum?;
> Has someone told you that they see you in that forum?;
> o Why do you think that they saw you there?
> Has someone told you that they do not see you in that forum?;
> o Why do you think that they did not see you there?
> Rank the forums in order of your preference.
> o Why did you choose your highest and lowest rank?

Joanna Smith, J.D. 2006

"When I decided to go to law school, I thought that after graduation I might practice law representing individual clients. While in law school, I served as a research assistant for a professor researching and drafting Supreme Court amicus briefs. I was also an editor of the Law Review and completed an externship for a federal appellate judge. That work helped me realize how much I enjoyed working with judges and lawyers on important issues of the day. So, after graduation, I accepted a staff attorney position researching and writing for state appellate and trial-court judges, work that I continue to enjoy."

Community Service—*Involving*

Your ethics and professional identity can also connect you with the community where you live and serve during your law career. Community service involves contributing your time and talent outside of your specific legal skills. Some lawyers hardly seem a part of their larger communities, while other **lawyers seem to do as much for the communities in which they live and work as they do for the clients whom they serve.** Study of lawyer happiness suggests that lawyers are most disappointed not with their pay, intellectual challenge, or professional relationships but with connecting their work to the public good. *See* NANCY LEVIT & DOUGLAS O. LINDER, THE HAPPY LAWYER: MAKING A GOOD LIFE IN THE LAW 52 (Oxford Univ. Press 2010). Lawyers who are prominent community leaders are often also highly productive within their law practices and firms. One feeds the other. A lawyer's community service brings the lawyer into contact with non-lawyers, some of whom are professionals who may refer matters to the lawyer and others of whom are potential clients. Community service is not only a means of marketing. It is also a way to:

- strengthen old skills;
- build new skills;
- develop new resources;
- maintain balance;
- meet friends; and
- build social support,

> "Individuals involved in community service enjoy a rich professional network. Law students should strive to cultivate relationships not only with their classmates but with individuals outside of law school. Community extends beyond geography and includes groups. Define your community, get involved, and be enriched by the experience."
>
> **Assistant Dean Cynthia Ward**

There are many forms of community service in which lawyers participate. Some service involves boards and committees of charitable organizations. Other service involves the charitable work itself. Uncompensated government service on boards and commissions is common among lawyers, including writing and administering community grants. Lawyers are frequently found serving as elders, teachers, and other leaders in faith organizations. Lawyers commonly serve as board members and volunteers supporting business and trade associations, wildlife organizations, and environmental and public-interest organizations. Other lawyers like to be involved in community work involving manual labor, perhaps rebuilding playgrounds or cleaning up parks and beaches. **Consider the following short list among many other types of organizations whom lawyers serve at local, regional, and national levels:**

- Goodwill, Salvation Army, and other charitable organizations;
- parent-teacher associations, and school boards and committees;
- YMCA, YWCA, and other recreational organizations;

- Chamber of Commerce, Rotarians, and other business associations;
- church, synagogue, and other faith organizations;
- planning commissions, zoning boards, and other government work;
- World Affairs Councils and other international organizations;
- Hispanic Chamber, Urban League, and other social organizations;
- League of Women Voters and other election organizations;
- Republican and Democratic Parties, and other political organizations;
- Trout Unlimited, Bird Watchers, and other wildlife organizations;
- environmental and public-interest organizations;
- Boy Scouts, Girl Scouts, and other youth organizations;
- coaching, refereeing, and administering sports teams and leagues.

Performing community service while in law school carries at least two advantages. First, **community service proves one's ethics and professional identity more clearly than the strongest recommendation letter or reference.** The adage to watch what one does rather than what one says could never be more true than when considering the value and impact of community service. **List your community service on your resume.** Your interviewer may be performing a similar service. Many law firms value community service. Those firms tend to highly value community service already performed by job candidates as a measure of commitment to future service. Community service tends to be a lifelong habit, not something that one picks up and discards with the needs or interests of an employer. Firms like to hire proven community servants. Give them that opportunity by performing community service while in law school and listing it on your resume. You may even find that the community leaders with whom you serve while you are in law school will give you job leads and write you job recommendations more helpful than traditional sources.

Another advantage to community service that you perform during law school is that it helps you identify and connect with a service community after graduation. All other things being equal, you may choose to live in a community after graduation where you have meaningful service outlets. It is one thing to find a fitting job. It adds another dimension to your opportunity when you find a fitting job in a fitting service community. Professional service is meaningful, yet **community service lends meaning to a life beyond what a profession can alone do.** Community service demonstrates citizenship, responsibility, integrity, and compassion in a way that a job alone does not always do, even when the job is law practice. Indeed, a new job in a new profession can be self absorbing. If you have already developed a community service before graduation, then you are likely to be able to more readily connect it to your new community after graduation even as you take on the new responsibilities of law practice.

> "As a law student, I volunteered to work on a local community service project with one of my professors. Several months after the project ended, I interviewed for a job as a law clerk to general counsel of a national organization. As it turned out, the general counsel was also involved in the same community service project on which I worked. During the interview, we shared stories of our community service experience, and I got the job."
>
> **Assistant Dean Cynthia Ward**

Find community service through your law school and its volunteer programs, especially if you want to deepen and enrich relationships with law students, faculty, and staff. Law schools have many community projects and connections. Also, find community service through your faith or community organization if you prefer to make new acquaintances outside of law school. Record what you do in the way of community service in an electronic journal to help you develop your personal vision and values. Include the organization's name, the name and contact information for the program manager, the activities you performed, and the skills you used, improved, or developed. Also, summarize it on your draft resume. Finally, keep in mind that community service is one of those few activities that one can legitimately call an end in itself, even in the unlikely chance that it does nothing for your legal skills, law career, or personal life or balance. There are some things that are just the right thing to do.

Exercise. Review again the list of types of community service that lawyers often perform. Then complete the following exercises:

> Which of the activities on the list of common community services that lawyers perform have you done in the past?;
  o Are any of them available in the community in which you are thinking of practicing?
> Which of the activities on the list of common community services that lawyers perform have you not done but would like to do?;
  o Are any of them available in the community in which you are thinking of practicing?

Benjamin Symko, J.D. 2008

"Community service turned my life around and set me on the path to law school. After I started law school, I began volunteering at a public defender's office, drawing on my community-service skills and experience to help the office counsel indigent clients. I joined that office as an associate defender after graduation. Soon after, I won a national award for public service. I am now in private practice with a small firm doing similar defense work and still volunteer for community service."

Pro-Bono Service—*Maturing*

Your ethics and professional identity can also connect you with pro-bono service that will promote your career and professional development. Pro-bono service differs from community service in that it involves using your legal knowledge, skills, and identity to provide clients with free or reduced-fee legal services. You must while in law school be sure to avoid the unauthorized practice of law, meaning that your pro-bono service should be in an approved clinic setting (beyond the hours for which you receive academic credit because pro-bono service does not generally include services for which you receive income or credit) or by assisting a licensed lawyer who is providing the direct service. Yet within that limitation, **pro-bono service can make a difference to you in choosing the right field, finding the right employment, continuing your professional development after graduation from law school, and promoting your reputation and career while in law practice.** Pro-bono service can promote your career and professional development in at least these general areas:

- improving your intercultural skills while serving unlike others;

- helping you identify achievable goals for diverse service populations;
- introducing you to social-service and other agency resources;
- broadening your knowledge, skills, and ethics in alternative fields;
- increasing your competence and confidence in specific matters;
- connecting you with other lawyers around meaningful service; and
- improving your relationship with judges around assignments.

There may be few more immediate and meaningful ways to build a law practice than through pro-bono service. Pro-bono service introduces you to populations whose members are in constant and acute need of legal services. The lawyers whom you find serving those populations either through pro-bono service, low-bono (below-market compensation for) services, or public or private programs are often among the most skilled and caring of lawyers. *See* Leslie C. Levin, *Pro Bono and Low Bono in the Solo and Small Law Firm Context*, in ROBERT GRANFIELD & LYNN MATHER, EDS., PRIVATE LAWYERS & THE PUBLIC INTEREST 156, 159 (Oxford Univ. Press 2009). They have found methods, practices, programs, and reasons to apply their skills for those most in need of and least likely to receive legal services. **Among pro-bono clients and the lawyer who serve them, you can find the heart, mind, soul, and strength of law practice, in ways that connect with and define your ethics and professional identity.** The populations whom pro-bono lawyers serve include among others:

- children;
- the disabled;
- servicemembers;
- immigrants;
- prisoners;
- recently released prisoners;
- the homeless;
- debtors;
- separated and divorcing spouses;
- foreclosed homeowners; and
- servicemembers.

Record your pro-bono service in an electronic journal, just as you do your community service. Indicate where you served, whom you served, the agency that supported your service, the lawyers who supervised you, what you did to serve, and the skills that you used, improved, or developed. Ask the lawyers and law professors whose pro-bono service you support to write you recommendation letters and give you positive references for your pro-bono contributions. Also, describe your pro-bono service on your resume. Lawyers who interview you as a job candidate have the same ethical responsibility to serve pro bono as you do. *See* ABA MODEL RULE OF PROFESSIONAL CONDUCT 6.1. Although the responsibility is everyone's, not everyone is fulfilling it. Pro-bono service connects you with interviewers who do perform pro-bono service, while distinguishing you from other candidates who do not. **Tell prospective employers about the value of your pro-bono work in improving your knowledge and skills, and developing your professional identity.** Have an example story ready. Law firms value pro-bono service particularly when the lawyers who perform it integrate it into their career and professional development.

> "Having practiced law for the better part of four decades, I have tried to apply in my work a principle I learned as a Rotarian: 'Service Above Self.' It is important to keep in mind that law is truly a service business. We lawyers are retained to serve the best interest of our clients. In dealing with the tension that can sometimes arise between the client's needs and personal goals, we must always put the client's interests first."
>
> *Former State Bar President Scott Brinkmeyer,*
> *Mika Meyers Beckett & Jones*

Use your pro-bono service to overcome questions that prospective employers may have about your readiness for practice and your lack of experience. Like clerkships, internships, and externships, pro-bono service can help you level the playing field against candidates who have practice experience. Do not be afraid to work outside of your comfort zone when supporting pro-bono service, so long as you and your lawyer supervisor ensure that your work is competent. One of the greater benefits of pro-bono service is that it gives you opportunities to expand your experience, learning new fields and skills. Especially, be willing to encounter and appreciate the challenges that pro-bono clients face in their legal and other matters.

You may meet individuals whom you never would otherwise have met, who lack the finances, education, citizenship, freedom, and other rights, resources, and benefits that you share with other law students, lawyers, and their paying clients.

Take advantage of pro-bono training programs, forms, manuals, and similar resources. Law schools, state and local bar associations, courts, legal-services programs, and other organizations offer training to lawyers who will provide pro-bono services and law students who will support them. Investigate and participate in those programs, listing them on your resume when you complete them. The same organizations often offer free or low-cost malpractice insurance covering pro-bono programs. Ensure that malpractice insurance covers your pro-bono work, whether as a student or graduate.

Exercise. Investigate the pro-bono programs that your law school offers. If its offerings are limited and do not provide you with a meaningful opportunity, then investigate the pro-bono programs of the local bar association, legal-services office, courts, or other organizations in your area. Then answer the following questions to help you choose a program in which to participate:

> ➤ Which program would most improve your skills in an area where you need improvement?;
> ➤ Which program serves a population with which you most identify out of compassion?;
> ➤ Which program serves a population in the greatest need of what you are able to do?;
> ➤ Which program offers service opportunities most fitting with your school and other schedule?

Samantha Hull, J.D. 2007

"In law school, I helped provide pro-bono service to immigrants at a Justice for Our Neighbors program, where I worked on asylum claims and other relief. I also clerked my last year at a local law firm. I am sure that my service learning helped me earn a job offer right out of law school at my current firm, where I handle family-law and probate matters."

Conclusion

Your prospects for gainful employment as a lawyer are good. Labor experts predict that the employment of lawyers will grow 13% in the next decade, at the same rate as the labor market for all occupations. Legal fields are changing as much now as they ever have, just as are law firms. Changes in the organization and delivery of legal services creates opportunity for you as a new lawyer. Law itself is changing as rapidly as it ever has, making the currency of your legal education even more valuable to law firms and other employers of lawyers. Technology is also changing rapidly, meaning that firms and other employers will benefit from your current technology skills. If you are among the law school graduates who never planned to enter the legal field or have decided that the legal field is not for you, then your law degree and legal-service skills give you advantages in other fields where law compliance is increasingly important. It is a good time to be a law school graduate.

When it comes to your career, though, it is never a time to stand still. You have seen from this text that there is a formula to career and professional development. Law school affects what you know (knowledge), what you do (skills), and who you become (identity) as a lawyer. Reliable professional-development tools articulate your law-practice knowledge, skills, and identity into your best career opportunities. Those tools are not like the pellets flung in spreading chaos from a shotgun. Rather, those tools are an organized set of practices that help you discern your desired employer and reflect your qualities to its representatives in the most cohesive and attractive fashion. Treat your career and professional development with thought. When it comes to your law career, do not forget to envision, plan, prepare, implement, and assess.

Yet do not give over your career and professional development entirely to formulas. Be ready to explore. Know your passion. Ultimately, career and professional development is not a formula. Oh, yes, law schools organize their curricula and offer the professional-development tools just as the text describes above. Every one of those tools has its own place and value. To flourish as a lawyer, though, you must connect your professional self to more than a job. There are larger perspectives than a specific role in a certain office of a certain employer. You must also connect your professional self to a community, profession, nation, and things beyond. For your community, you should become its friend, confidant, and pillar. For your profession, you should become its servant champion. For your nation, you should become a steward of the greatest democratic republic ever, helping it to remain that way for you, your children, and your grandchildren.

As for things beyond, you need not take aim for them because they will come and get you. When they come, you need only recognize, receive, honor, and embrace them. Do not worry about when they will come because they are with you now, helping you overcome the challenges of law school. They will be with you in job interviews when you do not know and cannot express who you are, because they made you for justice's purpose. They are with you when you face the seeming uncertainty of job searching, because they know everything that there is for you, knowing too that it is more than you could ever imagine. Ultimately, what career and professional development require is the same thing that life requires, that you live in faith, hope, and love, knowing that love is the greatest. Connect your law career to the great story of justice, and you will have made for yourself your greatest career.

References

Navigating Law School:

ABA Section on Legal Education & Admission to the Bar, *Legal Education and Professional Development—An Educational Continuum, Report of the Task Force on Law Schools and the Profession: Narrowing the Gap* (ABA 1992) (the "MacCrate Report");

COOPER, CHARLES, LATER IN LIFE LAWYERS: TIPS FOR THE NON-TRADITIONAL LAW STUDENT (The Fine Print Press 2006);

CURRIER, KATHERINE A., AND THOMAS E. EIMERMANN, THE STUDY OF LAW: A CRITICAL THINKING APPROACH (Aspen 2005);

KISSAM, PHILIP C., THE DISCIPLINE OF LAW SCHOOLS: THE MAKING OF MODERN LAWYERS (Carolina Academic Press 2003);

LE BRUN, MARLENE, AND RICHARD JOHNSTONE, THE QUIET REVOLUTION—IMPROVING STUDENT LEARNING IN LAW (The Law Book Co. 1994);

LITOWITZ, DOUGLAS, THE DESTRUCTION OF YOUNG LAWYERS: BEYOND ONE L 30-38 (Univ. of Akron Press 2006);

MAHARG, PAUL, TRANSFORMING LEGAL EDUCATION—LEARNING AND TEACHING LAW IN THE EARLY TWENTY-FIRST CENTURY (Ashgate 2007);

SCHAUER, FREDERICK, THINKING LIKE A LAWYER—A NEW INTRODUCTION TO LEGAL REASONING (Harvard Univ. Press 2009);

SEDBERRY, STEVEN R., LAW SCHOOL LABYRINTH—A GUIDE TO MAKING THE MOST OF YOUR LEGAL EDUCATION (Kaplan Pub. 2009);

SULLIVAN, WILLIAM M., ANNE COLBY, JUDITH WELCH WEGNER, LLOYD BOND, & LEE S. SHULMAN, EDUCATING LAWYERS: PREPARATION FOR THE PROFESSION OF LAW (Jossey-Bass 2007);

THOMSON, DAVID I.C., LAW SCHOOL 2.0: LEGAL EDUCATION FOR A DIGITAL AGE (LexisNexis 2009);

TIMMER, AMY, AND NELSON MILLER, REFLECTIONS OF A LAWYER'S SOUL—THE INSTITUTIONAL EXPERIENCE OF PROFESSIONALISM AT THOMAS M. COOLEY LAW SCHOOL (William S. Hein & Co. 2008);

TONSING, DENNIS, 1000 DAYS TO THE BAR (William S. Hein & Co. 2010).

Bar Registration and Admission:

American Bar Association Section of Legal Education and Admission to the Bar (www.abanet.org/legaled) provides an overview of bar admissions;

BarBri (www.barbri.com) offers commercial bar-preparation courses with state schedules;

Kaplan PMBR Bar Review (www.kaptest.com) offers commercial bar-preparation courses with state schedules;

Micromash (www.micromash.net) offers commercial bar-preparation courses with state schedules;

National Conference of Bar Examiners (www.ncbex.org) provides registration and bar-exam information for all states;

Self Assessment:

BOLLES, RICHARD NELSON, WHAT COLOR IS YOUR PARACHUTE? A PRACTICAL MANUAL FOR JOB-HUNTERS & CAREER-CHANGERS (Ten Speed Press 2010);

JANDA, LOUIS, CAREER TESTS: 25 REVEALING SELF-TESTS TO HELP YOU FIND AND SUCCEED AT THE PERFECT CAREER (Barnes & Noble 2004);

MORRIS, KATHY, AND JILL ECKERT, ASK THE CAREER COUNSELORS: ANSWERS FOR LAWYERS ON THEIR LIVES AND LIFE'S WORK (ABA 2004);

MORRIS, KATHY, AND JILL ECKERT, DIRECT EXAMINATION: A WORKBOOK FOR LAWYER CAREER SATISFACTION (ABA 2001);

SCHNEIDER, DEBORAH, AND GARY BELSKY, SHOULD YOU REALLY BE A LAWYER? THE GUIDE TO SMART CAREER CHOICES BEFORE, DURING & AFTER LAW SCHOOL (LawyerAvenue Press 2d. ed. 2010).

Career Options:

ARRON, DEBORAH, WHAT CAN YOU DO WITH A LAW DEGREE? (Lawyer Avenue Press 5th ed. 2003);

BATDORF, TIMOTHY D., THE LAWYER'S GUIDE TO BEING HUMAN—HOW TO BRING WHO YOU ARE TO WHAT YOU DO (iUniverse, Inc. 2007);

CANNON, K. CHARLES, THE ULTIMATE GUIDE TO YOUR LEGAL CAREER: WHAT EVERY LAWYER MUST KNOW TO AVOID THE MISTAKES AND MAXIMIZE THE VALUE OF A CAREER IN LAW (Da Capo Press 2007);

CAREY, CHRISTIAN CIVILETTO, FULL DISCLOSURE: THE NEW LAWYER'S MUST-READ CAREER GUIDE (ALM Publishing 2001);

FRIEDLAND, STEVEN I., THE ESSENTIAL RULES FOR BAR EXAM SUCCESS (Thomson West 2008);

FURI-PERRY, URSULA, FIFTY UNIQUE LEGAL PATHS: HOW TO FIND THE RIGHT JOB (ABA 2008);

HERMANN, RICHARD L., MANAGING YOUR LEGAL CAREER—BEST PRACTICES FOR CREATING THE CAREER YOU WANT (ABA 2010);

MANTIS, HILLARY, ALTERNATIVE CAREERS FOR LAWYERS (Princeton Review 1997);

NATIONAL ASSOCIATION OF LAW PLACEMENT, THE OFFICIAL GUIDE TO LEGAL SPECIALTIES: AN INSIDER'S GUIDE TO EVERY MAJOR PRACTICE AREA (The BarBri Group 2000);

STRAUSSER, JEFFREY, JUDGMENT REVERSED: ALTERNATIVE CAREERS FOR LAWYERS (Barrons Educ. Series 1997);

WALTON, KIMM ALAYNE, GUERRILLA TACTICS FOR GETTING THE LEGAL JOB OF YOUR DREAMS (BarBri 2d ed. 1999).

Email, Cover Letters, and Resumes:

KAPLAN, ROBBIE MILLER, HOW TO SAY IT IN YOUR JOB SEARCH: CHOICE WORDS, PHRASES, SENTENCES AND PARAGRAPHS FOR RESUMES, COVER LETTERS AND INTERVIEWS (Prentice Hall Press 2001);

National Association of Law-Placement Professionals, *Before You Hit Send: Guidelines for Using E-mail Effectively for Job Search-Related Correspondence* (2010);

Balance in Work and Personal Life:

ELWORK, AMIRAM, STRESS MANAGEMENT FOR LAWYERS—HOW TO INCREASE PERSONAL & PROFESSIONAL SATISFACTION IN THE LAW (Vorkell Group 3d ed. 2007);

KAUFMAN, GEORGE W., THE LAWYER'S GUIDE TO BALANCING LIFE & WORK—TAKING THE STRESS OUT OF SUCCESS (ABA Law Practice Management Section 2006);

LE VAN, GERALD, LAWYERS' LIVES OUT OF CONTROL—A QUALITY OF LIFE HANDBOOK (WorldComm Press 1992);

LEVIT, NANCY, & DOUGLAS O. LINDER, THE HAPPY LAWYER: MAKING A GOOD LIFE IN THE LAW (Oxford Univ. Press 2010);

STEFANIC, JEAN, & RICHARD DELGADO, HOW LAWYERS LOSE THEIR WAY—A PROFESSION THAT FAILS ITS CREATIVE MINDS (Duke Univ. Press 2005);

TAMMINEN, JULIE M., ED., LIVING WITH THE LAW—STRATEGIES TO AVOID BURNOUT AND CREATE BALANCE (ABA Law Practice Management Section 1997).

The Changing Profession:

ABBOTT, IDA O., THE LAWYER'S GUIDE TO MENTORING (National Association for Law Placement 2000);

Bryant, Susan, *The Five Habits: Building Cross-Cultural Competence in Lawyers*, 8 CLIN. L. REV. 33 (2001);

CARRINGTON, PAUL D., STEWARDS OF DEMOCRACY: LAW AS A PUBLIC PROFESSION (Westview Press 1999);

Daicoff, Susan, *Lawyer, Know Thyself: A Review of Empirical Research on Attorney Attributes Bearing on Professionalism*, 46 AM. U. L.REV. 1337 (1997);

DOWNEY, MICHAEL, INTRODUCTION TO LAW FIRM PRACTICE (ABA Law Practice Management Section 2010);

DUFFEY, WILLIAM S., JR., AND RICHARD A. SCHNEIDER, EDS., A LIFE IN THE LAW—ADVICE FOR YOUNG LAWYERS (ABA 2009);

GALBENSKI, DAVID, UNBOUND: HOW ENTREPRENEURSHIP IS DRAMATICALLY TRANSFORMING LEGAL SERVICES TODAY (Lumen Legal 2009);

LAURITSEN, MICHAEL, THE LAWYER'S GUIDE TO WORKING SMARTER WITH KNOWLEDGE TOOLS (ABA Law Practice Management Section 2010);

MILLER, BARBARA, AND MARTIN CAMP, THE LAW FIRM ASSOCIATE'S GUIDE TO CONNECTING WITH YOUR COLLEAGUES (ABA Law Practice Management Section 2009);

PAUL, RICHARD W., CRITICAL THINKING—WHAT EVERY PERSON NEEDS TO SURVIVE IN A RAPIDLY CHANGING WORLD (Foundation for Critical Thinking, 3rd ed. 1993).

Job-Posting Websites:

Already Bored (www.alreadybored.com) provides salary information and some job listings;

America's Job Bank (www.ajb.dni.us) is a federal-state partnership listing full-time private-sector job postings from all over the nation and all types of work;

CareerBuilder (www.careerbuilder.com) has general job postings including law jobs from all over the nation, searchable by keyword, job type, and geographic area;

Chicago Daily Law Bulletin (www.lawbulletin.com) has law-job postings in that and other Midwest geographic areas;

Chronicle of Higher Education (www.chronicle.com/jobs) lists academic jobs searchable by keyword, location, and position type;

CollegeGrad (www.collegegrad.com) lists job postings for recent college graduates including law jobs and summer-associate programs;

Complaw Attorney Job Listings (www.complaw.com) lists intellectual-property, Internet, and computer law postings;

Counsel.Net Attorney Job Center (www.counsel.net) lists job postings by geographic area and includes an email-notice function;

EmplawyerNet (www.emplawyernet.com) is a paid-membership service that includes thousands of listings matching your criteria;

Find Law (www.careers.findlaw.com) performs searches for summer and full-time jobs fitting your geographic and practice-area interests;

Hieros Gamos Comprehensive Legal and Government Portal (www.hg.org) includes general information on entering practices including job-search and resume-posting sections;

Law Forum Employment Opportunities (www.lawforum.net) is a directory of law-related websites including an employment section;

LawJobs (www.lawjobs.com) permits job-posting browsing by practice area, geographic area, and employer;

Monster (www.monster.com) lists job postings nationwide searchable by job title, skills, keyword, and location;

Nation Job Network (www.nationjob.com) is a general job-search website with a section for legal-field jobs;

National Lawyers Guild (www.nlg.org) is a website for lawyers interested in social-justice issues that includes job, internship, and fellowship postings;

United States Office of Personnel Management (www.usajobs.opm.gov) lists federal job postings searchable by keywords and geographic area;

United States Patent and Trademark Office (www.uspto.gov) has a section for job announcements available in the Office.

Appendices

Appendix A
Index of Activities

Following is an alphabetical list of the activities that the Guide recommends that you explore while thinking of them as your career and professional-development curriculum[sp1]:

Appendix B
Checklist of Activities in Order of Execution

Following is a checklist of the activities that the Guide recommends that you explore while thinking of them as your career and professional-development curriculum. In reality, you would start many of these activities as soon as you began planning for law school and continue them throughout your legal education and into a law career. Identifying your vision and values, planning finances, consulting advisors, and having models and mentors are examples. Others of these activities you would begin or think of together, like memberships and networking, or character, fitness, and ethics rules, or adapting your communications, dress, and demeanor to professional norms.

Appendix C
Checklist of Activities by Category

Following is a checklist of activities that the Guide recommends that you explore while thinking of them as your career and professional-development curriculum. Like the Guide itself, the checklist divides the activities into the three areas Knowledge, Skills, and Ethics. In reality, you would start many of these activities as soon as you began planning for law school and continue them throughout your legal education and into a law career. Identifying your vision and values, planning finances, consulting advisors, and having models and mentors are examples. Others of these activities you would begin or think of together, like memberships and networking, or character, fitness, and ethics rules, or adapting your communications, dress, and demeanor to professional norms.

Knowledge
- ☐ Schedule an appointment with a career advisor to begin identifying your career goals and to plan volunteer, legal employment, job search, and externship strategies;
- ☐ Begin thinking about the work and professional environment that best suits your personality and career goals;
- ☐ Research types of legal employers, types of legal positions available to law students, and the timing for applying for legal positions;
- ☐ Research the states that require law student registration and register where applicable;
- ☐ Determine when you will graduate and take your state's bar exam;
- ☐ Choose and register for a commercial bar-preparation course fitting to your state's bar exam;
- ☐ Consult the career library to learn more about your career options and job search resources;
- ☐ Investigate and attend career programs like speaker series and job excursions to learn more about practice areas and settings;

- ☐ Learn the timelines and criteria necessary to participate in interview programs, judicial clerkships, and job fairs;
- ☐ Read classified advertisements, job-bulletin exchange lists, national employment listings, and legal newspapers for volunteer, summer, part-time, fellowship, and full-time employment opportunities;
- ☐ Plan for summer or term-off employment opportunities.

Skills

- ☐ Draft a tailored cover letter and legal resume, and have a career advisor review both, revising and updating as appropriate;
- ☐ Gain legal and non-legal volunteer experience through school, bar, and community programs;
- ☐ Meet with a career advisor to finalize your career options and job search strategies;
- ☐ Develop and finalize a list of targeted law firms or other employers for summer, externship, and long-term employment possibilities;
- ☐ Join as a student member of the state bar of your choice;
- ☐ Attend state bar and professional association meetings, receptions, and seminars;
- ☐ Conduct informational interviews with attorneys, alumni, and professors in practice areas that interest you;
- ☐ Gain legal employment as a summer associate, law clerk, or volunteer;
- ☐ Choose and update your professional references, providing them with a copy of your resume and updated resumes;
- ☐ Select your writing sample for prospective employers, updating your writing sample as you progress through law school;
- ☐ Purchase and tailor a business suit for your job interviews;
- ☐ Participate in a mock job interview;
- ☐ Participate in job fairs and interviews;
- ☐ Apply for post-graduate judicial clerkships.

Ethics

- ☐ Ensure that your law school application is complete and accurate including all requested disclosures;
- ☐ Update your law school application as events occur requiring supplemental disclosure;

- ☐ Form mentor relationships with attorneys in the geographic region and practice settings that most interest you;
- ☐ Register for the Multistate Professional Responsibility Exam to coordinate with your state bar exam schedule, if required by your state bar;
- ☐ Take and pass the Multistate Professional Responsibility Exam if required;
- ☐ Obtain your state bar's application;
- ☐ Investigate and obtain all accurate character-and-fitness information with which to complete your state bar's application;
- ☐ Prepare and submit your bar application.

www.ingramcontent.com/pod-product-compliance
Lightning Source LLC
Chambersburg PA
CBHW081808200326
41597CB00023B/4186